Kochie's Best Jokes

DAVID KOCH

Published by
Wilkinson Publishing Pty Ltd
ACN 006 042 173
2 Collins Street
Melbourne Vic 3000
Ph: (03) 9654 5446

First published 2005

National Library of Australia
Cataloguing-in-Publication data:

Koch, David
Kochie's Best Jokes

ISBN 1 875889 78 7

1.   Wit and humour.   I. Title

808.882

Joke Complilation: David Koch
Cover & Page design: qgraphics
Illustrations/Cartoons: Wayne Harrison, Advanced Airbrush, Minchinbury, NSW
Printed in Australia by McPherson's Printing Group, Maryborough

David Koch

David Koch is well-known to millions of Australians as co-host of Australia's No. 1 breakfast show, *Sunrise,* on Channel 7. He also hosts *My Business Show* on the same channel, and is the resident Business and Finance expert for Seven and Prime TV Networks.

His popular segments *A Minute on Your Business* and *A Minute on Your Money* are broadcast on more than 50 regional radio stations.

David's knowledge of money and business is extensive, and in a survey conducted by *Money Management* newspaper his peers recognised him as one of the ten most influential people in the financial services industry. He also has a strong interest in small business issues, is in demand as a presenter and regularly addresses a wide range of corporate events and groups.

Wayne Harrison

Late last year, Wayne Harrison of Advanced Airbrush was invited by David Koch to spend a morning on *Sunrise*, drawing cartoons of Mel and Kochie. Kochie enjoyed it so much, he kept the caricature of himself – the very one that is now on the cover of this book, *Kochie's Best Jokes*. And moving on from there, Wayne was the obvious choice to create the kind of funny and clever cartoons needed for the book.

Wayne Harrison has been airbrushing for more than 25 years, and his artworks have won awards in USA and Australia. His artwork has also received a lot of major awards for Top Graphics and Airbrush Art (Murals) at various automotive shows, and was placed in the top five airbrush artists in Australia.

In 1995 Wayne entered his first overseas competition 'AIRSTORM 95' in Atlanta, USA and won 1st place in the Alternative Section. He is widely recognised for his work as seen on Virgin Blue planes and many promotional vehicles around Australia.

TaBle of contents

INTRODUCTION

Australia is one of the best countries in the world. People love to visit us, not just because of our scenery and animals, but also because of us. Yep, I know it's un-Australian to acknowledge anything good about ourselves, but people do seem to like us. And a lot of that is because of our sense of humour ... we're easy to get along with and are quite happy to take the 'Mickey' out of ourselves.

To the rest of the politically correct we're seen as refreshing ... of having good, old-fashioned values and sense of humour.

Every weekday morning that Aussie sense of humour is reflected in the *Sunrise* segment 'Kochie's Joke of the Day' on Channel 7. I receive thousands of jokes a year from *Sunrise* viewers about every subject under the sun. Some of them get me into trouble, some aren't seen as funny by my colleagues ... but all of them reflect the humour that is distinctly ours.

As a result 'Joke of the Day' has become an institution within the *Sunrise* program with many viewers arranging their breakfast routine around catching the day's 'funny'.

It has always been said that laughter is the best medicine ... and I reckon in this day and age it can be a miracle cure to the depressing bombardment of bad news we encounter every day.

I hope you like this small cross-section of the jokes which tickled my fancy.

Kochie

ADULt

A college teacher reminds her class of tomorrow's final exam.

'Now class, I won't tolerate any excuses for you not being here tomorrow. I might consider a nuclear attack or a serious personal injury or illness, or death in your immediate family but that's it, no other excuses whatsoever!'

A smart-ass guy in the back of the room raised his hand and asks, 'What would you say if tomorrow I said I was suffering from complete and utter sexual exhaustion?'

The entire class does its best to stifle their laughter and snickering. When silence is restored, the teacher smiles sympathetically at the student, shakes her head, and sweetly says, 'Well, I guess you'd have to write the exam with your other hand.'

A woman hears her husband cussing up a storm from behind the bathroom door.

She knocks and asks, 'Honey, what is it?'

Her husband emerges from the bathroom and says, 'The doctor prescribed suppositories for this stomach problem I've been having and no matter what I do, I just can't get the little sucker up my ass. Even the doctor had to shove the first one in to show me how it was done, and I tell you it took him forever to get it up there, and it hurt!'

'Poor baby,' says the wife. 'You were probably nervous and tense and he probably wasn't very gentle with you. Here, let me give you the suppository, I don't mind.'

Still grumbling, the husband bends over. His wife puts her left hand on his shoulder to brace him and with the right hand, quickly and easily slips the suppository up her husband's rear end. The husband lets out a bloodcurdling scream.

'My God,' says the wife. 'What happened? Did I hurt you?'

'No!' cries the man, 'but I just realised that when the doctor did it, he had BOTH his hands on my shoulders!'

An elderly Irish woman goes to the doctor and asks his help to revive her husband's sex drive. 'What about trying Viagra?' asks the doctor.

'Not a chance,' says Mrs. Murphy, 'he won't even take an aspirin for a headache.'

'No problem,' replies the doctor. 'Drop it into his coffee and he won't even taste it. Try it and then call me in a week to let me know how things go.'

A week later, Mrs. Murphy calls the doctor and he enquired as to how things went.

'Oh, faith, bejaysus and begorrah, it was terrible doctor!'

'What happened?' asked the doctor.

'Well, I did as you advised and slipped the Viagra into his coffee. The effect was immediate. He jumped straight up, with a gleam in his eye and with his pants bulging fiercely! He swept the cutlery off the table, at the same time ripping my clothes and then proceeded to make wild, mad, passionate love to me on the tabletop. It was TERRIBLE!'

'What was terrible?' asked the doctor. 'Was the sex not good?'

'Oh no, doctor, the sex was the best I've had in 25 years, but I'll never be able to show me face in Starbucks again.'

A man bumps in to a woman in a hotel lobby and as he does, his elbow goes in to her breast. They are both quite startled.

The man turns to her and says, 'Ma'am if your heart is as soft as your breast, I know you'll forgive me.'

She replies, 'If your dick is as hard as your elbow, I'm in room 22.'

A lonely older lady, aged 75, decided it was time to get married, so she put a wanted ad in the local paper that read, 'HUSBAND WANTED. Must be in my age group, must not beat me, must not run around on me, and must still be good in bed! All applicants must apply in person.'

On the second day of the ad she heard the doorbell ring. There sat a man in a wheelchair. He had no arms or legs. She asked sardonically, 'You're not expecting me to consider you, are you? Just look at you — you have no legs!'

The old man smiled, 'Therefore no chance to run around on you!'

She snorted, 'You have no arms either!'

'Therefore, no chance to beat you.'

The old lady raised her eyebrows and gazed at him intensely. 'Are you still good in bed?' she asked.

The old man smirked and said, 'I rang the doorbell didn't I?'

Two men were talking. 'So, how's your sex life?'

'Oh, nothing special. I'm having Social Security sex.'

'Social Security sex?'

'Yeah, you know: I get a little each month, not enough to live on!'

One night, a father overheard his son saying his prayers.

'God bless Mum,' prayed the boy, 'and bless Dad and Gran also. But goodbye Grandad and rest in peace.' The father thought the last bit of his prayer was strange, but soon forgot about it. The next day, the grandfather died.

About a month later, the father again overheard his son's prayers.

'God bless Mum and Dad,' the boy prayed. 'But, goodbye Grandma and rest in peace.'

The next day, the grandmother died. The father began to worry about the situation. Two weeks later, the father again heard his son praying.

'God bless Mum,' the boy prayed. 'But, goodbye Dad and rest in peace.'

This alone almost gave him a heart attack, so the next morning, without saying a thing, the father got up early and went to work. He stayed in his office all day.

Finally, after midnight, he went home. 'I'm still alive!' he congratulated himself. He crawled into bed with his wife and apologised for being late.

'I had a really bad day,' he moaned.

'You had a bad day?' his missus yelled. 'The postman dropped dead on our veranda this morning!'

Tired of a listless sex life, the man came right out and asked his wife during a recent lovemaking session, 'How come you never tell me when you have an orgasm?'

She glanced at him casually and replied, 'You're never home!'

One particular Christmas a long time ago, Santa was getting ready for his annual trip ... but there were problems everywhere.

Four of his elves got sick, and the trainee elves did not produce the toys as fast as the regular ones so Santa was beginning to feel the pressure of being behind schedule.

Then Mrs. Claus told Santa that her Mom was coming to visit. This stressed Santa even more. When he went to harness the reindeer, he found that three of them were about to give birth and two had jumped the fence and were out, heaven knows where. More stress.

Then when he began to load the sleigh one of the boards cracked and the toy bag fell to the ground and scattered the toys. So, frustrated, Santa went into the house for a cup of coffee and a shot of whiskey. When he went to the cupboard, he discovered the elves had hid the liquor and there was nothing to drink.

In his frustration, he accidentally dropped the coffee pot and it broke into hundreds of little pieces all over the kitchen floor. He went to get the broom and found that mice had eaten the straw it was made from. Just then the doorbell rang and Santa cursed on his way to the door. He opened the door and there was a little angel with a great big Christmas tree.

The angel said, very cheerfully, 'Merry Christmas Santa. Isn't it just a lovely day? I have a beautiful tree for you. Isn't it just a lovely tree? Where would you like me to stick it?'

Thus began the tradition of the little angel on top of the Christmas tree.

A wife went in to see a therapist and said, 'I've got a big problem, doctor. Every time we're in bed and my husband climaxes, he lets out this ear splitting yell.'

'My dear,' the shrink said, 'that's completely natural. I don't see what the problem is.'

'The problem is,' she complained, 'it wakes me up!'

A couple is lying in bed. The man says, 'I am going to make you the happiest woman in the world.'

The woman says … 'I'll miss you.'

Ethel was a bit of a demon in her wheelchair, and loved to charge around the nursing home, taking corners on one wheel and getting up to maximum speed on the long corridors.

Because the poor woman was one sandwich short of a picnic, the other residents tolerated her, and some of the males actually joined in.

One day, Ethel was speeding up one corridor when a door opened and Kooky Clarence stepped out with his arm outstretched.

'STOP!' he shouted in firm voice. 'Have you got a licence for that thing?'

Ethel fished around in her handbag and pulled out a Kit Kat wrapper and held it up to him.

'OK,' he said, and away Ethel sped down the hall.

As she took the corner near the TV lounge on one wheel, Weird Harold popped out in front of her and shouted, 'STOP! Have you got proof of insurance?'

Ethel dug into her handbag, pulled out a drink coaster and held it up to him. As Ethel neared the final corridor before the front door, Crazy Craig stepped out in front of her, stark naked, holding a very sizeable erection in his hand.

'Oh, good grief,' said Ethel, 'Not the breathalyser again!'

Chinese proverbs

Virginity like bubble, one prick, all gone.

Man who run in front of car get tired.

Man who run behind car get exhausted.

Man with hand in pocket feel cocky all day.

Foolish man give wife grand piano, wise man give wife upright organ.

Man who walk through airport turnstile sideways going to Bangkok.

Man with one chopstick go hungry.

Man who scratch ass should not bite fingernails.

Man who eat many prunes get good run for money.

Baseball is wrong: man with four balls cannot walk.

Panties not best thing on earth, but next to best thing on earth!

War does not determine who is right, war determine who is left.

Wife who put husband in doghouse soon find him in cathouse.

Man who fight with wife all day get no piece at night.

It take many nails to build crib, but one screw to fill it.

Man who drive like hell, bound to get there.

Man who stand on toilet is high on pot.

Man who live in glass house should change clothes in basement.

Man who fish in other man's well often catch crabs.

Man who fart in church sit in own pew.

Crowded elevator smell different to midget.

Mother Superior was on her way to late morning prayers when she passed two novices just leaving early morning prayers, on their way to classes. As she passed the young ladies, Mother Superior said, 'Good morning ladies.'

The novices replied, 'Good morning, Mother Superior, may God be with you.'

But after they had passed, Mother Superior heard one say to the other, 'I think she got out of the wrong side of the bed this morning.'

This startled Mother Superior, but she chose not to pursue the issue. A little further down the hall, Mother Superior passed two of the Sisters who had been teaching at the convent for several years. She greeted them with, 'Good morning Sister Martha, Sister Jessica, may God give you wisdom for our students today.'

'Good morning, Mother Superior. Thank you, and may God be with you.' But again, after passing, Mother Superior overheard, 'She got out of the wrong side of bed today.'

Baffled, she started to wonder if she had spoken harshly, or with an irritated look on her face. She vowed to be more pleasant.

Looking down the hall, Mother Superior saw retired Sister Mary approaching, step by step, with her walker. As Sister Mary was rather deaf, Mother Superior had plenty of time to arrange a pleasant smile on her face before greeting Sister Mary.

'Good morning, Sister Mary. I'm so happy to see you up and about. I pray God watches over you today, and grants you a wonderful day.'

'Ah, good morning, Mother Superior, and thank you. I see you got up on the wrong side of bed this morning.'

Mother Superior was floored!

'Sister Mary, what have I done wrong? I have tried to be pleasant, but three times already today people have said that about me.'

Sister Mary stopped her walker, and looked Mother Superior in the face. 'Oh, don't take it personal, Mother Superior. It's just that you're wearing Father Murphy's slippers!'

My husband came home with a jar of Vaseline and said, 'This will make you happy tonight.'

He was right. When he went out of the bedroom, I squirted it all over the doorknobs. He couldn't get back in.

Three nuns were talking. The first nun said, 'I was cleaning the Fathers' room the other day and do you know what I found? A bunch of pornographic magazines.'

'What did you do?' the others asked.

'Well, of course I threw them in the trash.'

The second nun said, 'Well I can top that. I was in the Fathers' room putting away the laundry and I found a bunch of condoms.'

'Oh my,' gasped the others. 'What did you do?' they asked.

'I poked holes in all of them,' she replied.

The third nun said 'Oh, damn!!!'

A man walks into the dentist's office and after the dentist examines him, he says, 'That tooth has to come out. I'm going to give you a shot of Novocain and I'll be back in a few minutes.'

The man grabs the doc's arm, 'No way. I hate needles. I'm not having a shot!'

So the dentist says, 'Okay, we'll have to go with the gas.'

The man replies, 'Absolutely not. It makes me very sick for a couple of days. I'm not having gas.'

So the dentist steps out and comes back with a glass of water, 'Here,' he says. 'Take this pill.'

The man asks, 'What is it?'

The doc replies, 'Viagra.'

The man looks surprised, 'Will that kill the pain?' he asks.

'No,' replies the dentist, 'but it will give you something to hang on to while I pull your tooth!'

A guy falls asleep on the beach for several hours and gets a horrible sunburn. He goes to the hospital and is promptly admitted after being diagnosed with second-degree burns. He was already starting to blister and in agony.

The doctor prescribed continuous intravenous feeding with saline and electrolytes, a sedative, and a Viagra pill every four hours.

The nurse, rather astounded, said, 'What good will Viagra do him?'

The doctor replied, 'It'll keep the sheets off his legs.'

She married and had 13 children. Her husband died. She married again and had seven more children. Again, her husband died. But, she remarried and this time had five more children. Alas, she finally died.

Standing before her coffin, the preacher prayed for her. He thanked the Lord, for this very loving woman and said, 'Lord, they're finally together.'

One mourner leaned over and asked her friend, 'Do you think he means her first, second or third husband?'

The friend replied, 'I think he means her legs.'

A bloke is walking along a beach when he comes across a lamp partially buried in the sand. He picks up the lamp and gives it a rub. Two genies appear and they tell him he has been granted three wishes. The guy makes his three wishes and the genies disappear.

Next thing he knows he's in a bedroom in a mansion surrounded by fifty beautiful women. He makes love to all of them and begins to explore the house.

Suddenly he feels something soft underfoot, he looks down and the whole of the floor is covered in $100 bills. Next thing there is a knock at the door. He answers the door and standing there outside are two persons dressed in Ku Klux Klan outfits.

They drag him outside to the nearest tree, throw a rope over a limb and hang him by the neck until he is dead.

As the two Klansmen are walking away they remove their hoods, it's the two genies. One genie says to the other: 'Hey, I can understand the first wish, having all those beautiful women in a big mansion to make love to. I can also understand wanting to be a millionaire.'

'But why he wanted to be hung like a black man is beyond me.'

A man went into a local tavern and took a seat at the bar next to a woman patron. He turned to her and said, 'This is a special day, I'm celebrating.'

'What a coincidence,' said the woman, 'I'm celebrating, too.' She clinked glasses with him and asked, 'What are you celebrating?'

'I'm a chicken farmer,' he replied. 'For years all my hens were infertile, but today they're finally fertile.'

'What a coincidence, the woman said. 'My husband and I have been trying to have a child. Today, my gynaecologist told me I'm pregnant!

'How did your chickens become fertile?' she asked.

'I switched cocks,' he replied.

'What a coincidence,' she said.

A woman meets a gorgeous man in a bar. They talk, they connect, and they end up leaving together. They get back to his place, and as he shows her around his apartment, she notices that his bedroom is completely packed with sweet cuddly teddy bears.

Hundreds of cute small bears on a shelf all the way along the floor, cuddly medium-sized ones on a shelf a little higher, and huge enormous bears on the top shelf along the wall. The woman is surprised that this guy would have a collection of teddy bears, especially one that's so extensive, but she decides not to mention this to him, and actually is quite impressed by his sensitive side.

She turns to him, they kiss, and then they rip each other's clothes off and make hot steamy love.

After an intense night of passion with this sensitive guy, they are lying there together in the afterglow, the woman rolls over and asks, smiling, 'Well, how was it?'

The guy says, 'Help yourself to any prize from the bottom shelf.'

A man enters a restaurant and sits at a table. Looking around, he notices a gorgeous woman sitting at a table nearby, all alone. He calls the waiter over and asks him to send their most expensive bottle of Merlot over to her, knowing that if she accepts it she is his.

The waiter gets the bottle and takes it over to the girl, saying, 'This is from the gentleman over there,' indicating to him. She regards the wine coolly for a second and decides to send a note over to the man.

The waiter conveyed it to the gentleman. The note read: *'For me to accept this bottle, you need to have a Mercedes in your garage, a million dollars in the bank, and seven inches in your pants.'*

After reading the note, the man decided to compose one of his own in return. He handed it to the waiter and instructed him to return it to the lady.

It read: *'For your information - I happen to have a Ferrari Maranello, a Mercedes CL600 and a Lear Jet in my garage; plus I have over twenty million dollars in various banks. But, not even for a woman as beautiful as you, would I cut off three inches. Just send the bottle back please.'*

A wife came home just in time to find her husband in bed with another woman. With super-human strength borne of fury, she dragged him down the stairs, out the back door, and into the tool shed in the back yard and put his penis in a vice. She then secured it tightly and removed the handle.

Next she picked up a hacksaw. The husband was terrified, and screamed, 'Stop! Stop! You're not going to cut it off, are you?'

The wife, with a gleam of revenge in her eye, put the saw in her husband's hand and said … 'Nope. I'm going to set the shed on fire. You do whatever you have to!'

A Scottish soldier dressed in all his regalia went into a chemist in Glasgow, he walked up to the counter, opened up his sporran and pulled out a shredded condom and asked the chemist if he could repair it.

The chemist stifled a giggle and said, 'I'm sorry, sir, but we don't repair these things.' So the soldier picked up the condom and stormed out of the shop. The following day the soldier returned, walked up to the chemist opened up his sporran and started counting pennies out onto the counter.

The chemist asked, 'What can I do for you, sir?' and the soldier replied … 'The Regiment have decided to buy a new one!'

Four Catholic ladies are having coffee together, discussing how important their children are.

The first one tells her friends, 'My son is a priest. When he walks into a room, everyone calls him Father.'

The second Catholic woman chirps, 'Well, my son is a bishop. Whenever he walks into a room, people say, Your Grace.'

The third Catholic woman says smugly, 'Well, not to put you down, but my son is a cardinal. Whenever he walks into a room, people say, Your Eminence.'

The fourth Catholic woman sips her coffee in silence.

The first three women give her this subtle 'Well ...?'

She replies, 'My son is a gorgeous, 6'2", hard bodied, well-hung, male stripper. Whenever he walks into a room women say, My God!'

A man was in a terrible accident, and his 'manhood' was mangled and torn from his body. His doctor assured him that modern medicine could give him back his manhood, but that his insurance wouldn't cover the surgery, since it was considered cosmetic.

The doctor said the cost would be $3,500 for small, $6,500 for medium, $14,000 for large.

The man was sure he would want a medium or large, but the doctor urged him to talk it over with his wife before he made any decision.

The man called his wife on the phone and explained their options. The doctor came back into the room, and found the man looking dejected.

'Well, what have the two of you decided?' asked the doctor.

The man answered, 'She'd rather remodel the kitchen.'

As a mother passed her daughter's closed bedroom door, she heard a strange buzzing noise coming from within. Opening the door, she observed her daughter giving herself a real workout with a vibrator. Shocked, she asked, 'What in the world are you doing?'

The daughter replied, 'Mom, I'm thirty-five years old, unmarried, and this thing is about as close as I'll ever get to a husband. Please, go away and leave me alone.'

The next day, the girl's father heard the same buzz coming from the other side of the closed bedroom door. Upon entering the room, he observed his daughter making passionate love to her vibrator. When he questioned her as to what she was doing, the daughter said, 'Dad, I'm thirty-five years old, unmarried, and this thing is about as close as I'll ever get to a husband. Please, go away and leave me alone.'

A couple days later, the wife came home from a shopping trip, placed the groceries on the kitchen counter, and heard the by now familiar buzzing noise coming from, of all places, the family room. She cautiously entered that area and observed her husband sitting on the couch, staring at the TV with the vibrator next to him buzzing like crazy. The wife shrieked, 'What the hell are you doing?'

The husband replied, 'I'm watching the footy with my son-in-law.'

A wealthy man was having an affair with an Italian woman for several years.

One night, during one of their rendezvous, she confided in him that she was pregnant. Not wanting to ruin his reputation or his marriage, he paid a large sum of money if she would go to Italy to secretly have the child. If she stayed in Italy to raise the child, he would also provide child support until the child turned 18.

She agreed, but asked how he would know when the baby was born. To keep it discreet, he told her to simply mail him a postcard, and write 'spaghetti' on the back. He would then arrange for child support payments to begin.

One day, about eight months later, he came home to his confused wife.

'Honey,' she said, 'you received a very strange post card today.'

'Oh, just give it to me and I'll explain it,' he said. The wife obeyed, and watched as her husband read the card, turned white and fainted.

On the card was written, 'Spaghetti, Spaghetti, Spaghetti. Two with meatballs, one without.'

A golfer was involved in a terrible car crash and was rushed to the hospital. Just before he was put under, the surgeon popped in to see him.

'I have some good news and some bad news,' says the surgeon. 'The bad news is that I have to remove your right arm!'

'Oh God no!' cries the man. 'My golfing is over! Please Doc, what's the good news?'

'The good news is, I have another one to replace it with, but it's a woman's arm. I'll need your permission before I go ahead with the transplant.'

'Go for it, doc' says the man. 'As long as I can play golf again.'

The operation went well and a year later the man was out on the golf course when he bumped into the surgeon.

'Hi, how's the new arm?' asks the surgeon.

'Just great,' says the businessman. 'I'm playing the best golf of my life. My new arm has a much finer touch and my putting has really improved.'

'That's great,' said the surgeon.

'Not only that,' continued the golfer, 'my handwriting has improved, I've learned how to sew my own clothes and I've even taken up painting landscapes in watercolours.'

'Unbelievable!' said the surgeon, 'I'm so glad to hear the transplant was such a great success. Are you having any side effects?'

'Well, just one problem,' said the golfer, 'every time I get an erection, I also get a headache.'

John invited his mother over for dinner. During the meal, his mother couldn't help noticing how beautiful John's flat mate was. She had long been suspicious of a relationship between John and his flat mate and this only made her more curious.

Over the course of the evening, while watching the two interact, she started to wonder if there was more between John and the flat mate than met the eye. Reading his mom's thoughts, John volunteered, 'I know what you must be thinking, but I assure you, Julie and I are just flat mates.'

About a week later, Julie came to John and said, 'Ever since your mother came to dinner, I've been unable to find the beautiful silver gravy ladle. You don't suppose she took it, do you?'

John said, 'Well, I doubt it, but I'll write her a letter and ask just to be sure.'

So, he sat down and wrote: *'Dear Mother, I'm not saying you "did" take a gravy ladle from my house and I'm not saying you "did not". But the fact remains that one has been missing ever since you were here for dinner.'*

Several days later, John received a letter from his mother which read: *'Dear Son, I'm not saying that you "do" sleep with Julie, and I'm not saying that you "do not" sleep with Julie. But the fact remains that if she were sleeping in her own bed, she would have found the gravy ladle by now. Love, Mom.'*

An old man was sitting on a bench at the mall.

A young man walked up to the bench and sat down. He had spiked hair in all different colours: green, red, orange, blue and yellow. The old man just stared ... Over time, the young man noticed the old man was staring at him.

The young man finally said sarcastically, 'What's the matter, old man, never done anything wild in your life?'

Without batting an eye, the old man replied, 'Got drunk once when I was in the Marines, on a tropical island, and had sex with a parrot. I was just wondering if you were my son.'

Paul returned from a doctor's visit one day and told his wife Alma that the doctor said he only had 24 hours to live. Wiping away her tears, he asked her to make love to him. Of course she agreed and they made passionate love.

Six hours later, Paul went to her again, and said, 'Honey, now I only have 18 hours left to live. Maybe we could make love again?'

Alma agrees and again they make love. Later, Paul is getting into bed when he realised he now had only eight hours of life left. He touched Alma's shoulder and said, 'Honey? Please? Just one more time before I die.' She agreed, then afterward she rolled over and fell asleep.

Paul, however, heard the clock ticking in his head, and he tossed and turned until he was down to only four more hours. He tapped his wife on the shoulder to wake her up. 'Honey, I only have four hours left! Could we ...?'

His wife sat up abruptly, turned to him and said, 'Listen Paul, I have to get up in the morning! You don't.'

A young Japanese girl had been taught all her life that when she married she was to please her husband and never upset him. So the first morning of her honeymoon the young Japanese bride crawled out of bed after making love, stooped down to pick up her husband's clothes, and accidentally lets out a big fart.

She looked up and said: 'Aww, so sorry ... excuse please, front hole so happy back hole laugh out loud.'

One night a guy takes his girlfriend home. They are about to kiss each other goodnight, but the guy is feeling a little horny. With an air of confidence, he leans with his hand against the wall and, smiling, he says to her, 'Darling, would you give me a blow job?' Horrified, she replies, 'Are you mad? My parents will see us!'

Him: 'Oh come on! Who's gonna see us at this hour?'

Her: 'No, please. Can you imagine if we get caught?'
Him: 'Oh come on, there's nobody around, they're all sleeping!'
Her: 'No way. It's just too risky!'
Him (horny as hell): 'Oh please, please, I love you so much?!?'
Her: 'No, no, and no. I love you too, but I just can't!'
Him: 'Oh yes you can. Please?'
Her: 'No, no. I just can't!'
Him: 'I beg you ...'

Out of the blue, the light on the stairs goes on, and the girl's sister shows up in her pyjamas, hair disheveled, and in a sleepy voice she says, 'Dad says to go ahead and give him a blow job. Or I can do it. Or if need be, he'll come down himself and do it. But for God sake tell him to take his hand off the intercom!!!'

A man with a winking problem is applying for a position as a sales rep for a large company.

The interviewer looks over the man's application and says, 'You've graduated from the best schools, your recommendations are wonderful and your experience is unparalleled. Normally, we'd hire you without a second thought. However, a sales rep has a highly visible position and we're afraid that your constant winking will scare off potential customers. I'm sorry but we can't hire you.'

'But wait,' the sales rep says. 'If I take two aspirins I'll stop winking.'

'Really?' says the interviewer. 'Show me.'

The applicant reaches into his jacket and begins pulling out all sorts of condoms; red ones, blue ones, ribbed ones and even flavoured condoms. Finally, he finds a packet of aspirin. He tears it open, swallows two pills and stops winking.

'Well,' the interviewer says, 'that's all well and good, but this is a respectable company and we will not have an employee womanising all over the country.'

'Womanising?' the sales rep says. 'What do you mean? I'm happily married.'

'Well then,' the interviewer asks, 'how do you explain all these condoms?'

'Oh, that,' the sales rep sighs. 'Have you ever walked into a pharmacy, winking, and asked for aspirin?'

An airline passenger cabin was being served by an obviously gay flight attendant, who seemed to put everyone into a good mood as he served them food and drinks. As the plane prepared to descend, he came swishing down the aisle and announced to the passengers, 'Captain Marvey has asked me to announce that he'll be landing the big scary plane shortly, lovely people, so if you could just put up your trays that would be super.'

On his trip back up the aisle, he noticed that a well-dressed rather exotic looking woman hadn't moved a muscle.

'Perhaps you didn't hear me over those big brute engines. I asked you to raise your trazy-poo so the main man can pitty-pat us on the ground.'

She calmly turned her head and said, 'In my country, I am called a Princess. I take orders from no-one.'

To which the flight attendant replied, without missing a beat, 'Well, sweet-cheeks, in my country, I'm called a Queen, so I outrank you. Tray-up, bitch.'

The young new army Captain was assigned to a unit in a remote part of the Iraqi desert. During his first inspection, he noticed two camels hitched up behind the mess tent. He asked the Sergeant why the camels were kept there.

'Well, sir,' was the nervous reply, 'as you know, there are 250 men here and no women, and sir, sometimes the men have ... m-m-m ... urges. That's why we have the camels, sir.'

The Captain said, 'I can't say that I condone this, but I understand about urges, so the camels can stay.'

About a month later, the Captain started having a real problem with his own urges. Crazy with passion, he asked the Sergeant to bring a camel to his tent. Putting a stool behind the camel, the Captain stood on it, pulled down his pants, and had wild, insane sex with the camel. When he was done, panting heavily, he asked the Sergeant, 'Is that how the men do it?'

'Uh, no sir,' the Sergeant replied, 'they just ride the camels into town where the girls are.'

A young man and his date were parked on a back road some distance from town. They were about to make love when the girl stopped.

'I really should have mentioned this earlier, but I'm actually a hooker and I charge $20 for sex.'

The man reluctantly paid her, and they did their thing. After a cigarette, the man just sat in the driver's seat looking out the window.

'Why aren't we going anywhere?' asked the girl.

'Well, I should have mentioned this before, but I'm actually a taxi driver, and the fare back to town is $25 ...'

A young boy asks his father, 'Dad, is it OK for us guys to notice all the different kinds of boobs?'

Surprised, the father answers, 'Well, sure son, we wouldn't be normal if we didn't. There are all kinds of breasts, depending on a woman's age. In her twenties, a woman's breasts are like melons, round and firm. In her thirties to forties, they are like pears, still nice but hanging a bit. After fifty, they are like onions.'

'Onions, Dad?' the boy asks.

'Yeah' his Dad replies, 'you see them and they make you cry.'

Not to be outdone, his sister asks her mother, 'Mom, how many kinds of penises are there?'

The mother, delighted to have equal time, answers, 'Well, daughter, a man goes through three phases. In a man's twenties, his penis is like an oak, mighty and hard. In his thirties and forties, it is like a birch, flexible but reliable. After his fifties, it is like a Christmas tree.'

'A Christmas tree?' the daughter asks.

'Yep,' her Mom replies, 'all dried up and the balls are only there for decoration.'

A man boarded an aircraft at Heathrow and took his seat. As he settled in, he noticed a very beautiful woman boarding the plane. He realised she was heading straight towards his seat and bingo! She took the seat right beside him.

Eager to strike up a conversation, he blurted out, 'Business trip or vacation?'

She turned, smiled enchantingly and said, 'Business. I'm going to the Annual Nymphomaniac Convention in the United States.'

He swallowed hard. Here was the most gorgeous woman he had ever seen sitting next to him, and she was going to a meeting for nymphomaniacs. Struggling to maintain his composure, he calmly asked, 'What's your business role at this convention?'

'Lecturer,' she responded. 'I use my experience to debunk some of the popular myths about sexuality.'

'Really,' he smiled, 'what myths are those?'

'Well,' she explained, 'one popular myth is that African American men are the most well-endowed when, in fact, it's the Native American Indian who is most likely to possess that trait. Another popular myth is that French men are the best lovers, when actually it is the men of Greek descent. We have also found that the best potential lovers in all categories are the Irish.'

Suddenly the woman became uncomfortable and blushed. 'I'm sorry,' she said, 'I really shouldn't be discussing this with you, I don't even know your name.'

'Tonto,' the man said ... 'Tonto Papadopoulos, but my friends call me Paddy.'

Two old friends were just about to tee off at the first hole of their local golf course when a chap carrying a golf bag called out to them, 'Do you mind if I join you? My partner didn't turn up.'

'Sure,' they said, 'You're welcome.'

So they started playing and enjoyed the game and the company of the newcomer. Part way around the course, one of the friends asked the newcomer, 'What do you do for a living?'

'I'm a hit man,' was the reply.

'You're joking!' was the response.

'No, I'm not,' he said, reaching into his golf bag, and pulling out a beautiful Martini sniper's rifle with a large telescopic sight. 'Here are my tools.'

'That's a beautiful telescopic sight,' said the other friend. 'Can I take a look? I think I might be able to see my house from here.'

So he picked up the rifle and looked through the sight in the direction of his house.

'Yeah, I can see my house all right. This sight is fantastic. I can see right in the window. Wow, I can see my wife in the bedroom. Ha ha, I can see she's naked! What's that? Wait a minute, that's my neighbour in there with her ... he's naked as well! The bitch!'

He turned to the hit man. 'How much do you charge for a hit?'

'I do a flat rate, for you, one thousand dollars every time I pull the trigger.'

'Can you do two for me now?'

'Sure, what do you want?'

'First, shoot my wife, she's always been mouthy, so shoot her in the mouth. Then the neighbour, he's a mate of mine, a bit of a dickhead, so just shoot his cock off to teach him a lesson.'

The hit man took the rifle and took aim, standing perfectly still for a few minutes.

'Are you going to do it or not?' said the friend impatiently.

'Just wait a moment, be patient,' said the hit man calmly, 'I think I can save you a thousand bucks here ...'

There was this couple that had been married for 20 years. Every time they made love the husband always insisted on turning off the light. Well, after 20 years the wife felt this was ridiculous. She figured she would break him out of this crazy habit.

So one night, while they were in the middle of a wild, screaming, romantic session, she turned on the lights.

She looked down ... and saw her husband was holding a battery-operated pleasure device ... a vibrator! Soft, wonderful and larger than a real one. She went completely ballistic.

'You impotent bastard,' she screamed at him. 'How could you be lying to me all of these years? You better explain yourself!'

The husband looks her straight in the eyes and says calmly, 'I'll explain the toy ... you explain the kids.'

Lulu was a prostitute, but she didn't want her grandma to know. One day, the police raided a whole group of prostitutes at a sex party in a hotel, and Lulu was among them.

The police took them outside and had all the prostitutes line up along the driveway when suddenly, Lulu's grandma came by and saw her granddaughter.

Grandma asked, 'Why are you standing in line here, dear?'

Not willing to let her grandmother know the truth, Lulu told her that the policemen were passing out free oranges and she was just lining up for some.

'Why, that's awfully nice of them. I think I'll get some for myself,' Grandma said, and she proceeded to the back of the line.

A policeman was going down the line asking for information from all of the prostitutes. When he got to Grandma, he was bewildered and exclaimed, 'Wow, still going at it at your age? How do you do it?'

Grandma replied, 'Oh, it's easy, dear. I just take my dentures out, rip the skin back and suck them dry.'

The policeman fainted.

In Pharmacology all drugs have two names, a trade name and a generic name.

For example, the trade name of Tylenol also has a generic name of Acetaminophen. Aleve is also called Naproxen.

Amoxil is also called Amoxicillin, and Advil is also called Ibuprofen.

The FDA has been looking for a generic name for Viagra. After careful consideration by a team of government experts, it recently announced that it has settled on the generic name of mycoxafloppin. Also considered were mycoxafailin, mydixadrupin, mydixarizin, mydixadud, dixafix and of course, ibepokin.

A lady goes on vacation alone to the Caribbean wishing her husband had been able to join her. Upon arriving, she meets a black man, and after a night of passionate lovemaking she asks him, 'What is your name?'

'I can't tell you!' the black man says.

Every night they meet and every night she asks him again what his name is and he always responds the same, he cannot tell her. On her last night there she asks again, 'Can you please tell me your name?'

'I can't because you will make fun of me!' the black man says.

'There is no reason for me to laugh at you,' the lady says.

'Fine, my name is Snow,' the black man replies.

And the lady bursts into laughter, and the black man gets mad and says, 'I knew you would make fun of it.'

The lady replied, 'It's my husband that won't believe me when I tell him that I had ten inches of Snow every day in the Caribbean!'

A man was not really happy about his manhood ... it was actually too long, 50cm long. He did not know what to do and went to a witch to ask for advice.

The witch thought for a long time before she said, 'Walk into the forest and you will meet a frog. Ask the frog if it wants to marry you. If it says "No" your manhood will shrink 10cm, but if it says "Yes" it will grow 10cm, so the risk is yours.'

The man thought about this for a while but decided it was worth the risk. He walked into the forest, found the frog and asked it, 'Will you marry me little frog?'

'No,' said the frog.

The man ran home and measured his manhood. Happily he found that it had shrunk down to 40cm. The man was so excited about the results that he ran back into the forest and asked the frog again. 'Will you marry me little frog?'

'No,' said the frog.

The man ran home and measured his manhood. Again he found that it had shrunk 10cm down to 30cm. The man was thinking '20cm, that would be the perfect size,' and ran back into the forest.

He met the frog again and asked him again, 'Will you marry me little frog?'

The frog answered him, 'Heavens man, what is wrong with you? I already told you NO! NO! NO!'

It was George the mailman's last day on the job after 35 years of carrying the mail through all kinds of weather to the same neighbourhood. When he arrived at the first house on his route, he was greeted by the whole family who roundly and soundly congratulated him and sent him on his way with a tidy gift envelope.

At the second house, they presented him with a box of fine cigars. The folks at the third house handed him a selection of terrific fishing lures.

At the fourth house he was met at the door by a strikingly beautiful woman in a revealing negligee. She took him by the hand, gently led him through the door and up the stairs to the bedroom where she blew his mind with the most passionate love he had ever experienced! When he had enough, they went downstairs where she fixed him a giant breakfast; eggs, potatoes, ham, sausage, blueberry waffles, and fresh-squeezed orange juice. When he was truly satisfied she poured him a cup of steaming coffee.

As she was pouring, he noticed a dollar bill sticking out from under the cup's bottom edge.

'All of this was just too wonderful for words,' he said, 'but what's the dollar for?'

'Well,' she said, 'last night, I told my husband that today would be your last day and that we should do something special for you. I asked him what to give you, and he said, "Screw him. Give him a dollar." The breakfast was my idea!!'

Bob joins a very exclusive nudist colony. On his first day he takes off his clothes and starts wandering around. A gorgeous petite blonde walks by him and he immediately gets an erection. The woman notices his erection, comes over to him grinning sweetly and says, 'Sir, did you call for me?'

Bob replies, 'No, what do you mean?'

She says, 'You must be new here; let me explain. It's a rule here that if I give you an erection, it implies you called for me.'

Smiling, she then leads him to the side of a pool, lays down on a towel, eagerly pulls him to her and happily lets him have his way with her.

Bob continues exploring the facilities. He enters a sauna, sits down, and farts. Within a few seconds a huge, horribly corpulent, hairy man with a firm erection lumbers out of the steam towards him.

The huge man says, 'Sir, did you call for me?'

Bob replies, 'No, what do you mean?'

The huge man, 'You must be new here; it is a rule that when you fart, it implies you called for me.' The huge man then easily spins Bob around, bends him over the bench and has his way with him.

Bob rushes back to the colony office. He is greeted by the smiling naked receptionist, 'May I help you?'

Bob says, 'Here is your card and key back. You can keep the $500 joining fee.'

Receptionist, 'But Sir, you've only been here a couple of hours; you only saw a small fraction of our facilities ...'

Bob replies, 'Listen lady, I am 58 years old, I get a hard-on twice a month, but I fart 15 times a day!'

One day, in line at the company cafeteria, Jack says to Mike behind him, 'My elbow hurts like hell. I guess I'd better see a doctor.'

'Listen, you don't have to spend that kind of money,' Mike replies. 'There's a diagnostic computer down at K-Mart. Just give it a urine sample and the computer will tell you what's wrong and what to do about it. It takes ten seconds and costs $10 ... a hell of a lot cheaper than a doctor.'

So Jack deposits a urine sample in a small jar and takes it to K-Mart. He deposits $10, and the computer lights up nd asks for the urine sample. He pours the sample into the slot and waits.

Ten seconds later, the computer ejects a printout:

You have tennis elbow. Soak your arm in warm water and avoid heavy activity. It will improve in two weeks.

That evening while thinking how amazing this new technology was, Jack began wondering if the computer could be fooled. He mixed some tap water, a stool sample from his dog, urine samples from his wife and daughter, and masturbated into the mixture for good measure. Jack hurries back to K-Mart, eager to check the results. He deposits $10, pours in his concoction, and awaits the results.

The computer prints the following:

1. *Your tap water is too hard. Get a water softener.*
2. *Your dog has ringworm. Bathe him with anti-fungal shampoo.*
3. *Your daughter has a cocaine habit. Get her into rehab.*
4. *Your wife is pregnant ... twin girls. They aren't yours. Get a lawyer.*
5. *If you don't stop playing with yourself, your elbow will never get better.*

Two men are in the doctor's office waiting to get vasectomies. A nurse comes in and asks the men to strip and put on their medical gowns while they wait for the doctor. A few minutes later she comes back, reaches under one man's gown and begins to masturbate him.

Shocked, he says, 'My God, what are you doing?'

To which she replies, 'We have to vacate the sperm from your system to have a clean procedure.' Not wanting to cause a problem, the man relaxes and enjoys it as she completes her task.

The second man watches all of this and by the time the nurse turns to him, he is quite ready for his turn. To his surprise, she drops to her knees, opens her lips and begins to give him a blow job.

The first man says, 'Hey, what is this? Why is it that I get a hand job and he gets a blow job?'

The nurse says, 'That, my dear sir, is the difference between Medicare and private insurance!!'

A female TV reporter arranged for an interview with a farmer living just outside town, to find the main cause of the Mad Cow Disease.

'Good evening, Sir, I'm here to collect information on the possible source of Mad Cow Disease. Can you offer any reason for this disease?'

The farmer stared at the reporter and said, 'Do you know that a bull mounts a cow only once a year!'

The lady reporter (obviously embarrassed), 'Well, Sir, that's a new piece of information, but what's the relation between this phenomenon and Mad Cow Disease?'

The farmer, 'And, madam, do you know that we milk a cow twice a day?'

The reporter, 'Sir, this is really valuable information, but what about getting to the point?'

The farmer, 'Just a minute, I am getting to the point, madam. Just imagine, if I was playing with your tits twice a day and only screwing you once a year, wouldn't you get mad … eh ?'

A chicken and an egg are lying in bed. The chicken is leaning against the headboard smoking a cigarette, with a satisfied smile on its face.

The egg, looking a bit frustrated, grabs the sheet, rolls over, and says, 'Well, I guess we finally answered THAT question.'

My neighbour found out her dog could hardly hear so she took it to the veterinarian.

He found that the problem was hair in its ears so he cleaned both ears and the dog could hear fine. The vet then proceeded to tell the lady that if she wanted to keep this from recurring she should go to the store and get some 'Nair' hair remover and rub it in its ears once a month.

The lady goes to the drug store and gets some 'Nair' hair remover.

At the register the druggist tells her, 'If you're going to use this under your arms don't use deodorant for a few days.'

The lady says, 'I'm not using it under my arms.'

The druggist says, 'If you're using it on your legs don't shave for a couple of days.'

The lady says, 'I'm not using it on my legs either; if you must know, I'm using it on my schnauzer.'

The druggist says, 'Stay off your bicycle for a week.'

They took a survey of 10,000 women in Washington DC, and asked, 'Would you have sex with Bill Clinton?'

86% said, 'Never again.'

A man suspected his wife of seeing another man. So, he hires a famous Asian detective to observe and inform him of any activities that might develop. A few days later, he received this report:

Most Honourable Sir,

You leave house. He come house. I watch.

He and she leave house. I follow.

He and she get on train. I follow.

He and she go in hotel. I climb tree - look in window.

He kiss she. She kiss he.

He strip she. She strip he.

He play with she. She play with he.

I play with me. I fall out tree, not see.

NO FEE!

ADULT JOKES

A guy took a blonde out on a date. Eventually they ended up parked at a 'Lovers' Point' where they started making out. After things started getting pretty good, he thought he might get lucky, so he asked her, 'Do you want to go in the back seat?'

'NO!' she answered.

Okay, he thought, maybe she's not ready yet. Now he has her shirt and skirt off, the windows are steamed, and things are getting really hot, so he asks again, 'Do you want to go in the back seat?'

'NO!' she answers again.

Now he has her bra off, they're both very sweaty, and she even has his pants unzipped. Okay, he thinks, she HAS to want it now. 'Do you want to go in the back seat NOW?' he asks again.

'NO!' she answers yet again.

Frustrated, he demands 'Well, why not!'

'Because I want to stay in the front with you!'

A guy walks into a bar with a pet alligator by his side. He puts the alligator up on the bar. He turns to the astonished patrons.

'I'll make you a deal. I'll open this alligator's mouth and place my genitals inside. Then the gator will close his mouth for one minute. He'll then open his mouth and I'll remove my unit unscathed. In return for witnessing this spectacle, each of you will buy me a drink.'

The crowd murmured their approval. The man stood up on the bar, dropped his trousers, and placed his privates in the alligator's open mouth. The gator closed his mouth as the crowd gasped. After a minute, the man grabbed a beer bottle and rapped the alligator hard on the top of its head. The alligator opened his mouth and the man removed his genitals unscathed as promised.

The crowd cheered and the first of his free drinks were delivered. The man stood up again and made another offer.

'I'll pay anyone $100 who's willing to give it a try.' A hush fell over the crowd. After a while, a hand went up in the back of the bar. A blonde woman timidly spoke up.

'I'll give it a go … but don't hit me on the head so hard with the beer bottle!'

———————— ¡ ¿ ¡ ————————

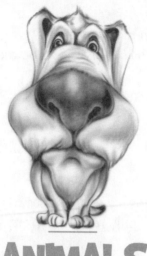

ANIMALS

A talking frog goes into a bank and approaches the teller. He sees right away from her window nameplate that her name is Patricia Whack. (He can read, too!)

'Miss Whack, I'd like to get a $30,000 loan to take a holiday.'

Patty looks at the frog in disbelief. In staying with the bank policy pertaining to customer relations, she kindly asks him his name.

The frog says his name is Kermit Jagger, adds the fact that his dad is Mick Jagger, and that it's OK to give him a loan because he knows the bank manager personally.

Patty explains that he will need to secure the loan with some collateral. The frog says, 'Sure. No problem. I have this,' and produces a tiny porcelain elephant, about half an inch tall, bright pink and perfectly formed.

Very confused, Patty explains that she'll have to consult with the bank manager and disappears into a back office.

She finds the manager and says, 'There's a frog at my window who says his name is Kermit Jagger, he claims to know you, says his dad is Mick Jagger, and wants to borrow $30,000, AND he wants to use this as collateral.'

She holds up the tiny pink elephant. 'I mean, what in the world is this thing?'

The bank manager looks back at her and says ... 'It's a knickknack, Patty Whack. Give the frog a loan. His old man's a Rolling Stone.'

(You're singing it, aren't you?!! - I knew you would!)

A librarian was working at her duties when she heard a strange scratching noise coming from the front of her desk, leaning over she saw a small red hen which said 'Buurrk, Buk, Buk, Buk.'

The librarian passed over a book which the little red hen tucked under her wing and walked out of the library. This occurred each day for a week and by this time the Librarian could not contain her curiosity any longer. So she followed the little red hen who walked around the rear of the building and down into the ornamental gardens where she placed the book at the edge of a pond. A few minutes later a small green frog hopped onto a stone at the water's edge, glanced briefly at the book and said ... 'Redit, Redit, Redit.'

A duck walks into a pub and says to the barman: 'Got any bread?'
Barman: 'No.'
Duck: 'Got any bread?'
Barman: 'No.'
Duck: 'Got any bread?'
Barman: 'No, we have no bread.'
Duck: 'Got any bread?'
Barman: 'No, we haven't got any f@#$%^g bread.'
Duck: 'Got any bread?'
Barman: 'No, are you deaf, we haven't got any f@#$%^g bread, ask me again and I'll nail your f@#$%^g beak to the bar, you irritating bast**d bird!'

Duck: 'Got any nails?'
Barman : 'No.'
Duck: 'Got any bread?

———————— ᛁᛘᛁ ————————

Once upon a time there was a frog that lived in a lake all by himself. A local witch had given him special powers. One day he finally ventured out of the lake to get his first glimpse of the world outside. The first thing he saw was a bear chasing a rabbit and so he called out to them and asked them to stop.

Then he said to them, 'I am a magical frog and since you are the first two animals I have ever seen, I am going to grant you both three wishes. You will each take turns using them and you have to use them now.'

The bear, which was obnoxious and greedy, went first, 'I would like for every bear in this forest to be female except for me.' A magical sound and it was done.

Then the rabbit said, 'I would like a helmet.' This confused both the frog and the bear, but after a magical sound there was a helmet.

It was the bear's turn again. 'I would like for every bear in the neighbouring forest to be female.' A magical sound and it was done.

The rabbit went again. 'I would like a motorcycle.' Both the frog and the bear wondered why the rabbit didn't just ask for a lot of money with which he could buy himself a motorcycle, but after a magical sound there was a motorcycle.

The bear took his last wish. 'I would like for all the bears in the world to be female except for me.' A magical sound and it was done.

The rabbit then put on his helmet, started up the motorcycle, and said, 'I wish the bear was gay,' and sped off.

———————— ᛁᛘᛁ ————————

Three handsome male dogs are walking down the street when they see a beautiful, enticing, female Poodle. The three male dogs fall all over themselves in an effort to reach her first. The males are speechless before her beauty, hoping for just a glance from her in return.

Aware of her charms and her obvious effect on the three suitors, she decides to be kind and tells them, 'The first one who can use the words "liver and cheese" together in an imaginative, intelligent sentence can go out with me.'

The sturdy, muscular black Lab speaks up quickly and says, 'I love liver and cheese.'

'Oh, how childish,' said the Poodle. 'That shows no imagination or intelligence whatsoever.' She turns to the tall, shiny Golden Retriever and says, 'How well can you do?'

'Um ... I HATE liver and cheese,' blurts the Golden Retriever.

'My, my,' said the Poodle. 'It's hopeless. That's just as dumb as the Lab's sentence.'

She then turns to the last of the three dogs and says, 'How about you, little guy?'

The last of the three, tiny in stature but big in fame and finesse, is the Taco Bell Chihuahua. He gives her a smile, a sly wink, turns to the Golden Retriever and the Lab and says ...

'Liver alone. Cheese mine.'

Two cows were standing next to each other in a field.

Daisy said to Dolly, 'I was artificially inseminated this morning.'

'I don't believe you,' said Dolly.

'It's true, honest, no bull!'

Donald and Daisy Duck finally got married. On the wedding night it got to the moment to consummate the marriage.

Daisy advised Donald that she was not using any form of contraception and that he should go down to the hotel pharmacy and buy a condom. So Donald goes to the hotel pharmacy and asks the chemist for a condom. The chemist turns takes a condom off the shelf and says to Donald, 'Will I put this on your bill?'

Donald shocked replies, 'No thank you very much!! What sort of a duck do you think I am?'

An out-of-towner drove his car into a ditch in a desolated area. Luckily, a local farmer came to help with his big strong horse named Buddy.

He hitched Buddy up to the car and yelled, 'Pull, Nellie, pull!'

Buddy didn't move.

Then the farmer hollered, 'Pull, Buster, pull!'

Buddy didn't respond.

Once more the farmer commanded, 'Pull, Coco, pull!' Nothing.

Then the farmer nonchalantly said, 'Pull, Buddy, pull!' And the horse easily dragged the car out of the ditch.

The motorist was most appreciative and very curious. He asked the farmer why he called his horse by the wrong name three times.

'Well ... Buddy is blind and if he thought he was the only one pulling, he wouldn't even try!'

ANIMAL JOKES

A duck walks into a pub and orders a pint of lager and a ham sandwich. The publican looks at him and says, 'But you're a duck'.

'I see your eyes are working,' replies the duck.

'And you talk!' exclaims the publican.

'I see your ears are working,' says the duck. 'Now can I have my beer and my sandwich please? I'm working on the building site across the road as a plasterer.'

Then the duck drinks his beer, eats his sandwich and leaves.

This continues for two weeks. Then one day the circus comes to town. The ringleader of the circus comes into the pub and the publican says to him, 'You're with the circus aren't you? I know this duck that would be just brilliant in your circus, he talks, drinks beer and everything!'

'Sounds marvellous,' says the ringleader. 'Get him to give me a call.'

So the next day when the duck comes into the pub the publican says, 'Hey Mr. Duck, I reckon I can line you up with a top job, paying really good money!'

'Yeah?' says the duck. 'Sounds great, where is it?'

'At the circus,' says the publican.

'The circus?' the duck enquires.

'That's right,' replies the publican.

'The circus? That place with the big tent? With all the animals? With the big canvas roof with the hole in the middle?' asks the duck.

'That's right!' says the publican.

The duck looks confused, 'What on earth would they want with a plasterer?'

A man went to visit his 90-year-old grandfather, who lived in a very remote, secluded rural area. After spending the night at the house, his grandfather prepared a breakfast of eggs and bacon.

As the man was eating he noticed a film like substance on the plate, and he asked, 'Grandfather, are these plates clean?'

His grandfather replied, 'They're as clean as cold water can get 'em, so go on and finish your meal.'

Later on that day, Grandfather prepared a lunch of hamburger steak and new potatoes. As the man was eating he noticed tiny specks around the edge of his plate, and a substance that looked like dried egg yolk. Concerned about his health, he asked again, 'Grandfather, are you sure that these plates are clean?'

Without looking up from his plate, his grandfather replied, 'I told you before, those dishes are as clean as cold water can get 'em, now don't ask me about it any more!'

That evening, the man decided to go out to a restaurant for dinner in a nearby town. As he walked toward his car, his Grandfather's dog started growling and would not let him pass.

'Grandfather,' the man complained, 'your dog won't let me by.'

Without diverting his attention from the TV, grandfather shouted, 'Coldwater! Get up and move out of the way and let the boy pass!'

―――――――― ₰ ₰ ₰ ――――――――

Q.: What is a shitzu?
A.: A zoo without any animals!

―――――――― ₰ ₰ ₰ ――――――――

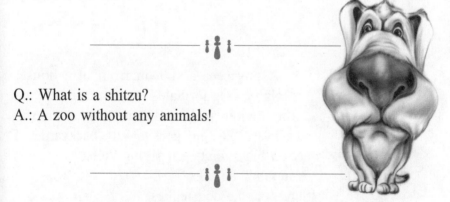

A few days before Christmas, a man enters a pet store, looking for a unique gift for his wife. The manager tells him he has just what he's looking for! A beautiful parrot named Chet that sings Christmas Carols.

He brings the husband over to a colourful but quiet bird. The man agrees that Chet certainly is pretty, but he doesn't seem to be much for singing. The manager tells him to watch, as he reaches into his pocket and pulls out a lighter. The pet store manager lights the lighter and holds it under Chet's left foot. Immediately Chet starts singing, *Silent Night*.

The man becomes very impressed with Chet's singing abilities and watches as the manager moves the lighter underneath Chet's right foot. Chet now starts singing *Jingle Bells*. The man says that Chet is perfect and that he'll take him.

He rushes home to his wife, and insists upon giving her this wonderful gift immediately. He presents Chet and starts to explain his special talent. Demonstrating, he holds a lighter under Chet's left foot and the bird sings *Silent Night* again. He then moves the lighter under Chet's right foot and again Chet lets loose with a round of *Jingle Bells*.

The wife is terribly impressed, and with a mischievous grin, asks her husband what happens if he holds the lighter between Chet's legs instead. Curious, the husband moves the lit lighter between the bird's legs, and the bird begins to sing ... *Chet's Nuts Roasting On An Open Fire*.

A guy sees a sign in front of a house, 'Talking Dog for Sale.' He rings the bell and the owner tells him the dog is in the backyard. The guy goes into the backyard and sees a black mutt just sitting there.

'You talk?' he asks.

'Sure do,' the dog replies.

'So, what's your story?'

The dog looks up and says, 'Well, I discovered my gift of talking pretty young and I wanted to help the government, so I told ASIO about my gift and in no time they had me jetting from country to country, sitting in rooms with spies and world leaders, because no one figured a dog would be

eavesdropping. I was one of their most valuable s[...]
running.

'The jetting around really tired me out, and [...]
getting any younger and I wanted to settle dow[...]
for a job at the airport to do some undercov[...]
mostly wandering near suspicious characters and listening [...]
uncovered some incredible dealings there and was awarded a
bunch of medals. Had a wife, a load of puppies, and now I'm
just retired.'

The guy is amazed. He goes back in and asks the owner what
he wants for the dog. The owner says, 'Ten Bucks.'

The guy says, 'This dog is amazing. Why on earth are you
selling him so cheap?'

'Cause he's a b#))$* liar. He didn't do any of that.'

A wealthy man decided to go on a safari in Africa. He took
his faithful pet dachshund along for company.

One day, the dachshund starts chasing butterflies and before
long the dachshund discovers that he is lost. So, wandering about,
he notices a leopard heading rapidly in his direction with the
obvious intention of having lunch.

The dachshund thinks 'OK, I'm in deep trouble now!'

Then he noticed some bones on the ground close by, and
immediately settles down to chew on the bones with his back
to the approaching cat. Just as the leopard is about to leap, the
dachshund exclaims loudly, 'Boy, that was one delicious leopard.
I wonder if there are any more around here?'

Hearing this, the leopard halts his attack in mid-stride, as a
look of terror comes over him, and slinks away into the trees.

'Whew,' says the leopard. 'That was close. That dachshund
nearly had me.'

Meanwhile, a monkey who had been watching the whole
scene from a nearby tree figures he can put this knowledge to
good use and trade it for protection from the leopard. So, off

goes. But the dachshund saw him heading after the leopard with great speed, and figured that something must be up.

The monkey soon catches up with the leopard, spills the beans and strikes a deal for himself with the leopard. The leopard is furious at being made a fool of and says, 'Here monkey, hop on my back and see what's going to happen to that conniving canine.'

Now the dachshund sees the leopard coming with the monkey on his back, and thinks, 'What am I going to do now?'

But instead of running, the dog sits down with his back to his attackers, pretending he hasn't seen them yet.

Just when they get close enough to hear, the dachshund says, 'Where's that monkey? I sent him off half an hour ago to bring me another leopard.'

Baby Bear goes downstairs and sits in his small chair at the table, he looks into his small bowl. It is empty. 'Who's been eating my porridge?!!' he squeaks.

Papa Bear arrives at the big table and sits in his big chair. He looks into his big bowl, and it is also empty. 'Who's been eating my porridge?!!' he roars.

Momma Bear puts her head through the serving hatch from the kitchen and yells, 'For Christ's sake, how many times do we have to go through this with you idiots? It was Momma Bear who got up first, it was Momma Bear who woke everyone in the house, it was Momma Bear who made the coffee, it was Momma Bear who unloaded the dishwasher from last night, and put everything away, it was Momma Bear who went out in the cold early morning air to fetch the newspaper, it was Momma Bear who set the damn table, it was Momma Bear who put the friggin cat out, cleaned the litter box, and filled the cat's water and food dish, and, now that you've decided to drag your sorry bear-asses downstairs, and grace Momma Bear's kitchen with your grumpy presence, listen good, I'm only going to say this one more time.'

'I haven't made the f@#$%^g porridge yet!!'

A lady goes to her priest one day and tell[] have a problem. I have two female parrots, b[] how to say one thing.'

'What do they say?' the priest inquired.

'They say, "Hi, we're hookers! Do you want to have some fun?"'

'That's obscene!' the priest exclaimed.

Then he thought for a moment. 'You know,' he said, 'I may have a solution to your problem. I have two male talking parrots, which I have taught to pray and read the Bible. Bring your two parrots over to my house, and we'll put them in the cage with Francis and Job. My parrots can teach your parrots to praise and worship and your parrots are sure to stop saying ... that phrase ... in no time.'

'Thank you,' the woman responded, 'this may very well be the solution.'

The next day, she brought her female parrots to the priest's house.

As he ushered her in, she saw that his two male parrots were inside their cage, holding rosary beads and praying. Impressed, she walked over and placed her parrots in with them. After a few minutes, the female parrots cried out in unison, 'Hi, we're hookers! Do you want to have some fun?'

There was stunned silence. Shocked, one male parrot looked over at the other male parrot and exclaimed, 'Put the beads away, Frank. Our prayers have been answered!'

A hunter walking through the jungle found a huge dead dinosaur with a pygmy standing beside it. Amazed, he asked, 'Did you kill that?'

The pygmy said, 'Yes.'

The hunter asked, 'How could a little fella like you kill a huge beast like that?'

Said the pygmy, 'I killed it with my club.'

The astonished hunter asked, 'How big is your club?'

The pygmy replied, 'There's about 90 of us.'

There's a bear and a rabbit in the forest by a bush doing number 2's. The bear turns around to the rabbit and asks him if he has trouble with poo sticking to his fur.

The rabbit said, 'No'. So the bear wiped his bum with the rabbit!

A guy walks into a bar with an octopus.

He sits the octopus down on a stool and tells everyone in the bar that this is a very talented octopus. 'He can play any musical instrument in the world.'

Everyone in the bar laughs at the man, calling him an idiot. So he says that he will wager $50 to anyone who has an instrument that the octopus can't play.

A customer walks up with a guitar and sets it beside the octopus. Immediately the octopus picks up the guitar and starts playing better than Jimmy Hendrix. The guitar owner pays up the $50.

Another customer walks up with a trumpet. This time the octopus plays the trumpet better than Miles Davis. The trumpet owner coughs up the $50.

Then Jim, a Scotsman plonks some bagpipes on the table. The octopus fumbles with the bagpipes for a minute and then backs off with a confused look.

'Ha!' the Scot says. 'Can ye nae plae it?'

The octopus looks up at him and says, 'Play it? I'm going to make love to it as soon as I figure out how to get its pyjamas off.'

A guy named David received a parrot for his birthday. The parrot was fully-grown, with a bad attitude and an even worse vocabulary. Every other word was a curse word. Those that weren't curse words were, to say the least, rude.

David tried hard to change the bird's attitude and was constantly saying polite words, playing soft music, anything he could think of to try and set a good example. Nothing worked. He yelled at the bird and the bird yelled back. He shook the bird and the bird just got angrier and ruder.

Finally, in a moment of desperation, David put the parrot in the freezer. For a few moments he heard the bird squawk and kick and scream! Then suddenly there was quiet. Not a sound for half a minute. David was frightened that he might have hurt the bird and quickly opened the freezer door.

The parrot calmly stepped out onto David's extended arm and said, 'I believe I may have offended you with my rude language and actions. I will endeavor at once to correct my behavior. I really am truly sorry and beg your forgiveness.'

David was astonished at the bird's change in attitude and was about to ask what had made such a dramatic change when the parrot continued, 'May I ask what the turkey did?'

Little Nancy was in the garden filling in a hole when her neighbor peered over the fence. Interested in what the cheeky-faced youngster was doing, he politely asked, 'What are you up to there, Nancy?'

'My goldfish died,' replied Nancy tearfully, without looking up, 'and I've just buried him.'

The neighbor was concerned, 'That's an awfully big hole for a goldfish, isn't it?'

Nancy patted down the last heap of earth then replied, 'That's because he's inside your f@#$%^ cat.'

A horse and a chicken are playing in a meadow. The horse falls into a mud hole and is sinking. He calls to the chicken to go and get the farmer to help pull him out to safety. The chicken runs to the farm but the farmer can't be found. So he drives the farmer's Mercedes back to the mud hole and ties some rope around the bumper. He then throws the other end of the rope to his friend, the horse, and drives the car forward saving him from sinking!

A few days later, the chicken and horse were playing in the meadow again and the chicken fell into the mud hole. The chicken yelled to the horse to go and get some help from the farmer.

The horse said, 'I think I can stand over the hole!' So he stretched over the width of the hole and said, 'Grab for my "thingy" and pull yourself up.' The chicken did so and pulled himself to safety.

The moral of the story is, if you are hung like a horse, you don't need a Mercedes to pick up chicks.

Three tortoises, Mick, Andy and Roy, decide to go on a picnic. So Mick packs the picnic basket with beer and sandwiches. The trouble is the picnic site is 10km away so it takes them 10 days to get there.

When they get there Mick unpacks the food and beer. 'OK Roy give me the bottle opener.'

'I didn't bring it,' says Roy. 'I thought you packed it.'

Mick gets worried. He turns to Andy and asks, 'Did you bring the bottle opener?' But he didn't bring it either. So they're stuck ten miles from home without a bottle opener.

Mick and Andy beg Roy to go back for it. But he refuses as he says they will eat all the sandwiches. After two hours, and after they have sworn on their tortoise lives that they will not eat the sandwiches, he finally agrees.

So Roy sets off down the road at a steady pace. 20 days pass and he still isn't back and Mick and Andy are starving, but a promise is a promise. Another five days and he still isn't back, but a promise is a promise.

Finally they can't take it any longer so they take out a sandwich each and just as they are about to eat it, Roy pops up from behind a rock and shouts, 'I knew it … I'm not bloody going!!!!!'

An atheist was taking a walk through the woods. 'What majestic trees! What powerful rivers! What beautiful animals!' he said to himself.

As he was walking alongside the river he heard a rustling in the bushes behind him. He turned to look. A seven foot grizzly charge towards him. He ran as fast as he could up the path. He looked over his shoulder and saw that the bear was closing in on him. He looked over his shoulder again, and the bear was even closer. His heart was pumping frantically and he tried to run even faster.

He tripped and fell on the ground. He rolled over to pick himself up but saw the bear right on top of him, reaching for him with his left paw and raising his right paw to strike him. At that instant the atheist cried out, 'Oh my God!'

Time stopped. The bear froze. The forest was silent as a bright light shone upon the man, a voice came out of the sky, 'You deny my existence for all of these years, teach others I don't exist, and even credit creation to a cosmic accident. Do you expect me to help you out of this predicament? Am I to count you as a believer?'

The atheist looked directly into the light, 'It would be hypocritical of me to suddenly ask you to treat me as a Christian now, but, perhaps, you could make the BEAR a Christian?'

There was a pause and then the voice said, 'Very well.'

The light went out. And the sounds of the forest resumed. And then the bear dropped his right paw, brought both paws together, bowed his head and spoke, 'Lord, Bless this food which I am about to receive and for which I am truly thankful.'

Today some French scientists announced that they have cloned a rat. Thank God! This will solve that big rat shortage.

Dear Cat Owner,
How to bath your cat!
1. *Thoroughly clean toilet.*
2. *Lift both lids and add shampoo.*
3. *Find and soothe cat as you carry him to bathroom.*
4. *In one swift move, place cat in toilet, close both lids and stand on top, so cat cannot escape.*
5. *The cat will self-agitate and produce ample suds. (Ignore ruckus from inside toilet, cat is enjoying this.)*
6. *Flush toilet three or four times. This provides power rinse, which is quite effective.*
7. *Have someone open outside door, stand as far from toilet as possible and quickly lift both lids.*
8. *Clean cat will rocket out of toilet and outdoors, where he will air dry.*
   Sincerely,
   The Dog

This guy lived on his own and he was feeling a bit lonely, so he goes to the pet shop to get something to keep him company. The pet shop owner suggested an unusual pet, a talking centipede. OK, thought the man, I'll give it a go, so he bought one and took it home.

That night he decided to test out his new pet, so he opened the box and said, 'I'm going to the pub for a drink, do you want to come too?' But there was no reply.

He tried again, 'Oi, centipede, wanna come to the boozer with me?' Again, no response.

So the man ranted and raved for a bit, but after a while decided to give it one more try before he took the thing back to the shop. So he took the lid off the box and repeated, 'I said I'm going to the pub for a drink do you want to come?'

'For f@#$s sake, I heard you the first time,' snapped the centipede. 'I'm just putting my shoes on.'

A Hawaiian woodpecker and a Californian woodpecker were arguing about which place had the toughest trees. The Hawaiian woodpecker said Hawaii had a tree that no woodpecker could peck. The Californian woodpecker accepted his challenge, and promptly pecked a hole in the tree with no problem. The Hawaiian woodpecker was in awe.

The Californian woodpecker then challenged the Hawaiian woodpecker to peck a tree in California that was absolutely unpeckable. The Hawaiian woodpecker expressed confidence he could do it, so accepted the challenge.

After flying to California, the Hawaiian woodpecker successfully pecked the tree with no problem.

So the two woodpeckers were now confused. How is it that the Californian woodpecker was able to peck the Hawaiian tree and the Hawaiian woodpecker was able to peck the Californian tree, but neither one was able to peck the tree in their own state?

After much woodpecker-pondering, they both came to the same conclusion ... Your pecker is always harder when you're away from home.

A burglar broke into a house one night. He shone his flashlight around looking for valuables, and when he picked up a CD player to place in his sack, a strange disembodied voice echoed from the dark saying, 'Jesus is watching you.'

He nearly jumped out of his skin, clicked his flashlight out and froze.

When he heard nothing more after a bit, he shook his head, clicked the light back on and began searching for more valuables. Just as he pulled the stereo out so he could disconnect the wires, clear as a bell he heard, 'Jesus is watching you.'

Freaked out, he shone the light around frantically looking for the source of the voice. Finally in the corner of the room his flashlight came to rest on a parrot.

'Did you say that?' he hissed at the parrot.

'Yep,' the parrot confessed, 'I'm just trying to warn you.'

The burglar relaxed, 'Warn me huh? Who are you?'

'Moses,' replied the parrot.

'Moses!' the burglar laughed. 'What kind of stupid people would name a parrot Moses?'

The parrot says, 'The same kind of stupid people that would name a Rottweiler Jesus.'

BLONDES

One day three blondes were walking along and came upon a raging, violent river. They needed to get to the other side, but had no idea of how to do it.

The first blonde prayed to God saying, 'Please God, give me the strength to cross this river.'

Poof! God gave her big arms and strong legs, and she was able to swim across the river in about two hours.

Seeing this, the second blonde prayed to God saying, 'Please God, give me the strength and ability to cross this river.' Poof! God gave her a rowboat and she was able to row across the river in about three hours.

The third blonde had seen how this worked out for the other two, so she also prayed to God saying, 'Please God, give me the strength, ability, and intelligence to cross this river.' And Poof! God turned her into a man. He looked at the map, then walked upstream and across the bridge.

BLONDE JOKES

Fifteen minutes into the flight from Melbourne to Sydney, the captain announced, 'Ladies and gentlemen, one of our engines has failed. There is nothing to worry about. Our flight will take an hour longer than scheduled, but we still have three engines left.'

Thirty minutes later the captain announced, 'One more engine has failed and the flight will take an additional two hours. But don't worry ... we can fly just fine on two engines.'

An hour later the captain announced, 'One more engine has failed and our arrival will be delayed another three hours. But don't worry ... we still have one engine left.'

A young blonde passenger turned to the man in the next seat and remarked, 'If we lose one more engine, we'll be up here all day'

Q.: Why did the blonde take a ladder into the bar?
A.: She heard the drinks were on the house.

A young blonde was on vacation in the depths of Louisiana. She desperately wanted a pair of genuine alligator shoes, but was very reluctant to pay the high prices the local vendors were asking.

After becoming very frustrated with the 'no haggle' attitude of one of the shopkeepers, the blonde shouted, 'Maybe I'll just go out and catch my own alligator so I can get a pair of shoes at a reasonable price!'

The shopkeeper said, 'By all means, be my guest. Maybe you'll luck out and catch yourself a big one!' Determined, the blonde turned and headed for the swamps, set on catching herself an alligator.

Later in the day, the shopkeeper was driving home, when he spotted the young woman standing waist deep in the water, shotgun in hand. Just then, he saw a huge 9-foot alligator swimming quickly toward her. She took aim, killed the creature, and with a great deal of effort hauled it on to the swamp bank.

Lying nearby were several more of the dead creatures. The shopkeeper watched in amazement. Just then the blonde flipped the alligator on its back, and frustrated, shouts out, 'Damn it, this one isn't wearing any shoes either!'

A young ventriloquist is touring the clubs and one night he's doing a show in a small club in a small country town. With his dummy on his knee, he's going through his usual dumb blonde jokes when a blonde woman in the fourth row stands on her chair and starts shouting.

'I've heard enough of your stupid blonde jokes. What makes you think you can stereotype women that way? What does the colour of a person's hair have to do with her worth as a human being? It's guys like you who keep women like me from being respected at work and in the community and from reaching our full potential as a person, because you and your kind continue to perpetuate discrimination against, not only blondes, but women in general ... and all in the name of humor!'

The ventriloquist is embarrassed and begins to apologise, when the blonde yells, 'You stay out of this, mister! I'm talking to that little jerk on your knee!'

Q.:　What do a blonde and a car have in common?
A.:　They can both drive you crazy.

Q.:　What do you call a hundred blondes stacked up on each other?
A.:　An air mattress.

A blonde and a brunette are out driving, and the brunette tells the blonde to look out for cops—especially cops with their lights on. After they've been driving for a while, the brunette asks the blonde if she's seen any cops.

'Yes,' says the blonde.

'Are their lights on?'

The blonde has to think for a moment, then says, 'Yes. No. Yes. No. Yes. No.'

Q.:   Did you hear about the blonde that tried to blow up her husband's car?

A.:   She burned her lips on the tailpipe!

Q.:   How does a blonde turn the light on after having sex?

A.:   She kicks the car door open.

A blonde guy and a brunette girl were happily married and about to have a baby. One day, the wife started having contractions, so the husband rushed her to the hospital. He held her hand as she went through a trying birth. In the end, there were two little baby boys.

The blonde guy turned to his wife and angrily said, 'All right, who's the other father!?!'

One day, a blonde's neighbour goes over to her house, sees the blonde crying, and asks her what happened. The blonde said that her mother had passed away.

The neighbor made her some coffee and calmed her down a little and then left. The next day the neighbour went back over to the house and found the blonde crying again. She asked her why she was crying this time.

'I just got off of the phone with my sister, her mother died too!'

A blonde, a brunette, and a man are driving in their pick-up truck. The brunette was sitting up front with the man and the blonde was in the back. While driving across a bridge the man lost control of the truck and drove over the side of the bridge. After the truck had sunk, the man and brunette fought their way out of the cab and surfaced. A couple of minutes later the blonde came out of the water, panting and breathless.

'Where have you been?' asked the man.

'I can't believe you left me down there! I couldn't get the tailgate open!'

Q.: Why did the blonde quit his restroom attendant job?
A.: He couldn't figure out how to refill the hand dryer!

Q.: Why did the three blondes jump off the building?
A.: They wanted to see if their maxi-pads really had wings.

A blonde was shopping at K-Mart and came across a shiny silver thermos. She was quite fascinated by it, so she picked it up and took it over to the clerk to ask what it was.

The clerk said, 'Why, that's a thermos ... it keeps hot things hot and cold things cold.'

'Wow,' said the blonde, 'that's amazing ... I'm going to buy it!'

So she bought the thermos and took it to work the next day.

Her boss, who was also blonde, saw it on her desk. 'What's that?' she asked.

'Why, that's a thermos ... it keeps hot things hot and cold things cold,' she replied.

'Wow, that's amazing,' said the boss, 'what do you have in it?'

'Two ice creams and some coffee.'

Two blondes are walking down the street. One notices a compact on the sidewalk and leans down to pick it up.

She opens it, looks in the mirror and says, 'Hmm, this person looks familiar.'

The second blonde says, 'Here, let me see!'

So the first blonde hands her the compact.

The second one looks in the mirror and says, 'You dummy, it's me!'

Q.: Why are blonde jokes so short?

A: So men can remember them.

Q.: Why is it difficult to find men who are sensitive, caring and good looking?
A.: They already have boyfriends.

Q.: What do you call a woman who knows where her husband is every night?
A.: A widow.

Q.: Why are married women heavier than single women?
A.: A single woman comes home and sees what's in the fridge and goes to bed. A married woman comes home, sees what's in bed and goes to the fridge.

A married couple was asleep when the phone rang at 2am in the morning.

The wife (undoubtedly blonde), picked up the phone, listened a moment and said, 'How should I know, that's 200 miles from here!' and hung up.

The husband said, 'Who was that?'

The wife said, 'I don't know, some woman wanting to know if the coast is clear.'

A blonde suspects her boyfriend of cheating on her, so she goes out and buys a gun. She goes to his apartment unexpectedly and when she opens the door she finds him in the arms of a redhead. Well, the blonde is really angry.

She opens her purse to take out the gun, and as she does so, she is overcome with grief. She takes the gun and puts it to her head.

The boyfriend yells, 'No, honey, don't do it!!!'

The blonde replies, 'Shut up, you're next!'

A blonde was bragging about her knowledge of state capitals. She proudly says, 'Go ahead, ask me, I know all of them.'
A friend says, 'OK, what's the capital of Wisconsin?'
The blonde replies, 'Oh, that's easy: W.'

Q.: What did the blonde ask her doctor when he told her she was pregnant?
A.: 'Is it mine?'

Q.: Why didn't the blonde's legs know each other?
A.: Because they never met.

A blonde and a brunette woman were walking along the road when the brunette says, 'Hey look a dead bird,' so the blonde woman looks up and goes 'Where?!?!'

A sweet young thing gets to a soft drink machine just ahead of a businessman who wants to quench his thirst.
She opens her purse and puts in 50 cents, studies the buttons for a short time, pushes a Diet Coke selection and out comes a Diet Coke. She puts it on the counter by the machine.
She reaches into her purse again, takes out a dollar and inserts it in the machine. She examines the buttons carefully, then pushes the button for Coke Classic. Out comes a Coke Classic

and 50 cents change.

She immediately takes the change and puts it in the machine, studies the buttons for a moment and pushes the Solo button. Out pops a Solo.

As she is reaching into her purse again, the thirsty businessman says, 'Excuse me, miss, but why are you putting more money in?'

She looks at him and replies indignantly, 'Well, duhhh. I'm still winning.'

A blonde walks into an appliance store and says to the clerk, 'I want to buy that TV over there.'

He says in return, 'I'm sorry, we don't sell stuff to blondes.'

The next day, she comes in with red hair and says, 'I want to buy that TV over there.'

He says, 'I'm sorry, we don't sell things to blondes.'

The next day, she comes in with brown hair and says, 'I want to buy that TV over there.'

He says, 'I'm sorry, we don't sell things to blondes.'

Frustrated, she says, 'How do you know I'm a blonde?'

He replies, 'That's not a TV. It's a microwave.'

Q.:   What do you call a blonde with a dollar on top of her head?
A.:   All you can eat under a buck.

Q.:   How can you tell a blonde had a bad day?
A.:   Her tampon is behind her ear and she doesn't know what she did with her cigarette.

Q.: What is the difference between a blonde and a penny?
A : A penny has more cents.

Q.: What do UFOs and smart blondes have in common?
A.: You keep hearing about them, but never see any.

Q.: What does a blonde say during a porn movie?
A.: 'There I am!'

Q.: Why can't blondes dial 911?
A.: They can't find the eleven on the phone.

Q.: Did you hear about the blonde who died drinking milk?
A.: The cow fell on her.

Q.: What do you call a blonde in college?
A.: A visitor.

Q.: Why do blondes have TGIF written on their shoes?
A.: Toes Go In First.

Q.: What do you call a blonde with half a brain?
A.: Gifted.

I know a blonde so dumb that she got locked in a bathroom and peed in her pants!

A young redhead goes into the doctor's office and says that her body hurts wherever she touches it. 'Impossible,' says the doctor. 'Show me.'

She takes her finger and pushes her elbow and screams in agony. She pushes her knee and screams, pushes her ankle and screams. Everywhere she touches makes her scream.

The doctor says, 'You're not really a redhead, are you?'

'No,' she says, 'I'm actually a blonde.'

'I thought so,' the doctor says. 'Your finger is broken.'

A blonde was speeding in an 80km zone when a local police cruiser pulled her over and walked up to the car. The police officer also happened to be a blonde and she asked for the blonde's driver's licence.

The driver searched frantically in her purse for a while and finally said to the blonde policewoman, 'What does a driver's licence look like?'

Irritated, the blonde cop said, 'You dummy, it's got your picture on it!'

The blonde driver frantically searched her purse again and found a small rectangular mirror down at the bottom. She held it up to her face and said, 'Aha! This must be my driver's licence,' and handed it to the blonde policewoman.

The blonde cop looked in the mirror, handed it back to the driver and said, 'You're free to go. And, if I had known you were a police officer too, we could have avoided all this hassle.'

A plane is on its way to Melbourne when a blonde in Economy Class gets up and moves to the First Class section and sits down.

The flight attendant watches her do this and asks to see her ticket. She then tells the blonde passenger that she paid for Economy and that she will have to go and sit in the back. The blonde replies, 'I'm blonde, I'm beautiful, I'm going to

Melbourne and I'm staying right here!'

The flight attendant goes into the cockpit and tells the pilot and co-pilot that there is some blonde bimbo sitting in First Class that belongs in Economy and won't move back to her seat.

The co-pilot goes back to the blonde and tries to explain that because she only paid for Economy she is only entitled to an Economy place and she will have to leave and return to her original seat.

The blonde replies, 'I'm blonde, I'm beautiful, I'm going to Melbourne and I'm staying right here!'

Exasperated the co-pilot tells the pilot that it was no use and that he probably should have the police waiting when they land to arrest this blonde woman that won't listen to reason. The pilot says, 'You say she's blonde? I'll handle this, I'm married to a blonde, and I speak blonde!'

He goes back to the blonde, whispers in her ear, and she says 'Oh, I'm sorry - I had no idea,' gets up and moves back to her seat in the Economy section. The flight attendant and co-pilot are amazed and asked him what he said to make her move without any fuss.

The pilot replied, 'I told her First Class isn't going to Melbourne.'

———— ⁙ ————

A girl was visiting her blonde friend who had acquired two new dogs and asked her what their names were.

The blonde responded by saying that one was named Rolex and one was named Timex.

Her friend asked, 'Whoever heard of someone naming dogs like that?'

'Hellooo,' answered the blonde. 'They're watch dogs!'

Q.: What's black and blue and brown and laying in a ditch?
A.: A brunette who's told too many blonde jokes.

Q.: What's the real reason a brunette keeps her figure?
A.: No one else wants it.

Q.: Why are so many blonde jokes one-liners?
A.: So brunettes can remember them.

Q.: What do you call a brunette in a room full of blondes?
A.: Invisible.

Q.: What's a brunette's mating call?
A.: 'Has the blonde left yet?'

Q.: Why didn't Indians scalp brunettes?
A.: The hair from a buffalo's butt was more manageable.

Q.: Why is brunette considered an evil colour?
A.: When was the last time you saw a blonde witch?

Q.: What do brunettes miss most about a great party?
A.: The invitation.

Q.: What do you call a good looking man with a brunette?
A.: A hostage.

Q.: Who makes bras for brunettes?
A.: Fisher-Price.

Q.: Why are brunettes so proud of their hair?
A.: It matches their moustache.

A girl came skipping home from school one day. 'Mommy, Mommy!' she yelled, 'we were counting today and all the other kids could only count to four, but I counted to ten. 1, 2, 3, 4, 5, 6, 7, 8, 9, 10! See?'

'Very good,' said her mother.

'Is it because I'm blonde, Mommy?'

'Yes, it's because you're blonde.'

The next day the girl came skipping home from school. 'Mommy, Mommy,' she yelled, 'we were saying the alphabet today, and all the other kids could only go to D, but I went all the way to G. A, B, C, D, E, F, G! See?'

'Very good,' said her mother.

'Is it because I'm blonde, Mommy?'

'Yes, it's because you're blonde.'

The next day the girl came skipping home from school. 'Mommy, Mommy,' she yelled, 'we were in gym class today, and when we showered, all the other girls had flat chests, but I have these!' And she lifted her tank top to reveal a pair of 36Cs.

'Very good,' said her embarrassed mother.

'Is it because I'm blonde, Mommy?'

'No, honey, it's because you're 24.'

A young blonde gets a job in a chemist at lunchtime. The chemist says, ' I'll be over the road in the food shop if you need help.' He comes back and says, 'Everything OK?'

'Yes,' she said, 'old Mr Brown came in for cough medicine. I couldn't see any so I told him to take a packet of laxatives.'

'You what?' said the chemist. 'That won't cure his cough.'

'Yes, it will,' she replied. 'Now he's too scared to cough.'

A blonde found herself in serious financial trouble after her business had gone bankrupt. She was so desperate that she decided to ask God for help. She prayed, 'God, please help me. I've lost my business and if I don't get some money, I'm going to lose my house as well. Please let me win the lottery.'

Lottery night came and the blonde didn't win.

She again prayed, 'God, please let me win the lottery. I've lost my business, my house and now I'm going to lose my car as well.'

Lottery night came and she still had no luck.

Once again, she prayed, 'My God, why have you forsaken me? I've lost my business, my house, and my car. My children are starving. I don't often ask you for help and I've always been a good servant to you. PLEASE, let me win the lottery just this one time so I can get my life back in order.'

Suddenly there was a blinding flash of light and the heavens opened.

The blonde was overwhelmed by the voice of God himself, 'Sweetheart, work with me on this ... buy a ticket.'

Two bone-weary public servants were working their little hearts and souls out. Their department was just too busy for staff to be able to take their flexi days off. But there had to be a way ...

One of the two public servants suddenly lifted his head. 'I know how to get some time off work,' the man whispered.

'How?' hissed the blonde at the next workstation.

Instead of answering, the man quickly looked around. No sign of his Director. He jumped up on his desk, kicked out a couple of ceiling tiles and hoisted himself up. 'Look!' he hissed, then swinging his legs over a metal pipe, hung upside down.

Within seconds, the Director emerged from the office at the far end of the floor. He saw the worker hanging from the ceiling, and asked him what on earth he thought he was doing.

'I'm a light bulb,' answered the public servant.

'I think you need some time off,' barked the Director. 'Get out of here that's an order - and I don't want to see you back here for at least another two days! You understand me?'

'Yes sir' the public servant answered meekly, then jumped down, logged off his computer and left, the blonde was hot on his heels.

'Where do you think you're going?' the boss asked.

'Home,' she said. 'I can't work in the dark.'

Three girls all worked in the same office with the same female boss. Each day, they noticed the boss left work early.

One day the girls decided that when the boss left, they would leave right behind her. After all, she never called or came back to work, so how would she know they went home early?

The brunette was thrilled to be home early. She did a little gardening, spent playtime with her son, and went to bed early.

The redhead was elated to be able to get in a quick workout at the gym before meeting a dinner date.

The blonde was happy to get home early and surprise her husband, but when she got to her bedroom, she heard a muffled noise from inside. Slowly and quietly, she cracked open the door and was mortified to see her husband in bed with her lady boss! Gently, she closed the door and crept out of her house.

The next day, at their coffee break, the brunette and redhead planned to leave early again and they asked the blonde if she was going to go with them.

'No way,' the blonde exclaimed. 'I almost got caught yesterday.'

A blonde walks into a pharmacy and asks the assistant for some rectum deodorant. The pharmacist, a little bemused, explains to the woman they don't sell rectum deodorant, and never have. Unfazed, the blonde assures the pharmacist that she has been buying the stuff from this store on a regular basis and would like some more.

'I'm sorry,' says the pharmacist, 'we don't have any.'

'But I always buy it here,' says the blonde.

'Do you have the container that it came in?' asks the pharmacist.

'Yes,' said the blonde, 'I'll go home and get it.'

She returns with the container and hands it to the pharmacist who looks at it and says to her, 'This is just a normal stick of underarm deodorant.'

Annoyed, the blonde snatches the container back and reads out loud from the container ... 'TO APPLY, PUSH UP BOTTOM.'

She was so blonde ...
- she thought a quarterback was a refund
- she thought General Motors was in the Army
- she thought Meow Mix was a CD for cats
- at the bottom of the application where it says 'sign here' she wrote Sagittarius

She was soo blonde ...
- she took a ruler to bed to see how long she slept
- she sent a fax with a stamp on it
- she thought TuPan Shakur was a Jewish holiday
- under 'education' on a job application, she put 'Hooked on Phonics'

She was sooo blonde ...

- she tripped over a cordless phone
- she spent 20 minutes looking at the orange juice because it said 'concentrate'
- she told me to meet her at the corner of 'walk' and 'don't walk'
- she asked for a price check at the Two Dollar Store
- she tried to put M&M's in alphabetical order

She was soooo blonde ...

- she studied for a blood test
- she sold her car for petrol money
- when she went to the Airport and saw a sign that read 'Airport Left', she turned around and went home

She was sooooo blonde ...

- when she heard that 90% of all crimes occurred around home, she moved
- she thinks Taco Bell is the Mexican phone company
- she thought if she spoke her mind she'd be speechless
- she thought she could not use her AM radio in the evening.

Q.: What do you call a blonde wearing a leather jacket riding a motorbike?

A.: Rebel without a clue.

Q.: Why don't blondes breast feed?

A.: Because it hurts to much when they boil their nipples.

Now who says blondes are not intelligent!!!!

Last year I replaced several windows in my house and they were the expensive double-pane energy efficient kind. But this week I got a call from the contractor complaining that his work has been completed for a whole year and I had yet to pay for them.

Boy, oh boy, did we go round. Just because I am female doesn't mean that I'm automatically stupid. So, I proceeded to tell him, just what his fast talking sales guy had told me last year ... "that in one year the windows would pay for themselves."

There was silence on the other end of the line so I just hung up and I haven't heard back. Guess I must have won that silly argument.

———— ⁞⁞ ————

A blonde walks into a bank and asks for the loan officer. She says she's going to Europe on business for two weeks and needs to borrow $5,000. The bank officer says the bank will need some kind of security for the loan, so the blonde hands over the keys to a new Rolls Royce. The car is parked on the street in front of the bank, she has the title and everything checks out. The bank agrees to accept the car as collateral for the loan.

The bank's executives all enjoy a good laugh at the blonde for using a $250,000 Rolls Royce as collateral against a $5,000 loan.

An employee of the bank then proceeds to drive the Rolls into the bank's underground garage and parks it there.

Two weeks later, the blonde returns, repays the $5,000 and the interest, which comes to $15.41. The loan officer says, 'Miss, we are very happy to have had your business, and this transaction has worked out very nicely, but we are a little puzzled. While you were away, we checked you out and found that you are a multi-millionaire. What puzzles us is, why would you bother to borrow $5,000?'

The blonde replies ... 'Where else can I park my car for two weeks for only $15.41 and expect it to be there when I return?'

A group of blondes walk into a bar. One of them tells the bartender to line up a row of drinks for all of them. They lift their glasses, make a toast, 'Here's to 51 days!' and put down their drinks.

Once again, they tell the bartender to 'line 'em up', and once again they toast 51 days and down their drinks.

The bartender says, 'I don't get it. Why in the world are you toasting 51 days?'

One of the blondes explains, 'We just finished a jigsaw puzzle that had "2 to 4 years" written on the box, and we finished it in 51 days.'

Q.: Why was there lipstick all over the blonde's steering wheel?

A.: She'd been trying to blow the horn!

Three blondes are training to be police officers. The police sergeant who is training them takes out a picture and asks the first blonde, 'What do you notice about the man in this picture?'

The blonde says, 'He only has one eye!.

The sergeant says 'No, no, it's a side view.'

Then he says to the second blonde, 'What do you notice about this man?'

The second blonde says, 'He only has one ear!'

The sergeant says 'Hello!!!! It's a side view!'

So the sergeant goes over to the last blonde and says, 'What do you notice about this man?'

The final blonde says, 'He wears contacts!'

The sergeant goes to the FBI computer and looks up the man in the picture - sure enough - he wears contacts!

The sergeant totally amazed says, 'How did you know that?'

The blonde says, 'Well, if he only has one eye and one ear, how can he wear glasses?'

Two groups charter a double decker bus for a weekend trip to the Gold Coast. One group is all brunette and the other is all blonde.

Once upon the bus, the blondes head upstairs and the brunettes hang out on the bottom level.

The brunette group has a ball. They're whooping it up and having a great time then one of them realises she doesn't hear anything from the blondes upstairs. She decides to go and check on them.

When she gets up to the top deck, she finds all of the blondes frozen in fear, staring straight ahead, each clutching the seat in front of them.

'Whoa, whoa — what's going on up here? We're having a GREAT time downstairs!'

One of the blondes replies through chattering frightened teeth, 'Yeah, but you guys have a driver!'

A blonde had just written off her car in a horrific accident. Miraculously, she managed to pry herself from the wreckage without a scratch and was applying fresh lipstick when the police arrived.

'My God!' the police officer gasped. 'Your car looks like an accordion that was stomped on by an elephant. Are you OK, ma'am?'

'Yes, officer, I'm just fine,' the blonde chirped.

'Well, how in the world did this happen?' the officer asked as he surveyed the wrecked car.

'Officer, it was the strangest thing!' the blonde began. 'I was driving along this road when from out of nowhere this TREE pops up in front of me. So I swerved to the right, and there was another tree! I swerved to the left and there was yet ANOTHER tree! I swerved to the right and there was another tree! I swerved to the left and there was ...'

'Uh, ma'am,' the officer said, cutting her off, 'there isn't a tree on this road for 30 miles. That was your air freshener swinging back and forth.'

I knew a blonde that was so stupid that ...

- She called me to get my phone number.
- She put lipstick on her forehead because she wanted to make up her mind.
- She tried to drown a fish.
- She got locked in a grocery store and starved to death.
- When she missed the 44 bus, she took the 22 bus twice instead.

A blonde girl enters a store that sells curtains. She tells the salesman, 'I would like to buy a pink curtain in the size of my computer screen.'

The surprised salesman replies, 'But, madam, computers do not have curtains!!'

And the blonde said, 'Helloooo ... I've got Windows!!'

A blonde guy gets home early from work and hears strange noises coming from the bedroom. He rushes upstairs to find his wife naked on the bed, sweating and panting.

'What's up?' he says.

'I'm having a heart attack,' cries the woman.

He rushes downstairs to grab the phone, but just as he's dialing, his 4-year-old son comes up and says, 'Daddy! Daddy! Uncle Ted's hiding in your closet and he's got no clothes on!'

The guy slams the phone down and storms upstairs into the bedroom, past his screaming wife, and rips open the wardrobe door. Sure enough, there is his brother, totally naked, cowering on the closet floor.

'You rotten bastard,' says the husband, 'my wife's having a heart attack and you're running around naked scaring the kids!'

Alma (a blonde), visiting a farm, saw something which puzzled her. She saw the farmer walk by and hailed him.

'Sir,' she inquired, 'why doesn't this cow have any horns?'

The farmer cocked his head for a moment, then began in a patient tone, 'Well, ma'am, cattle can do a powerful lot of damage with horns. Sometimes we keep 'em trimmed down with a hacksaw. Other times we can fix up the young 'uns by puttin' a couple drops of acid where their horns would grow in, and that stops 'em cold. Still, there are some breeds of cattle that never grow horns. But the reason this cow don't have no horns, ma'am, is 'cause it's a horse.'

A blonde pushes her BMW into a gas station. She tells the mechanic it died. After he works on it for a few minutes, it is idling smoothly.

She says, 'What's the story?'

He replies, 'Just crap in the carburetor.'

She asks, 'How often do I have to do that?'

A blonde is walking down the street with her blouse open and her right breast hanging out. A policeman approaches her and says, 'Ma'am, are you aware that I could cite you for indecent exposure?'

She says, 'Why, officer?'

'Because your breast is hanging out,' he says.

She looks down and says, 'Oh my God! I left the baby on the bus again!'

There's this blonde out for a walk. She comes to a river and sees another blonde on the opposite bank.

'Yoo-hoo!' she shouts, 'how can I get to the other side?'

The second blonde looks up the river then down the river and shouts back, 'You ARE on the other side.'

A Russian, an American, and a Blonde were talking one day. The Russian said, 'We were the first in space!'

The American said, 'We were the first on the moon!'

The Blonde said, 'So what? We're going to be the first on the sun!'

The Russian and the American looked at each other and shook their heads. 'You can't land on the sun, you idiot! You'll burn up!' said the Russian.

To which the Blonde replied, 'We're not stupid, you know. We're going at night!'

The blonde reported for her university final examination that consists of yes/no type questions. She takes her seat in the examination hall, stares at the question paper for five minutes and then, in a fit of inspiration, takes out her purse, removes a coin and starts tossing the coin, marking the answer sheet: Yes, for Heads, and No, for Tails.

Within half an hour she is all done whereas the rest of the class is still sweating it out. During the last few minutes she is seen desperately throwing the coin, muttering and sweating. The moderator, alarmed, approaches her and asks what is going on.

'I finished the exam in half an hour, but now I'm rechecking my answers.'

Two sisters, one blonde and one brunette, inherit the family ranch. Unfortunately, after just a few years, they are in financial trouble. In order to keep the bank from repossessing the ranch, they need to purchase a bull so that they can breed their own stock.

Upon leaving, the brunette tells her sister, 'When I get there, if I decide to buy the bull, I'll contact you to drive out after me and haul it home.'

The brunette arrives at the man's ranch, inspects the bull, and decides she wants to buy it. The man tells her that he will sell it for $599, no less. After paying him, she drives to the nearest town to send her sister a telegram to tell her the news.

She walks into the telegraph office, and says, 'I want to send a telegram to my sister telling her that I've bought a bull for our ranch. I need her to hitch the trailer to our pickup truck and drive out here so we can haul it home.'

The telegraph operator explains that he'll be glad to help her, then adds, 'It's just 99 cents a word.' Well, after paying for the bull, the brunette only has $1 left. She realises that she'll only be able to send her sister one word.

After thinking for a few minutes, she nods, and says, 'I want you to send her the word "comfortable".'

The telegraph operator shakes his head. 'How is she ever going to know that you want her to hitch the trailer to your pickup truck and drive out here to haul that bull back to your ranch if you send her the word "comfortable"?'

The brunette explains, 'My sister's blonde. The word's big. She'll read it very slowly - "com-for-da-bul".'

Three mothers were sitting having tea together. One was a redhead, one was a brunette, and the other was blonde.

The redhead said, 'I was cleaning my daughter's room today and I found a pack of cigarettes. I can't believe my daughter SMOKES!'

The brunette said, 'That's weird, I was cleaning my daughter's room the other day, and I found a bottle of beer. I can't believe she DRINKS!'

The blonde said, 'How strange, I was cleaning my daughter's room the other day, and I found a condom. I can't believe she has a PENIS!'

A blonde, wanting to earn some money, decided to hire herself out as a handyperson and started canvassing a well-to-do neighbourhood. She went to the front door of the first house and asked the owner if he had any jobs for her to do.

'Well, you can paint my porch. How much will you charge?'

The blonde said, 'How about $50?'

The man agreed and told her that the paint and other materials that she might need were in the garage.

The man's wife, inside the house, heard the conversation and said to her husband, 'Does she realise that the porch goes all the way around the house?'

The man replied, 'She should, she was standing on it.'

A short time later the blonde came to the door to collect her money.

'You're finished already?' he asked.

'Yes,' the blonde answered, 'and I had paint left over, so I gave it two coats.'

Impressed, the man reached in his pocket for the $50.

'And by the way,' the blonde added, 'it's not a Porch, it's a Lexus.

A fair young lady went to the doctor with two badly burnt ears. The doctor asked her how she got them.

'Well,' she replied, 'I was doing some ironing when the phone rang and I put the iron up to my ear.'

The doctor said he could understand that, but how did she get the other one burnt?

Her reply was, 'The silly idiot rang back.'

A blonde and a lawyer are seated next to each other on a flight from Sydney to Perth.

The lawyer asks if she would like to play a fun game? The blonde, tired, just wants to take a nap, politely declines and rolls over to the window to catch a few winks. The lawyer persists and explains that the game is easy and a lot of fun. He explains, 'I ask you a question, and if you don't know the answer, you pay me $5, and vice versa.'

Again, she declines and tries to get some sleep.

The lawyer, now agitated, says, 'Okay, if you don't know the answer, you pay me $5, and if I don't know the answer, I will pay you $500.'

This catches the blonde's attention and figuring there will be no end to this torment unless she agrees to play the game, says OK.

The lawyer asks the first question. 'What is the distance from the earth to the moon?'

The blonde doesn't say a word, reaches into her purse, pulls out a $5 bill and hands it to the lawyer.

'Okay,' says the lawyer, 'your turn.'

She asks the lawyer, 'What goes up a hill with three legs and comes down with four legs?'

The lawyer, puzzled, takes out his laptop computer and searches all his references, no answer. He taps into the air phone with his modem and searches the net and a library, no answer. Frustrated, he sends emails to all his friends and co-workers, but to no avail.

After an hour, he wakes the blonde, and hands her $500. The blonde says, 'Thank you,' and turns back to get some more sleep.

The lawyer, who is more than a little miffed, wakes the blonde and asks, 'Well, what's the answer?'

Without a word, the blonde reaches into her purse, hands the lawyer $5, and goes back to sleep.

A blonde calls her boyfriend and says, 'Please come over here and help me ... I have a killer jigsaw puzzle, and I can't figure out how to get it started.'

Her boyfriend asks, 'What is it supposed to be when it's finished?'

The blonde says, 'According to the picture on the box, it's a rooster.'

Her boyfriend decides to go over and help with the puzzle. She lets him in and shows him where she has the puzzle spread all over the table.

He studies the pieces for a moment, then looks at the box, then turns to her and says, 'First of all, no matter what we do, we're not going to be able to assemble these pieces into anything resembling a rooster.'

He held her hand and said, 'Second, I'd advise you to relax. Let's have a cup of coffee, and then ... ' he sighed, 'let's put all these Corn Flakes back in the box.'

Two blondes were driving through the beautiful Welsh countryside one day, when they came across a road sign that read:

'Llanfairpwllgwyngyllgogerychwymdrobwilllantsiliogogoch'.

(The longest town-name in the world!)

One of the blondes tries to say the name and the other laughs hysterically.

'That's not how you pronounce it,' she says and proceeds to say it herself. The first blonde nearly crashes the car laughing and they start debating how to correctly pronounce the name.

Well, the debate soon turns into a heated argument and coming up to lunchtime they pull into a restaurant in the town whose name is the subject of the argument.

As they are settling their bill, one of the blondes says to the cashier, 'Excuse me, but would you mind settling an argument between my friend and I? Could you possibly pronounce the name of where we are, only please could you do it very very slowly.'

The cashier leans forward and says ... 'BuuuuurrrrrggggggeeeeerrrrrKiiiiinnnnnggggg.'

Two bored casino dealers were waiting at a craps table.

A very attractive blonde woman arrived and bet $20,000 on a single roll of the dice. She said, 'I hope you don't mind, but I feel much luckier when I'm completely nude.'

With that, she stripped from her neck down, rolled the dice and yelled, 'Mama needs new clothes!' Then she hollered ... 'YES! YES! I WON! I WON!'

She jumped up and down and hugged each of the dealers. She then picked up all the money and her clothes and quickly departed.

The dealers just stared at each other dumbfounded. Finally, one of them asked, 'What did she roll?'

The other answered, 'I don't know, I thought YOU were watching the dice!'

Q.: How do you kill a blonde?
A.: Put a scratch and sniff sticker at the bottom of the swimming pool!

Q.: What do you call a bunch of blondes in a circle?
A.: A dope ring!!

Q.: What do you call a group of blondes in straight line?
A.: A wind tunnel!

Q.: What do you call a brunette standing between two blondes?
A.: An interpreter.

Q.: What happened to the blonde tap dancer?
A.: She fell in the sink.

Q.: What did the blonde say when her boyfriend blew in her ear?
A.: 'Thanks for the refill, honey.'

The sheriff in a small town walks out in the street and sees a very blonde cowboy, coming down the walk with nothing on but his cowboy hat, gun and his boots, so he arrests him for indecent exposure.

As he is locking him up, the sheriff asks him, 'Why in the world are you dressed like this?'

The cowboy says ,'Well it's like this Sheriff ... I was in the bar down the road, when this pretty little redhead asks me to go out to her motor home with her, and so I did ... We go inside and she pulls off her top and asks me to pull off my shirt, so I did. Then she pulls off her skirt and asks me to pull off my pants, so I did. Then she pulls off her panties and asks me to pull off my shorts, so I did. Then she gets on the bed and looks at me kind of hot and sexy and says, "Now go to town, cowboy,"... And so here I am.'

Medical Terminology a la Blonde!

Anally —	Occurring yearly
Artery —	Study of paintings
Bacteria —	Back door of cafeteria
Barium —	What doctors do when treatment fails
Bowel —	Letter like A.E.I.O.U
Caesarian section —	District in Rome
Cat scan —	Searching for kitty
Cauterise —	Made eye contact with her
Colic —	Sheep dog
Coma —	A punctuation mark
Congenital —	Friendly
Diarrhoea —	Journal of daily events
Dilate —	To live long
Enema —	Not a friend
Fester —	Quicker
Fibula —	A small lie
Genital —	Non-Jewish
G.I. Series —	Soldiers' ball game
Grippe —	Suitcase
Hangnail –	Coat hook
Impotent —	Distinguished, well known
Intense pain —	Torture in a teepee
Labour pain —	Got hurt at work
Medical staff —	Doctor's cane
Morbid —	Higher offer
Nitrate —	Cheaper than day rate
Node —	Was aware of
Outpatient —	Person who had fainted
Pap smear —	Fatherhood test
Pelvis —	Cousin of Elvis
Post operative —	Letter carrier
Protein —	Favouring young people
Rectum —	Damn near killed 'em
Recovery room —	Place to do upholstery
Rheumatic —	Amorous
Scar —	Rolled tobacco leaf

Secretion —	Hiding anything
Seizure —	Roman emperor
Serology —	Study of knighthood
Tablet —	Small table
Terminal illness —	Sickness at airport
Tibia —	Country in North Africa
Tumour —	An extra pair
Urine —	Opposite of you're out
Varicose —	Located nearby
Vein –	Conceited

A redhead, a brunette and a blonde perform a Post Office robbery. They are on the run from the police and they have to ditch their car and go cross-country. They are all getting tired and happen across an old farm with a huge barn. Sneaking inside the barn, they see three old flour sacks. They all hide in separate sacks.

The police enter the barn and upon seeing the sacks, kick the first one containing the redhead. The redhead says 'Woof!'

'Nothing in here but a dog, Sarge,' says the constable. 'We'd better move on.'

They kick the sack containing the brunette.

'Miaow!' she says.

'Nothing in here but a cat, Sarge. Better move on.'

They kick the sack containing the blonde and the blonde says, 'Potatoes!'

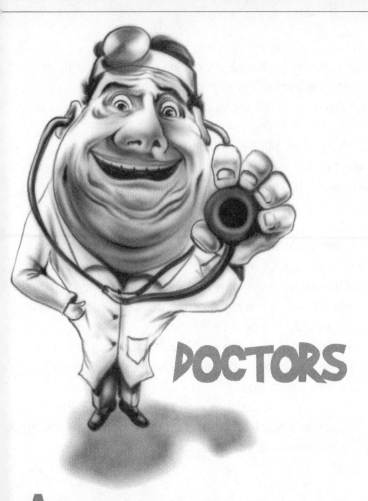

DOCTORS

A psychiatrist was conducting a group therapy session with four young mothers and their small children.

'You all have obsessions,' he observed. To the first mother he said, 'You are obsessed with eating. You've even named your daughter Candy.'

He turned to the second mother, 'Your obsession is with money. Again, it manifests itself in your child's name, Penny.'

He turns to the third mother, 'Your obsession is alcohol. This manifests itself in your child's name, Brandy.'

At this point, the fourth mother gets up, takes her little boy by the hand and whispers, 'Come on, Dick, we're leaving.'

The doctor cautiously placed his ear to the man's thigh only to hear, 'Gimme 20 bucks. I really need 20 bucks.'

'I've never seen or heard anything like this before, how long has this been going on?' the doctor asked.

'That's nothing Doc, put your ear to my knee.'

The doctor put his ear to the man's knee and heard it say, 'Man, I really need 10 dollars, just lend me 10 bucks!!'

'Sir, I really don't know what to tell you. I've never seen anything like this.' The doctor was dumbfounded.

'Wait Doc, that's not it. There's more, just put your ear up to my ankle,' the man urged him.

The doctor did as the man said and was blown away to hear his ankle plead, 'Please, I just need 5 dollars. Lend me 5 bucks, just 5 bucks. PLEASE, if you will.'

'I have no idea what to tell you,' the doctor said. 'There's nothing about it in my books,' he said as he frantically searched all his medical reference books.

'I can make a well educated guess though. Based on life and all my previous experience I can tell you that your leg seems to be broke in three places.'

A woman goes to her doctor for a check-up. The doctor says, 'Congratulations, you're in perfect health.'

The woman replies,'Yes I know I am, and the reason I know is because when I pass wind, it doesn't make a noise and it doesn't smell! For example, since I've been in your office, I've passed wind twice and you haven't even noticed!!'

The doctor raises his eyebrows ... 'Really?' he said. 'You know, that's not normal, I'd like to give you these tablets to take for a week and come back and see me again after that.'

A week later, the woman returns and immediately curses the doctor ... 'What on earth was in those tablets?' she asked. 'Now, whenever I pass wind, the smell is dreadful ... I can't bear it!'

The doctor smiled, 'I'm glad to hear that,' he said, 'now that I've fixed your sinuses, I'll get your hearing checked!!'

'Doc,' says Steve, 'I want to be castrated.'

'What on earth for?' asks the doctor in amazement.

'It's something I've been thinking about for a long time and I want to have it done,' replies Steve.

'But have you thought it through properly?' asks the doctor. 'It's a very serious operation and once it's done, there's no going back. It will change your life forever!'

'I'm aware of that and you're not going to change my mind — either you book me in to be castrated or I'll simply go to another doctor.'

'Well, OK,' says the doctor, 'but it's against my better judgment!'

So Steve has his operation, and the next day he is up and walking very slowly, legs apart, down the hospital corridor with his drip stand. Heading towards him is another patient, who is walking exactly the same way.

'Hi there,' says Steve. 'It looks as if you've just had the same operation as me.'

'Well,' said the patient, 'I finally decided after 37 years of life that I would like to be circumcised.'

Steve stared at him in horror and screamed, 'Damn! THAT'S the word!'

An older gentleman had an appointment to see the urologist who shared an office with several other doctors. The waiting room was filled with patients. As he approached the reception desk he noticed that the receptionist was a large unfriendly woman who looked like a Sumo wrestler.

He gave her his name. In a very loud voice, the receptionist said, 'Yes, I have your name right here you want to see the doctor about impotence, correct?'

All the patients in the waiting room snapped their heads around to look at the very embarrassed man. He recovered quickly, and replied in an equally loud voice.

'No, I've come to inquire about a sex change operation, but I don't want the same doctor that did yours.'

———————————— ⁞⁞⁞ ————————————

An 86-year-old man walked into a crowded doctor's office. As he approached the desk, the receptionist said, 'Yes sir, what are you seeing the doctor for today?' 'There's something wrong with my dick,' he replied.

The receptionist became irritated and said, 'You shouldn't come into a crowded office and say things like that.'

'Why not? You asked me what was wrong and I told you,' he said.

The receptionist replied, 'You've obviously caused some embarrassment in this room full of people. You should have said there is something wrong with your ear or something and then discussed the problem further with the doctor in private.'

The man replied, 'You shouldn't ask people things in a room full of others, if the answer could embarrass anyone.'

The man walked out, waited several minutes and then re-entered. The receptionist smiled smugly and asked, 'Yes?'

'There's something wrong with my ear,' he stated.

The receptionist nodded approvingly and smiled, knowing he had taken her advice. 'And what is wrong with your ear, Sir?'

'I can't piss out of it,' the man replied.

———————————— ⁞⁞⁞ ————————————

I was due later in the week for an appointment with the gynaecologist. Early one morning I received a call from the doctor's office to tell me that I had been rescheduled for early that morning at 9.30am.

I had only just packed everyone off to work and school, and it was already around 8.45 am. The trip to his office took about 35 minutes, so I didn't have anytime to spare. As most women do, I like to take a little extra effort over hygiene when making such visits, but this time I wasn't going to be able to make the full effort. So I rushed upstairs, threw off my dressing gown, wet the washcloth that was sitting next to the basin and gave myself a quick wash in 'that area' to make sure it was at least presentable. I threw the washcloth in the clothes basket, donned some clothes, hopped in the car and raced to my appointment.

I was in the waiting room only a few minutes when I was called in. Knowing the procedure, as I'm sure you do, I hopped up on the table, looked over at the other side of the room and pretended that I was in Paris or some other place a million miles away.

I was a little surprised when the doctor said, 'My, we have made an extra effort this morning, haven't we?' but I didn't respond.

When the appointment was over, I heaved a sigh of relief and went home. The rest of the day was normal ... some shopping, cleaning, cooking, etc. After school when my six-year-old daughter was playing, she called out from the bathroom, 'Mum, where's my washcloth?' I told her to get another one from the cupboard.

She replied, 'No, I need the one that was here by the basin. It had all my glitter and sparkles in it!'

Mrs Ward goes to the doctor's office to collect her husband's test results.

The lab tech says to her, 'I'm sorry, ma'am, but there has been a bit of a mix-up and we have a problem. When we sent the samples from your husband to the lab, the samples from another Mr Ward were sent as well and we are now uncertain which one is your husband's. Frankly, it is either bad or terrible.'

'What do you mean?' Mrs Ward asked.

'Well, one has tested positive for Alzheimer's and the other for AIDS. We can't tell which is your husband.'

'That's terrible! Can we do the test over?' questioned Mrs Ward.

'Normally, yes. But Medicare won't pay for these expensive tests more than once.'

'Well, what am I supposed to do now?'

'The people at Medicare recommend that you drop your husband off in the middle of town. If he finds his way home, don't sleep with him.'

Actual sentences found in patients' hospital charts
(Proves that those medical folks are right on top of things.)

1. *She has no rigors or shaking chills, but her husband states she was very hot in bed last night.*
2. Patient has chest pain if she lies on her left side for over a year.
3. *On the second day the knee was better, and on the third day it disappeared.*
4. The patient is tearful and crying constantly. She also appears to be depressed.
5. *The patient has been depressed since she began seeing me in 1993.*

6. Discharge status: Alive but without my permission.
7. *Healthy appearing decrepit, 69-year-old male, mentally alert but forgetful.*
8. The patient refused autopsy.
9. *The patient has no previous history of suicides.*
10. Patient has left white blood cells at another hospital.
11. *Patient's medical history has been remarkably insignificant with only 40 pound weight gain in the past three days.*
12. Patient had waffles for breakfast and anorexia for lunch.
13. *Between you and me, we ought to be able to get this lady pregnant.*
14. Since she can't get pregnant with her husband, I thought you might like to work her up.
15. *She is numb from her toes down.*
16. While in ER, she was examined, X-rated and sent home.
17. *The skin was moist and dry.*
18. Occasional, constant infrequent headaches.
19. *Patient was alert and unresponsive.*
20. Rectal examination revealed a normal size thyroid.
21. *She stated that she had been constipated for most of her life, until she got a divorce.*
22. I saw your patient today, who is still under our car for physical therapy.
23. *Both breasts are equal and reactive to light and accommodation.*
24. Examination of genitalia reveals that he is circus sized.
25. *The lab test indicated abnormal lover function.*
26. The patient was to have a bowel resection. However, he took a job as a stockbroker instead.
27. *Skin: somewhat pale but present.*
28. The pelvic exam will be done later on the floor.
29. *Patient was seen in consultation by Dr. Blank, who felt we should sit on the abdomen and I agree.*
30. Large brown stool ambulating in the hall.
31. *Patient has two teenage children, but no other abnormalities.*

DOCTOR JOKES

This girl walks into a chemist's shop and tells the pharmacist she wants to buy some arsenic. He says, 'What do you want with arsenic?'

She said 'I want to kill my husband because he cheats on me by having sex with another woman.'

The pharmacist says, 'I can't sell you arsenic so you can kill your husband lady, even if he is having sex with another woman.'

So she reaches into her pocket and pulls out a picture of her husband having sex with the pharmacist's wife.

The pharmacist says, 'Oh, I didn't realise you had a prescription.'

Doctor Bob had slept with one of his patients and felt guilty all day long. No matter how much he tried to forget about it, he couldn't. The guilt and sense of betrayal was overwhelming.

But every once in a while he'd hear that soothing voice, within himself, trying to reassure him.

'Bob, don't worry about it. You are not the first doctor to sleep with one of their patients and you won't be the last. And you're single. Let it go!'

But invariably the other voice would bring him back to reality ... 'Bob, you're a vet.'

Narelle is probably the ugliest woman that the planet has ever sustained, but her friends are too embarrassed to tell her why she can't pull a bloke. She enquires of her doctor, who is equally reluctant, but makes an appointment for her to see a Chinese doctor who is a specialist in personal relationships.

She duly presents herself, and is somewhat taken aback at the first instruction from Dr Huong Kwack, which is, 'Please take off all clothes.' She complies.

The next instruction is, 'Please turn with back to me, bend forward and place head between legs.'

She does as requested, and is delighted to hear the instant diagnosis. 'I see problem. You have Zackery's disease.'

'What do you mean?'

'Your face Zackery the same as your ass.'

A lady with a protruding stomach goes to the doctor and said 'I think I'm pregnant.' The doctor examined her and said, 'You merely have a chronic case of wind.'

A few months later the lady was pushing a pram down the street. The doctor saw her and said, 'What have we here?'

'A fart in a bonnet,' was the reply.

A man asked his doctor if he thought he'd live to be one hundred. The doctor asked the man 'Do you drink or smoke?'

'No,' he replied, 'I've never done either.'

'Do you gamble, drive fast cars and fool around with women?' inquired the doctor.

'No I've never done any of those things either.'

'Well then,' said the doctor, 'what do you want to live to one hundred for?'

DOCTOR JOKES

FEMALE

A man walked into a supermarket with his zipper down. A lady cashier walked up to him and said, 'Your barracks door is open.'

This is not a phrase we men normally use so he went on his way looking a bit puzzled. When he was about done shopping a man came up and said, 'Your fly is open.' He zipped up and finished his shopping.

He then intentionally got in the line to check out where the lady was who told him about his 'barracks door'. He was planning to have a little fun with her. When he reached her counter he said, 'When you saw my barracks door open did you see a soldier standing at attention in there?'

The lady thought for a moment and said, 'No, no I didn't, all I saw was a disabled veteran sitting on two duffle bags!!!'

A couple drove down a country road for several miles, not saying a word. An earlier discussion had led to an argument and neither of them wanted to concede their position.

As they passed a barnyard of mules, goats and pigs, the husband asked sarcastically, 'Relatives of yours?'

'Yes,' the wife replied, 'they're my in-laws.'

Relatives gathered in the waiting room of a hospital as their family member lay gravely ill. Finally, the doctor came in looking tired and sombre.

'I'm afraid I'm the bearer of bad news,' she said as she surveyed the worried faces. 'The only hope left for your loved one at this time is a brain transplant. It's an experimental procedure, very risky but it is the only hope. Insurance will cover the procedure, but you will have to pay for the brain yourselves.'

The family members sat silent as they absorbed the news. After a great length of time, someone asked her, 'Well, how much does a brain cost?'

The doctor quickly responded, '$5,000 for a male brain, and $200 for a female brain.'

The moment turned awkward. Men in the room tried not to smile, avoiding eye contact with the women, but some actually smirked.

A man, unable to control his curiosity, blurted out the question everyone wanted to ask, 'Why is the male brain so much more?'

The doctor smiled at the childish innocence and explained to the entire group, 'It's just standard pricing procedure. We have to mark down the price of the female brains, because they've actually been used.'

***

Some friends were sitting at the bar talking about their professions.

The first guy says, 'I'm a Y.U.P.P.I.E, you know ... Young, Urban, Professional, Peaceful, Intelligent, Ecologist.'

The second guy says, 'I'm a D.I.N.K, you know ... Double Income, No Kids.'

The third guy says, 'I'm a R.U.B., you know ... Rich, Urban, Biker.'

They turn to the woman and ask her, 'What are you?'

She replies: 'I'm a W.I.F.E, you know ... Wash, Iron, F@#k, Etc.

A second girl answers their question before they even ask it, 'B.I.T.C.H.'

'What exactly is a B.I.T.C.H?!?', they ask in unison.

'Babe In Total Control of Herself.'

So ladies, next time somebody calls you 'Bitch' - SMILE ... and say 'Thank You!!'

A fifteen year-old boy came home with a Porsche and his parents began to scream, 'Where did you get that car???!!!'

He calmly told them, 'I bought it today.'

'With what money?' demanded his parents. 'We know what a Porsche costs.'

'Well,' said the boy, 'this one cost me fifteen dollars.'

So the parents began to yell even louder. 'Who would sell a car like that for fifteen dollars?' they said.

'It was the lady up the street,' said the boy. 'I don't know her name - they just moved in. She saw me ride past on my bike and asked me if I wanted to buy a Porsche for fifteen dollars.'

'Dear God,' moaned the mother, 'she must be a child abuser. Who knows what she will do next? John, you go right up there and see what's going on.'

So the boy's father walked up the street to the house where the lady lived and found her out in the yard calmly planting petunias! He introduced himself as the father of the boy to whom she had sold a Porsche for fifteen dollars and demanded to know why she did it.

'Well,' she said, 'this morning I got a phone call from my husband. I thought he was on a business trip, but it seems he has run off to Hawaii with his secretary and doesn't intend to come back. He asked me to sell his new Porsche and send him the money. So I did.'

After 17 years of marriage, a man dumped his wife for a younger woman.

The downtown luxury apartment was in his name and he wanted to remain there with his new love, so he asked the wife to move out and then he would buy her another place. The wife agreed to this, but asked that she be given three days on her own there to pack up her things.

While he was gone the first day, she lovingly put her personal belongings into boxes and crates and suitcases.

On the second day she had the movers come and collect her things.

On the third day she sat down for the last time at their candlelit dining table, soft music playing in the background, and feasted on a kilo of prawns and a bottle of chardonnay.

When she had finished, she went into each room and deposited a few of the resulting prawn shells into the hollow of the curtain rods. She then cleaned up the kitchen and left.

The husband came back with his new girl and all was bliss for the first few days. Then it started, slowly but surely.

Clueless, the man could not explain why the place smelled so bad. They tried everything; cleaned and mopped and aired the place out. Vents were checked for dead rodents, carpets were steam cleaned, air fresheners were hung everywhere. Exterminators were brought in, the carpets were replaced, and on it went.

Finally, they could take it no more and decided to move.

The moving company arrived and did a very professional packing job, taking everything to their new home ... including the curtain rods.

In a crowded City bus stop, a beautiful young woman who was waiting for a bus was wearing a very tight mini skirt.

As the bus stopped and it was her turn to get on, she became aware that her skirt was too tight to allow her leg to come up to the height of the first step of the bus.

Slightly embarrassed and with a quick smile to the bus driver, she reached behind her to unzip her skirt a little, thinking that this would give her enough slack to raise her leg. Again, she tried to make the step only to discover she still couldn't.

So, a little more embarrassed, she once again reached behind her to unzip her skirt a little more, and for the second time attempted the step, and, once again, much to her chagrin, she could not raise her leg. With a little smile to the driver, she again reached behind to unzip a little more and again was unable to make the step.

About this time, a large cowboy who was standing behind her picked her up easily by the waist and placed her gently on the step of the bus.

She went ballistic and turned to the would-be Good Samaritan and yelled, 'How dare you touch my body! I don't even know who you are!'

The cowboy smiled and drawled, 'Well, ma'am, normally I would agree with you, but after you unzipped my fly three times, I kinda figured we was friends.'

A new employee was hired at the Tickle-Me-Elmo factory. The manager explained her duties and told her to report to work promptly at 8am. The next day the assembly line foreman tells the manager the new employee is causing problems. He says she's incredibly slow and the whole line is backing up.

They go down to the line to see the problem. Sure enough, Elmos are backed up all over the place. At the end of the line is the new employee. She has a roll of the material used for Elmos and a big bag of marbles. They both watch as she cuts a little piece of the fabric, wraps it around two marbles, and starts sewing the little package between Elmo's legs. The manager starts laughing hysterically.

After several minutes, he pulls himself together, walks over to the woman, and says, 'I'm sorry, I guess you misunderstood me yesterday. Your job is to give Elmo two test tickles!'

She's sitting at the table with her gourmet coffee.
Her son is on the cover of the Wheaties box.
Her daughter is on the cover of *Business Week*.
Her boyfriend is on the cover of *Playgirl*.
And her husband is on the back of the milk carton.

(104)

Dear Lord,
I pray for wisdom to understand my man,
Love to forgive him; and patience for his moods.
Because, Lord, if I pray for strength, I'll beat him to death.
Amen

A young man excitedly tells his mother he's fallen in love and is going to get married.

He says, 'Just for fun, Ma, I'm going to bring over two other female friends, in addition to my fiancée and you try and guess which one I'm going to marry.'

The next day he brings three beautiful women into the house and sits them down on the couch and they chat for a while. He says, 'Okay, Ma. Guess which one I'm going to marry.'

She immediately replies, 'The redhead in the middle.'

'That's amazing, Ma. You're right, how did you know?'

'I don't like her.'

Once upon a time, in a land far away, a beautiful, independent, self-assured princess happened upon a frog as she sat, contemplating ecological issues on the shores of an unpolluted pond in a verdant meadow near her castle.

The frog hopped into the princess' lap and said, 'Elegant Lady, I was once a handsome prince, until an evil witch cast a spell upon me. One kiss from you, however, and I will turn back into the dapper, young prince that I am and then, my sweet, we can marry and set up housekeeping in your castle with my mother, where you can prepare my meals, clean my clothes, bear my children, and forever feel grateful and happy doing so.'

That night, as the princess dined sumptuously on a feast of lightly sautéed frog legs seasoned in a white wine and onion cream sauce, she chuckled and thought to herself, 'I don't flipping think so.'

A very attractive lady goes up to a bar in a quiet rural pub. She gestures alluringly to the bartender who comes over immediately.

She seductively signals that he should bring his face closer to hers. When he does she begins to gently caress his full beard. 'Are you the manager?' she asks, softly stroking his face with both hands.

'Actually, no,' the man replied.

'Can you get him for me? I need to speak to him,' she says, running her hands beyond his beard and into his hair.

'I'm afraid I can't,' breathes the bartender. 'Is there anything I can do?'

'Yes, there is. I need you to give him a message,' she continues, running her forefinger across his lips and slyly popping a couple of fingers into his mouth allowing him to suck them gently.

'What should I tell him?' the bartender manages to say.

'Tell him,' she whispers, 'there is no toilet paper, hand soap, or paper towels in the ladies room.'

The CIA had an opening for an assassin. After all of the background checks, interviews, and testing were done there were three finalists ... Two men and a woman.

For the final test, the CIA agents took one of the men to a large metal door and handed him a gun. 'We must know that you will follow our instructions, no matter what the circumstances. Inside this room, you will find your wife sitting in a chair. Kill her!!!'

The man said, 'You can't be serious. I could never shoot my wife.'

The agent said, 'Then you're not the right man for this job.'

The second man was given the same instructions. He took the gun and went into the room. All was quiet for about five minutes. Then the man came out with tears in his eyes. 'I tried, but I can't kill my wife.'

The agent said, 'You don't have what it takes. Take your wife and go home.'

Finally, it was the woman's turn. She was given the same instructions to kill her husband. She took the gun and went into the room. Shots were heard, one shot after another. They heard screaming, crashing, banging on the walls. After a few minutes, all was quiet. The door opened slowly and there stood the woman.

She wiped the sweat from her brow, and said, 'This gun is loaded with blanks, so I had to beat him to death with the chair.'

A middle aged woman had a heart attack and was taken to the hospital. While on the operating table she had a near death experience. Seeing God she asked, 'Is my time up?'

God said, 'No, you have another 40 years, two months and eight days to live.'

Upon recovery, the woman decided to stay in the hospital and have a facelift, liposuction, and a tummy tuck. She even had someone come in and change her hair color. Since she had so much more time to live, she figured she might as well make the most of it. After her last operation, she was released from the hospital. While crossing the street on her way home, she was killed by an ambulance.

Arriving in front of God, she demanded, 'I thought you said I had another 40 years to go. Why didn't you pull me from out of the path of the ambulance?'

God replied, 'I didn't recognise you.'

The girl was supposed to write a short story in as few words as possible for her literary class and the instructions were that it had to discuss Religion, Sexuality and Mystery.

She was the only one who received an A+ and this is what she wrote, 'Good God, I'm pregnant, I wonder who did it?'

Words women use
Fine

This is the word women use to end
an argument when they feel they are
right and you need to shut up. Never
use 'Fine' to describe how a woman
looks - this will cause you to have
one of those arguments.

Five minutes

This is half an hour. It is equivalent
to the five minutes that your football
game is going to last before you take out
the rubbish, so it's an even trade.

Nothing

This means 'something,' and you should be on
your toes. 'Nothing' is usually used to describe the feeling a
woman has of wanting to turn you inside out, upside down, and
backwards. 'Nothing' usually signifies an argument that will last
'Five Minutes' and end with 'Fine'.

Go ahead (with raised eyebrows!)

This is a dare. One that will result in a woman getting upset
over 'Nothing' and will end with the word 'Fine'.

Go ahead (normal eyebrows)

This means 'I give up' or 'Do what you want because I don't
care.' You will get a 'Raised Eyebrow Go Ahead' in just a few
minutes, followed by 'Nothing' and 'Fine' and she will talk to
you in about 'Five Minutes' when she cools off.

Loud sigh

This is not actually a word, but is a non-verbal statement often
misunderstood by men. A 'Loud Sigh' means she thinks you are
an idiot at that moment, and wonders why she is wasting her
time standing there and arguing with you over 'Nothing'.

Soft sigh

Again, not a word, but a non-verbal statement. 'Soft Sighs' mean that she is content. Your best bet is to not move or breathe, and she will stay content.

That's okay

This is one of the most dangerous statements that a woman can make to a man. 'That's Okay' means that she wants to think long and hard before paying you back for whatever it is that you have done. 'That's Okay' is often used with the word 'Fine' and in conjunction with a 'Raised Eyebrow'.

Go ahead!

At some point in the near future, you are going to be in some mighty big trouble.

Please do

This is not a statement, it is an offer. A woman is giving you the chance to come up with whatever excuse or reason you have for doing whatever it is that you have done. You have a fair chance with the truth, so be careful and you shouldn't get a 'That's Okay'.

Thanks

A woman is thanking you. Do not faint! Just say 'You're welcome.'

Thanks a lot

This is much different from 'Thanks'. A woman will say, 'Thanks a Lot' when she is really ticked off at you. It signifies that you have offended her in some callous way, and will be followed by the 'Loud Sigh'. Be careful not to ask what is wrong after the 'Loud Sigh', as she will only tell you 'Nothing'.

FEMALE JOKES

A couple goes on vacation to a fishing resort. The husband likes to fish at the crack of dawn. The wife likes to read.

One morning the husband returns after several hours of fishing and decides to take a nap. Although not familiar with the lake, the wife decides to take the boat out. She motors out a short distance, anchors, and continues to read her book.

Along comes a game warden in his boat. He pulls up alongside the woman and says, 'Good morning Ma'am. What are you doing?'

'Reading a book,' she replies, (thinking, 'Isn't that obvious?')

'You're in a restricted fishing area,' he informs her.

'I'm sorry, officer, but I'm not fishing, I'm reading.'

'Yes, but you have all the equipment. For all I know you could start at any moment. I'll have to take you in and write you up.'

'If you do that, I'll have to charge you with sexual assault,' says the woman.

'But I haven't even touched you,' says the game warden.

'That's true, but you have all the equipment. For all I know you could start at any moment.'

'Have a nice day ma'am', he said as he left …

I know I'm not going to understand women. I'll never understand how you can take boiling hot wax, pour it onto your upper thigh, rip the hair out by the root, and still be afraid of a spider.

Top ten things only women understand

10.   Cats' facial expressions.

9.   *The need for the same style of shoes in different colors.*

8.   Why bean sprouts aren't just weeds.

7.   *Fat clothes.*
6.   Taking a car trip without trying to beat your best time.
5.   *The difference between beige, ecru, cream, off-white, and eggshell.*
4.   Cutting your bangs between haircuts.
3.   *Eyelash curlers.*
2.   The inaccuracy of every bathroom scale ever made.
     AND, the Number One thing only women understand:
1.   Other Women!

———— ⚮ ————

My Mother taught me

- My mother taught me to appreciate a job well done - *'If you're going to kill each other, do it outside, I've just finished cleaning.'*
- She taught me religion - *'You'd better pray that comes out of the carpet.'*
- My mother taught me about time travel - *'If you don't behave I'll knock you into next week.'*
- She taught me about logic - *'Because I said so, that's why.'*
- My mother taught me foresight - *Make sure that you wear clean underwear in case you're in an accident.'*
- She taught me irony - *'Keep laughing and I'll give you something to cry about.'*
- My mother taught me about the science of osmosis - *'Shut your mouth and eat your dinner.'*
- She taught me about being a contortionist - *'Will you look at all that dirt on the back of your neck.'*
- My mother taught me about stamina - *'You'll sit there until all that spinach is finished.'*
- She taught me about the weather - *'I't looks as though a tornado went through here.'*
- My mother taught me about hyperbole - *'If I've told you once, I've told you a million times, don't exaggerate!'*
- She taught me about behaviour modification - *'Stop acting like your father!!!'*

A man walking along the beach at Portsea was deep in prayer. Suddenly the clouds opened above his head and in a booming voice the Lord said, 'Because you have tried to be faithful to me in all ways, I will grant you one wish.'

The man said, 'That's a good idea! Can you build me a bridge to Tasmania so that I can drive over and go trout fishing anytime I like?'

The Lord said, 'Hang on a sec, your request is very materialistic, and not too easy either. Think of the logistics, the supports required to reach the bottom of Bass Strait; the concrete and steel it would take! I can do it, but it's pretty hard to justify on any sensible cost/benefit basis, and I'm not sure that it would really be a good idea to satisfy such a worldly request. Why don't you take a little more time, think about it a bit more and maybe come up with a wish more worthy of both of us.'

The man thought about it for a long time. Finally he said, 'Lord, I have been married and divorced four times. All of my wives said that I am uncaring and insensitive. I wish that I could understand women. I want to know how they feel inside, what they are thinking when they give me the silent treatment, why they cry, what they mean when they say 'nothing'. I would really like to be able to make just one woman truly happy.'

After a few minutes God said, 'You want two lanes or four on that bridge?'

Geriatric

Jacob, age 92, and Rebecca, age 89, are excited about their decision to get married.

They go for a stroll to discuss the wedding and on the way they pass a Chemist. Jacob suggests they go in.

Jacob addresses the man behind the counter: 'Are you the owner?' The pharmacist answers 'Yes'.

Jacob: 'We're about to get married. Do you sell heart medication?'

Pharmacist: 'Of course we do.'

Jacob: 'How about medicine for circulation?'

Pharmacist: 'All kinds.'

Jacob: 'Medicine for rheumatism, scoliosis?'

Pharmacist: 'Definitely.'

Jacob: 'How about Viagra?'

Pharmacist: 'Of course.'

Jacob: 'Medicine for memory problems, arthritis, jaundice?'

Pharmacist: 'Yes, a large variety ... the works!'

Jacob: 'What about vitamins, sleeping pills, antidotes for Parkinson's Disease?'

Pharmacist: 'Absolutely.'

Jacob: 'You sell wheelchairs and walkers?'

Pharmacist: 'All speeds and sizes ... why do you ask ... is there something I can help you with?'

Jacob: 'We'd like to nominate your store as our Bridal Gift Registry.'

The wise old Mother Superior from county Tipperary was dying. The nuns gathered around her bed trying to make her comfortable. They gave her some warm milk to drink, but she refused it.

Then one nun took the glass back to the kitchen. Remembering a bottle of Irish whiskey received as a gift at Christmas, she opened it and poured a generous amount into the warm milk.

Back at Mother Superior's bed, she held the glass to her lips. Mother drank a little, then a little more.

Before they knew it, she had drunk the whole glass ... down to the last drop. The nuns asked earnestly, 'Please give us some wisdom before you die.'

The wise Mother Superior raised herself up in bed with a pious look on her face and said, 'Don't sell that cow.'

Two elderly women were eating breakfast in a restaurant one morning. Ethel noticed something funny about Mabel's ear and she said, ' Mabel, did you know you've got a suppository in your left ear?'

Mabel answered, 'I have? A suppository?' She pulled it out and stared at it.

Then she said, 'Ethel, I'm glad you saw this thing. Now I think I know where my hearing aid is.'

Just before the funeral service, the undertaker came up to the very elderly widow and asked, 'How old was your husband?'

'98,' she replied. 'Two years older than me.'

'So you're 96,' the undertaker commented.

She responded, 'Hardly worth going home is it?'

A 97-year-old man goes into his doctor's office and says, 'Doc, I want my sex drive lowered.'

'Sir,' replied the doctor, 'you're 97. Don't you think your sex drive is all in your head?'

'You're damned right it is!' replied the old man. 'That's why I want it lowered!'

———————— ⁙ ————————

God, grant me the senility
To forget the people
I never liked anyway,
The good fortune
To run into the ones I do,
And the eyesight to tell the difference.

———————— ⁙ ————————

An elderly woman from Melbourne decided to prepare her will and make her final requests. She told her lawyer she had two final requests.

First, she wanted to be cremated, and second, she wanted her ashes scattered all over Myer.

'Myer!' the lawyer exclaimed. 'Why Myer?'

'Then I'll be sure my daughters visit me twice a week.'

———————— ⁙ ————————

A doctor gave a speech to a large audience about nutrition. He said, 'The material we put into our stomachs is enough to have killed most of us sitting here.'

'For example, red meat is awful. Soft drinks corrode our stomach lining. Chinese food is loaded with MSG. High-fat diets can be disastrous.'

'But there is one thing that is the most dangerous of all, and we all have, or will eat it. Would anyone care to guess what food causes the most grief and suffering for years after eating it?'

After several seconds of silence, a 75-year-old man raised his hand and said, 'Wedding cake.'

———— ⁂ ————

An old farmer had owned a large farm for several years. He had a large pond in the back, fixed up nice; picnic tables, horseshoe courts, basketball court, etc. The pond was properly shaped and fixed up for swimming when it was built.

One evening the old farmer decided to go down to the pond, as he hadn't been there for a while, and look it over. As he neared the pond, he heard voices shouting and laughing with glee. As he came closer he saw it was a bunch of young women skinny-dipping in his pond. He made the women aware of his presence and they all went to the deep end of the pond.

One of the women shouted to him, 'We're not coming out until you leave!'

The old man replied, 'I didn't come down here to watch you ladies swim or make you get out of the pond naked. I only came to feed the alligator.'

Moral: Old age and treachery will triumph over youth and inexperience ...

———— ⁂ ————

An 85-year-old man went to his doctor's office and while there the Doctor asked for a sperm count. The doctor gave the man a jar and said, 'Take this jar home and bring back a semen sample tomorrow.'

The next day the 85-year-old man reappeared at the doctor's office and gave him the jar, which was as clean and empty as on the previous day.

The doctor asked what happened and the man explained, 'Well, doc, it's like this. First I tried with my right-hand, but nothing. Then I tried with my left hand, but still nothing. Then I asked my wife for help. She tried with her right hand, then her left, still nothing. She tried with her mouth, first with the teeth in, then with her teeth out, and still nothing. We even called up Arleen, the lady next door and she tried too, first with both hands, then an armpit and she even tried squeezin' it between her knees, but still nothing.'

The doctor was shocked! 'You asked your neighbour?'

The old man replied, 'Yep. And no matter what we tried, we still couldn't get the jar open!'

Two old men decide they are close to their last days on earth and decide to have a last night on the town. After a few drinks they end up at the local brothel.

The madam takes one look at the two old geezers and whispers to her manager, 'Go up to the first two rooms and put an inflated doll in each bed. These two are so old and drunk. I'm not wasting two of my girls on them. They won't know the difference.'

Her manager does as he is told and the two old men go upstairs and take care of their business.

As they are walking home the first one says, 'You know, I think my girl was dead!

'Dead?' says his friend, 'why would you think that?'

'Well, she never moved or made a single sound all the time I was giving her the loving of her life.'

His friend says, 'I think mine was a witch.'

'A witch!!! Why the hell would you say that?

'Well, I was making love to her, kissing on her neck and I gave it a little bite, then she farted and flew out the window!!'

An old lady was standing at the railing of the cruise ship holding her hat on tightly so that it would not blow off in the wind.

A gentleman approached her and said, 'Pardon me, madam. I do not intend to be forward, but did you know that your dress is blowing up in this high wind?'

'Yes, I know,' said the lady, 'I need both hands to hold onto this hat.'

'But, madam, you must know that your privates are exposed!' said the gentleman in earnest.

The woman looked down, then back up at the man and replied, 'Sir, anything you see down there is 85 years old. I just bought this hat yesterday!'

Three old ladies were sitting side by side in their retirement home reminiscing. The first lady recalled shopping at the green grocers and demonstrated with her hands, the length and thickness of a cucumber she could buy for a dollar.

The second old lady nodded, adding that onions used to be much bigger and cheaper also, and demonstrated the size of two big onions she could buy for a dollar a piece.

The third old lady remarked, 'I can't hear a word you're saying, but I remember the guy your're talking about.'

Two elderly women were out driving in a large car. Both could barely see over the dashboard. As they were cruising along, they came to an intersection. The plight was red but they just went on through.

The woman in the passenger seat thought to herself, 'I must be losing it. I could have sworn we just went through red light.' After a few more minutes they came to another intersection, the light was red, and again they went right through.

This time, the passenger was almost sure that the light had been red, but was also concerned that she might be seeing things.

She was getting nervous and decided to pay very close attention. At the next intersection, sure enough, the light was definitely red and they blew right through it.

She turned to the other woman and said, 'Mildred! Did you know that you ran through three red lights in a row? You could have killed us.'

Mildred turned to her and said, 'Oh shit! Am I driving?'

Three retirees, each with a hearing loss, were playing golf one fine March day.

One remarked to the other, 'Windy, isn't it?'

'No,' the second man replied, 'it's Thursday.'

And the third man chimed in, 'So am I. Let's have a beer.'

Miss Bea, the church organist, was in her 80s and had never been married. She was much admired for her sweetness and kindness to all.

One afternoon the pastor came to call on her and she showed him into her quaint sitting room. She invited him to have a seat while she prepared tea. As he sat facing her old pump organ, the young minister noticed a cut glass bowl sitting on top of it, filled with water. In the water floated, of all things, a condom!

When she returned with tea and scones, they began to chat.

The pastor tried to stifle his curiosity about the bowl of water and its strange floater, but soon it got the better of him and he could no longer resist.

'Miss Bea,' he said, 'I wonder if you would tell me about this?' pointing to the bowl.

'Oh, yes,' she replied, 'isn't it wonderful? I was walking downtown a few months ago and I found this little package on the ground. The directions said to place it on the organ, keep it wet, and it would prevent the spread of disease. And you know I haven't had a cold all winter!'

A little old lady was going up and down the halls in a nursing home. As she walked, she would flip up the hem of her nightgown and say, 'Supersex! Supersex!' She walked up to an elderly man in a wheelchair.

Flipping her gown at him, she again said, 'Supersex.'

He sat silently for a moment or two looking up at her and finally answered, 'I'll take the soup.'

80-year-old Bessie bursts into the rec room at the retirement home. She holds her clenched fist in the air and announces, 'Anyone who can guess what's in my hand can have sex with me tonight!!'

An elderly gentleman in the rear shouts out, 'An elephant?'

Bessie thinks a minute and says, 'Close enough.'

Two widows, Martha and Edna, are talking.

Martha: 'That nice George Johnson asked me out for a date. I know you went out with him last week, and I wanted to talk with you about him before I give him my answer.'

Edna: 'Well, I'll tell you. He shows up at my apartment punctually at 7pm. And dressed like such a gentleman in a fine suit. And he brings me such beautiful flowers! Then he takes me downstairs, and what's there but a beautiful car ... a limousine, uniformed chauffeur and all. Then he takes me out for dinner ... marvellous dinner - lobster. Then we go see a show ... let me tell you, Martha, I enjoyed it so much I could have just died from pleasure! So then we are coming back to my apartment and he turns into an animal. Completely crazy, he tears off my expensive new dress and has his way with me two times!'

Martha: 'Goodness gracious! So are you telling me I shouldn't go out with him?'

Edna: 'Heavens no! I'm just saying, wear an old dress!'

Mother Superior calls all the nuns together and says to them, 'I must tell you all something ... We have a case of gonorrheae in the convent.'

'Thank God,' says an elderly nun at the back. 'I'm so tired of Chardonnay'.

Defence Counsel: *Will you please state your age?*
Little Old Lady: *I am 86 years old.*
Defence Counsel: *Will you tell us, in your own words, what happened the night of April 1st?*

Little Old Lady: *There I was, sitting there in my swing on my front porch on a warm spring evening, when a young man comes creeping up on the porch and sat down beside me.*

Defence Counsel: *Did you know him?*

Little Old Lady: *No, but he sure was friendly.*

Defence Counsel: *What happened after he sat down?*

Little Old Lady: *He started to rub my thigh.*

Defence Counsel: *Did you stop him?*

Little Old Lady: *No, I didn't stop him.*

Defence Counsel: *Why not?*

Little Old Lady: *It felt good. Nobody had done that since my Abner died some 30 years ago.*

Defence Counsel: *What happened next?*

Little Old Lady: *He began to rub my breasts.*

Defence Counsel: *Did you stop him then?*

Little Old Lady: *No, I did not stop him.*

Defence Counsel: *Why not?*

Little Old Lady: *His rubbing made me feel all alive and excited. I haven't felt that good in years!*

Defence Counsel: *What happened next?*

Little Old Lady: *Well, by then, I was feeling really 'spicy' so I just laid down and told him 'Take me, young man. Take me!'*

Defence Counsel: *Did he take you?*

Little Old Lady: *Hell, no! He just yelled, 'April Fool!!' And that's when I shot the little bastard.*

An elderly gentleman walks into the Daily Planet in Melbourne. He marches up to the Madam and says, 'I want a woman and I want her now.'

The Madam says, 'And how old would you be Sir?'

The elderly gentleman says, 'I'm 95 years young!'

The Madam says, 'Gawd, you've had it!'

The Gentleman says, 'Have I? How much do I owe you?'

Upon hearing that her elderly grandfather had just passed away, Katie went straight to her grandparents' house to visit her 95-year-old grandmother and comfort her.

When she asked how her grandfather had died, her grandmother replied, 'He had a heart attack while we were making love on Sunday morning.'

Horrified, Katie told her grandmother that two people nearly 100 years old having sex would surely be asking for trouble.

'Oh no, my dear,' replied granny. 'Many years ago, realising our advanced age, we figured out the best time to do it was when the church bells would start to ring. It was just the right rhythm. Nice and slow and even. Nothing too strenuous, simply in on the Ding and out on the Dong.'

She paused to wipe away a tear, and continued, 'And if the darned ice cream truck hadn't come along, he'd still be alive today.'

Ageing Mildred was a 93-year-old woman who was particularly despondent over the recent death of her husband Earl.

She decided that she would just kill herself and join him in death. Thinking it would be best to get it over with quickly, she took out Earl's old army pistol and made the decision to shoot herself in the heart since it was so badly broken in the first place.

Not wanting to miss the vital organ and become a vegetable and burden to someone, she called her doctor to inquire exactly where the heart would be.

'On a woman,' the doctor said, 'your heart would be just below your left breast.'

Later that night Mildred was admitted to hospital with a gunshot wound to her knee.

A little ol' lady, carrying a bag full of money, walked into a bank and demanded to speak with the president of the bank. The teller, in shock, immediately called for the president.

As he approached the little ol' lady, looking at her bag full of dollars, he led her to his office. He then proceeded to ask where she had gotten all this cash.

'I make bets,' she replied. Confused by her answer, he asked her to explain.

She again said 'I make bets and win!'

'What type of bets could you possibly make to win so much money? I don't believe you can win that much just by betting. Prove it!'

'Well, OK,' she said, 'I'll bet you $5,000 dollars that by 10am tomorrow morning, your balls will be square.'

He became totally confused and stated that he couldn't make a bet like that because it was not possible and he didn't want to hurt her.

But again, she offered the bet and then stated that if he was so sure of himself then just bet it! So, he did.

Later that night he went home, stripped and began to examine himself. He thought, 'That poor woman, but hey she wanted to bet!'

At 10am the next morning she entered his office. But there was a man with her. The president asked who he was and she said it was her lawyer to witness the bet. She then asked the president to drop his drawers. He did. She looked at his balls and then asked if she could hold them. He shrugged his shoulder, but then said, 'Hey, go ahead it's your loss.'

Just then he noticed that the lawyer was banging his head against the wall.

When the president asked why, the woman replied, 'Yesterday I bet him $10,000 dollars that by 10am today, I would have the president of the bank's balls in my hands.'

Night time prayer
Now I lay me
Down to sleep
I pray the Lord
My shape to keep

Please no wrinkles
Please no bags
And please lift my butt
Before it sags

Please no age spots
Please no gray
And as for my belly
Please take it away

Please keep me healthy
Please keep me young
And thank you Dear Lord
For all that you've done.
Amen

An old man decided his old wife was getting hard of hearing. So he called her doctor to make an appointment to have her hearing checked.

The doctor said he could see her in two weeks, and meanwhile there's a simple, informal test the husband could do to give the doctor some idea of the dimensions of the problem.

'Here's what you do. Start about 40 feet away from her, and speak in a normal conversational tone and see if she hears you. If not, go to 30 feet, then 20 feet, and so on until you get a response.'

So that evening she's in the kitchen cooking dinner, and he's in the living room, and he says to himself, 'I'm about 40 feet away, let's see what happens.'

'Honey, what's for supper?' No response.

So he moves to the other end of the room, about 30 feet away. 'Honey, what's for supper?' No response.

So he moves into the dining room, about 20 feet away. 'Honey, what's for supper?' No response.

On to the kitchen door, only 10 feet away. 'Honey, what's for supper?' No response.

So he walks right up behind her. 'Honey, what's for supper?' 'For the fifth time! Chicken!!!'

A teenage granddaughter comes downstairs for her date with a very sheer blouse on and no bra. Her grandmother has a fit, telling her not to dare go out like that!

The teenager tells her, 'Loosen up Grams. These are modern times. You gotta let your rose buds show!' and out she goes.

The next day the teenager comes downstairs, and the grandmother is sitting there with no top on. The teenager wants to die. She explains to her grandmother that she has friends coming over and that it is just not appropriate ...

The grandmother says, 'Loosen up, Sweetie. If you can show off your rosebuds, then I can display my hanging baskets.'

The preacher's Sunday sermon was Forgive Your Enemies.

He asked, 'How many of you have forgiven your enemies?' About half held up their hands.

He then repeated his question. Now about 80% held up their hands.

He then repeated his question again. All responded, except one elderly lady.

'Mrs. Jones, are you not willing to forgive your enemies?' asked the preacher.

'I don't have any,' she replied.

'Mrs. Jones, that is very unusual. How old are you?' asked the preacher.

'Ninety-three,' she replied.

'Mrs. Jones, please come down in front and tell the congregation how a person cannot have an enemy in the world,' asked the preacher.

The little sweetheart of a lady tottered down the aisle, and said, 'It's easy, I just outlived all those bitches.'

An elderly couple had been dating for some time. Finally they decided it was time for marriage. Before the wedding, they went out to dinner and had a long conversation regarding how their marriage might work.

They discussed finances, living arrangements and so on. Finally the old gentleman decided it was time to broach the subject of their physical relationship.

'How do you feel about sex?' he asked, rather trustingly.

'Well,' she says, responding very carefully, 'I'd have to say I would like it infrequently.'

The old gentleman sat quietly for a moment. Then looking over his glasses, looked her in the eye casually and asked, 'Was that one or two words?'

Two old ladies were outside their nursing home, having a smoke when it started to rain. One of the ladies pulled out a condom, cut off the end, put it over her cigarette and continued smoking.

Lady 1: *'What's that?'*

Lady 2: *'A condom. This way my cigarette doesn't get wet.'*

Lady 1: *'Where did you get it?'*

Lady 2: *'You can get them at any chemist shop.'*

The next day, Lady 1 hobbles into the local chemist shop and announces to the chemist that she wants a box of condoms. The chemist, obviously embarrassed, looks at her kind of strangely (she is, after all, over 80 years of age), but very delicately asks what brand she prefers.

Lady 1: 'Doesn't matter son, as long as it fits a Camel.'

The chemist fainted.

Morris, a man 85 years of age, married Lou Anne, a lovely 25-year-old. Since her new husband is so old, Lou Anne decides that after their wedding she and Morris should have separate bedrooms, because she is concerned that her new but aged husband may over-exert himself if they spend the entire night together.

After the wedding festivities Lou Anne prepares herself for bed and the expected 'knock' on the door. Sure enough the knock comes, the door opens and there is Morris, her 85-year-old groom ready for action. They unite as one. All goes well, Morris takes leave of his bride, and she prepares to go to sleep.

After a few minutes, Lou Anne hears another knock on her bedroom door, and it's Morris. Again he is ready for more action. Somewhat surprised, Lou Anne consents for more coupling.

When the newlyweds are done, Morris kisses his bride, bids her a fond goodnight and leaves.

She is set to go to sleep again, but, aha you guessed it - Morris is back again, rapping on the door, and is as fresh as a 25-year-old, ready for more action. And, once again they enjoy each other.

But as Morris gets set to leave again, his young bride says to him, 'I am thoroughly impressed that at your age you can perform so well and so often. I have been with guys less than a third of your age who were only good once. You are truly a great lover, Morris.'

Morris, somewhat embarrassed, turns to Lou Anne and says, 'You mean I was here already?'

It was the stir of the town when an 80-year-old man married a 20-year-old girl. After a year of marriage she went into hospital to give birth. The nurse came out to congratulate the fellow saying, 'This is amazing. How do you do it at your age?'

He answered, 'You've got to keep that old motor running.'

The following year the young bride gave birth again. The same nurse said, 'You really are amazing. How do you do it?'

He again said, 'You've got to keep that old motor running.'

The same thing happened the next year.

The nurse said, 'Well, well, well!! You certainly are quite a man!'

He responded 'You've got to keep that old motor running.'

The nurse then said, 'Well, you better change the oil. This one's black!'

A young man saw an elderly couple sitting down to lunch at Burger King. He noticed that they ordered one meal, and an extra drink cup.

As he watched, the gentleman carefully divided the hamburger in half, then counted out the fries. One for him, one for her, until each had half of them. Then he poured half of the soft drink into the extra cup, and set it in front of his wife. The old man began to eat, and his wife sat watching, with her hands folded in her lap.

The young man decided to ask if they would allow him to purchase another meal for them so that they didn't have to split theirs.

The old gentleman said, 'Oh, no. We've been married 50 years, and everything has always been and will always be shared, 50/50.'

The young man than asked the wife if she was going to eat, and she replied, 'Not yet. It's his turn using the teeth.'

A couple has been married for fifty years. They are sitting at the breakfast table one morning when the old gentleman says to his wife, 'Just think, honey, we've been married for fifty years.'

'Yes, she replies, 'just think, fifty years ago we were sitting here at this breakfast table together.'

'I know,' the old man says, 'we were probably sitting here naked as jaybirds fifty years ago.'

'Well,' says Granny snickering, 'what do you say ... should we get naked?'

So the two strip the buff and sit down at the table. 'You know, honey,' the little old lady whispers, 'my nipples are as hot for you today as they were fifty years ago.'

'I'm not surprised,' replies Gramps, 'one's in your coffee and the other is in your porridge.'

As a senior citizen was driving down the freeway, his car phone rang. Answering, he heard his wife's voice urgently warning him, 'Herman, I just heard on the news that there's a car going the wrong way on Interstate 77. Please be careful!'

'Hell,' said Herman, 'it's not just one car. It's hundreds of them!'

Three sisters, ages 92, 94, and 96 live in a house together. One night the 96-year-old runs a bath. She puts one foot in and pauses. She yells down the stairs, 'Was I getting in or out of the bath?'

The 94-year-old yells back, 'I don't know. I'll come up and see.'

She starts up the stairs and pauses. Then, she yells, 'Was I going up the stairs or down?'

The 92-year-old is sitting at the kitchen table having tea, listening to her sisters. She shakes her head and says, 'I sure hope I never get that forgetful.'

She knocks on wood for good measure. She then yells, 'I'll come up and help both of you as soon as I see who's at the door.'

An older couple were lying in bed one night. The husband was falling asleep but the wife was in a romantic mood and wanted to talk. She said, 'You used to hold my hand when we were courting.'

Wearily he reached across, held her hand for a second and tried to get back to sleep. A few moments later she said, 'Then you used to kiss me.'

Mildly irritated, he reached across, gave her a peck on the cheek and settled down to sleep. Thirty seconds later she said, 'Then you used to bite my neck.'

Angrily, he threw back the bedclothes and got out of bed. 'Where are you going?' she asked.

'To get my teeth!' was the reply.

One evening a family brings their frail, elderly mother to a nursing home and leaves her, hoping she will be well cared for. The next morning, the nurses bathe her, feed her a tasty breakfast, and set her in a chair at a window overlooking a lovely flower garden.

She seems OK, but after a while she slowly starts to lean over sideways in her chair. Two attentive nurses immediately rush up to catch her and straighten her up. Again, she seems OK, but after a while, she starts to tilt to the other side. The nurses rush back and once more bring her back upright.

This goes on all morning. Later the family arrives to see how the old woman is adjusting to her new home.

'So Ma, how is it here? Are they treating you all right?' they ask.

'It's pretty nice,' she replies. 'Except they won't let you fart.'

A little old man shuffled slowly into an ice cream parlour, crawled painfully onto a stool, and ordered a banana split.

The waitress asked, 'Crushed nuts?'

'No,' he replied, 'it's just arthritis.'

A travel agent looked up from his desk to see an older lady and an older gentleman peering in the shop window at the posters showing the glamorous destinations around the world. The agent had had a good week and the dejected couple looking in the window gave him a rare feeling of generosity.

He called them into his shop, 'I know that on your pension you could never hope to have a holiday, so I am sending you off to a fabulous resort at my expense, and I won't take no for an answer.'

He took them inside and asked his secretary to book two flights and book a room in a five star hotel. They, as can be expected, gladly accepted, and were off!

About a month later the little old lady came in to his shop. 'And how did you like your holiday?' he asked eagerly.

'The flight was exciting and the room was lovely,' she said. 'I've come to thank you. But, one thing puzzled me. Who was that old fart I had to share the room with?'

Heaven & Hell

Once upon a time in the Kingdom of Heaven, God went missing for six days. Eventually, Michael the archangel found him, resting on the Seventh day. He inquired of God, 'Where have you been?'

God sighed a deep sigh of satisfaction and proudly pointed downwards through the clouds. 'Look Michael, look what I've made.' Archangel Michael looked puzzled and said, 'What is it?'

'It's a planet,' replied God, 'and I've put LIFE on it. I'm going to call it Earth, and it's going to be a place of great balance.'

'Balance?' inquired Michael, still confused.

God explained, pointing to different parts of Earth. 'For example, Northern Europe will be a place of great opportunity and wealth while Southern Europe is going to be poor. The Middle East over there will be a hot spot. Over there I've placed a continent of white people and over there is a continent of black people,' God continued, pointing to different countries.

'And over there, I call this place America. North America will be rich and powerful and cold, while South America will be poor and hot and friendly. And the little spot in the middle is Central America, which is a hot spot. Can you see the balance?'

'Yes,' said the Archangel, impressed by God's work. Then he pointed to a large land mass and asked, 'What's that one?'

'Ah,' said God. 'That's Australia, the most glorious place on Earth. There are beautiful mountains, rainforests, rivers, streams and an exquisite coastline. The people are good-looking, intelligent and humorous, and they're going to be found travelling the world. They'll be extremely sociable, hard-working and high-achieving, and they will be known through the world as diplomats and carriers of peace. I'm also going to give them super-human, undefeatable sporting players and teams of cricket, rugby, tennis, golf and the like, who will be admired and feared by all who come across them.'

Michael gasped in wonder and admiration, but then exclaimed, 'But you said there would be BALANCE!'

God replied wisely, 'Wait until you see the ugly, whingeing, sheep-loving Kiwis I'm putting next to them!'

In the beginning, God created the earth and rested.
Then God created Man and rested,
Then God created Woman,
Since then, neither God nor Man has rested.

One day a guy died and found himself in hell. As he was wallowing in despair, he had his first meeting with a demon. The demon asked, 'Why so glum?'

The guy responded, 'What do you think? I'm in hell!'

'Hell's not so bad,' the demon said. 'We actually have a lot of fun down here. You a drinking man?'

'Sure,' the man said, 'I love to drink.'

'Well you're gonna love Mondays then. On Mondays all we do is drink. Whiskey, tequila, Guinness, wine coolers, vodka and Red Bull. We drink till we throw up and then we drink some more!'

The guy is astounded. 'Damn, that sounds great.'

'You a smoker?' the demon asked.

'You better believe it!'

'You're gonna love Tuesdays. We get the finest cigars from all over the world and smoke our lungs out. If you get cancer, no biggie. You're already dead, remember?'

'Wow,' the guy said, 'that's awesome!'

The demon continued, 'I bet you like to gamble.'

'Why yes, as a matter of fact I do.'

'Wednesdays you can gamble all you want. Craps, blackjack, roulette, poker, slots, whatever. If you go bankrupt, well, you're dead anyhow. You into drugs?'

'Are you kidding? I love drugs! You don't mean ...'

'That's right! Thursday is drug day. Help yourself to a great big bowl of crack, or smack. Smoke a doobie the size of a submarine. You can do all the drugs you want, you're dead, who cares!'

'Wow,' the guy said, starting to feel better about his situation, 'I never realised Hell was such a cool place!'

The demon said, 'You gay?'

'No way!'

'Ooooh, you're gonna hate Fridays!'

Two cannibals meet one day. The first cannibal says, 'You know I just can't seem to get a tender missionary. I've baked them, I've roasted them, I've stewed them, I've barbecued them, I've tried every sort of marinade. I just cannot seem to get them tender.'

The second cannibal says, 'What kind of missionary do you use?'

The other replied, 'You know, the ones that hang out at that place at the bend of the river. They have those brown cloaks with a rope around the waist and they're sort of bald on top with a funny ring of hair on their heads.'

'Aha!' the second cannibal replies. 'There's your problem; those are friars.'

Last night while I lay sleeping
I died or so it seems
Then I went to heaven
But t'was only in my dreams

But, it seems St. Peter met me
There at the pearly gate
He said, 'I must check your record
So stand right here and wait

I see where you drank whiskey
And used tobacco, too
Fact is you've done everything
That a good person shouldn't do

We can't have people like you up here
Your life was full of sin.'
Then he read the last of my record
Grasped my hand and said, 'Come in.'

He took me up to the Big Boss
Said 'Take him in and treat him well
He worked for a Telecommunications company, sir
He's already had his share of hell.'

⁙

One day, while a woodcutter was cutting a branch of a tree above a river, his axe fell into the river. When he cried out, the Lord appeared and asked, 'Why are you crying?'

The woodcutter replied that his axe has fallen into water, and he needed the axe to make his living. The Lord went down into the water and reappeared with a golden axe.

'Is this your axe?' the Lord asked.

The woodcutter replied, 'No.'

The Lord again went down and came up with a silver axe. 'Is this your axe?' the Lord asked.

Again, the woodcutter replied, 'No.'

The Lord went down again and came up with an iron axe. 'Is this your axe?' the Lord asked.

The woodcutter replied, 'Yes.'

The Lord was pleased with the man's honesty and gave him all three axes to keep, and the woodcutter went home happy. Some time later the woodcutter was walking with his wife along the riverbank, and his wife fell into the river. When he cried out, the Lord again appeared and asked him, 'Why are you crying?'

'Oh Lord, my wife has fallen into the water!'

The Lord went down into the water and came up with Jennifer Lopez.

'Is this your wife?' the Lord asked.

'Yes,' cried the woodcutter.

The Lord was furious. 'You lied! That is an untruth!'

The woodcutter replied, 'Oh, forgive me, my Lord. It is a misunderstanding. You see, if I had said "No" to Jennifer Lopez, you would have come up with Catherine Zeta-Jones. Then if I also said "No" to her, you would have come up with my wife. Had I then said "Yes", you would have given me all three. Lord, I am a poor man, and am not able to take care of three wives, so THAT'S why I said "Yes" to Jennifer Lopez.'

An Australian, Irishman and an Englishman were sitting in a bar. There was one other man at the bar. He had long hair and a medium length beard. The three men kept looking at this other man, for he seemed terribly familiar. They stared and stared, wondering where they had seen him before when suddenly the Irishman cried out, 'My God! I know who that man is - it's Jesus!'

The others looked again and sure enough, it was Jesus himself, sitting alone at a table.

The Irishman calls out across the lounge, 'Hey! Hey you! Are you Jesus?!'

Jesus looks over at him, smiles a small smile and nods his head. 'Yes, I am Jesus,' he says.

Well, the Irishman calls the bartender over and says to him, 'I'd like you to give Jesus over there a pint of Guinness from me.' The bartender pours Jesus a Guinness. Jesus looks over, raises his glass, thanks and drinks.

The Englishman then calls out, 'Er, excuse me Sir, but would you be Jesus?'

Jesus smiles and says 'Yes, I am Jesus.'

The Englishman beckons the bartender and tells him to send over a pint of Newcastle Brown Ale for Jesus, which the bartender duly does. As before, Jesus accepts the drink and smiles over at the table.

Then the Australian calls out, 'Oy, you! D'ya reckon you're Jesus or what?'

Jesus nods and says 'Yes, I am Jesus.'

The Australian is mighty impressed and has the bartender send over a schooner of VB for Jesus which Jesus accepts with pleasure.

Some time later, after finishing the drinks, Jesus leaves his seat and approaches our three friends. He reaches for the hand of the Irishman and shakes it, thanking him for the Guinness. When he lets go, the Irishman gives a cry of amazement, 'Oh God! The arthritis is gone! The arthritis I've had for years is gone! It's a miracle!'

Jesus then shakes the Englishman's hand, thanking him for the Newcastle. Upon letting go, the Englishman's eyes widen in shock, 'By jove, the migraine! The migraine I've had for 40 years is completely gone! It's a miracle!!!'

Jesus then goes to approach the Australian who says ... 'Back off mate! I'm on compo!!'

The Reverend Francis Norton woke up Sunday morning and realising it was an exceptionally beautiful and sunny early spring day, decided he just had to play golf. So ... he told the Associate

Pastor that he was feeling sick and convinced him to say Mass for him that day.

As soon as the Associate Pastor left the room, Father Norton headed out of town to a golf course about forty miles away. This way he knew he wouldn't accidentally meet anyone he knew from his parish. Setting up on his first tee, he was alone. After all, it was Sunday morning and everyone else was in church!

At about this time, Saint Peter leaned over to the lord while looking down from the heavens and exclaimed, ' You're not going to let him get away with this, are you?'

The lord sighed, and said, 'No, I guess not.'

Just then Father Norton hit the ball and it shot straight towards the pin, dropping just short of it, rolled up and fell into the hole. It was a 420 yard hole-in-one!

St Peter was astonished. He looked at the Lord and asked, 'Why did you let him do that?'

The Lord smiled and replied, 'Who's he going to tell?'

Three women die together in an accident and go to heaven. When they get there, St. Peter says, 'We only have one rule here in heaven … Don't step on the ducks!'

So they enter heaven, and sure enough, there are ducks all over the place. It is almost impossible not to step on a duck, and although they try their best to avoid them, the first woman accidentally steps on one.

Along comes St. Peter with the ugliest man she ever saw. St. Peter chains them together and says, 'Your punishment for stepping on a duck is to spend eternity chained to this ugly man!'

The next day, the second woman steps accidentally on a duck and along comes St. Peter, who doesn't miss a thing. With him is another extremely ugly man. He chains them together with the same admonishment as for the first woman.

The third woman has observed all this and, not wanting to be chained for all eternity to an ugly man, is very, very careful where

139

HEAVEN & HELL JOKES

she steps. She manages to go months without stepping on any ducks, but one day St. Peter comes up to her with the most handsome man she has ever laid eyes on ... very tall, long eyelashes, muscular, and thin.

St. Peter chains them together without saying a word. The happy woman says, 'I wonder what I did to deserve being chained to you for all of eternity?'

The guy says, 'I don't know about you, but I stepped on a duck!'

In the beginning God created day and night. He created day for footy matches going to the beach and barbecues. He created night for going prawning, sleeping and barbecues.

God saw that it was good.

Evening came and morning came and it was the Second Day. On the Second Day, God created water - for surfing, swimming and barbecues on the beach.

God saw that it was good.

Evening came and morning came and it was the Third Day. On the Third Day, God created the Earth to bring forth plants - to provide malt and yeast for beer and wood for barebecues.

God saw that it was good.

Evening came and morning came and it was the Fourth Day. On the Fourth Day, God created animals and crustaceans for chops, sausages, steak and prawns for barbecues.

God saw that it was good.

Evening came and morning came and it was the Fifth Day. On the Fifth day, God created a bloke - to go to the footy, enjoy the beach, drink the beer and eat the meat and prawns at bbq's.

God saw that it was good.

Evening came and morning came and it was the Sixth Day. On the Sixth Day, God saw that this bloke was lonely and needed someone to go to the footy, surf, drink beer, eat and stand around the barbie with. So God created Mates, and God saw that they were good blokes.

God saw that it was good.

Evening came and morning came and it was the Seventh Day. On the Seventh Day, God looked around at the twinkling barbie fires, heard the hiss of opening beer cans and the raucous laughter of all the Blokes, smelled the aroma of grilled chops and sizzling prawns and God saw that it was good ... well almost good.

God saw that the blokes were too tired to clean up and needed a rest.

So God created Sheilas - to clean the house, bear children, wash, and cook and clean the barbecue. God saw that it was not just good, it was better than that, it was Bloody Good! ... IT WAS AUSTRALIA!!!

———— ₤ ₤ ₤ ————

There was a Protestant boys' school alongside a Catholic boys' school. The boys' toilet in the Protestant school blocked up and couldn't be used, so the Principal went over to the Head Brother and asked if his boys could use their toilet. The Head brother said, 'By all means go ahead, you would do the same for us.'

One day, one of the Brothers from the Catholic school was walking past the toilet when he heard yelling and laughter coming from the toilet block. He went in to investigate and found the Protestant boys having a competition to see who could pee the highest up the wall (as all boys do at some time).

He scolded the boys and told them his Catholic boys would never behave like that, and he would report the matter to their Principal.

He went straight up to the Head Brother's office and said, 'Head Brother, I just saw a terrible thing, I saw those Protestant boys in our toilet having a competition to see who could pee the highest up the wall, I was so disgusted.'

The Head Brother was shocked and said, 'And what did you do about it?'

The Head Brother said, 'I was so angry I hit the roof.'

'Well done!' said the Head Brother, 'we can't have those Protestant boys beating us.'

Eve called out to God, 'Lord, I have a problem.'

'What's the problem, Eve?'

'I know that you created me and provided this beautiful garden and all of these wonderful animals, as well as that hilarious snake, but I'm just not happy.'

'And why is that Eve?'

'Lord, I am lonely, and I'm sick to death of apples.'

'Well Eve, in that case, I have a solution. I shall create a man for you.'

'What is that Lord?'

'It will be a flawed creature with many bad traits. He'll lie, cheat, and be vain; all in all, he'll give you a hard time. But, he'll be bigger, faster, and will like to hunt and kill things. He will look silly when he is aroused, but since you've been complaining, I'll create him in such a way that he will satisfy your physical needs. He will be witless and will revel in childish things like fighting and kicking a ball about. He won't be too smart, so he will also need your advice to think properly.'

'Sounds great,' said Eve, with ironically raised eyebrows, 'but what's the catch, Lord?'

'Well, you can have him on one condition.'

'And what's that Lord?'

'As I said, he'll be proud, arrogant, and self-admiring ... so you'll have to let him believe that I made him first. And it will have to be our little secret. You know, woman to woman.'

A woman arrived at the Gates of Heaven. While she was waiting for St. Peter to greet her, she peeked through the gates. She saw a beautiful banquet table. Sitting all around were her parents and all the other people she had loved and who had died before her. They saw her and began calling greetings to her 'Hello, how are you! We've been waiting for you! Good to see you.'

When St. Peter came by, the woman said to him, 'This is such a wonderful place! How do I get in?'

'You have to spell a word,' St. Peter told her.

'Which word?' the woman asked.

'Love.'

The woman correctly spelled 'Love' and St. Peter welcomed her into Heaven.

About a year later, St. Peter came to the woman and asked her to watch the Gates of Heaven for him that day.

While the woman was guarding the Gates of Heaven, her husband arrived. 'I'm pleased to see you,' the woman said. 'How have you been?'

'Oh, I've been doing pretty well since you died,' her husband told her. 'I married the beautiful young nurse who took care of you while you were ill. And then I won Tattslotto. I sold the little house you and I lived in and bought a huge mansion. And, my wife and I travelled all around the world. We were on vacation in Cancun and I went water skiing today. I fell and hit my head, and here I am. What a bummer. How do I get in?'

'You have to spell a word,' the woman told him.

'Which word?' her husband asked.

'Czechoslovakia.'

'Well, Bill,' said God, 'I'm really confused on this one. I'm not sure whether to send you to Heaven or Hell. After all, you helped society enormously by putting a computer in almost every home in the world, and yet you created that ghastly Windows. I'm going to do something I've never done before. I'm going to let you decide where you want to go.'

Mr. Gates replied, 'Well, thanks, God. What's the difference between the two?'

God said, 'You can take a peek at both places briefly if it will help you decide. Shall we look at Hell first?'

'Sure!' said Bill, 'Let's go!'

Bill was amazed! He saw a clean, white sandy beach with clear waters. There were thousands of beautiful men and women running around, playing in the water, laughing and frolicking about. The sun was shining and the temperature was perfect.

'This is great!' said Bill. 'If this is Hell, I can't wait to see Heaven.'

God replied, 'Let's go!' and so off they went to Heaven.

Bill saw puffy white clouds in a beautiful blue sky with angels drifting about playing harps and singing. It was nice, but surely not as enticing as Hell. Mr. Gates thought for only a brief moment and rendered his decision.

'God, I do believe I would like to go to Hell.'

'As you desire,' said God.

Two weeks later, God decided to check up on the late billionaire to see how things were going. He found Bill shackled to a wall, screaming amongst the hot flames in a dark cave. He was being burned and tortured by demons.

'How ya doin', Bill?' asked God.

Bill responded with anguish and despair, 'This is awful! This is not what I expected at all! What happened to the beach and the beautiful women playing in the water?'

'Oh THAT!' said God. 'That was the Screensaver.'

At the wake, a woman told her priest that ever since she was a child, she and her father had discussed life after death. They had agreed that whoever went first would try to contact the other. They had discussed it again only two weeks before his death. He died in her home, and a few hours later, the smoke alarm in her garage went off. She had lived there for 28 years and it had never gone off before. She didn't know how to stop it and had to call the security company.

The next morning, the smoke alarm sounded again - and the reason finally dawned on her. She said aloud, 'OK, Dad, I missed the signal yesterday, but I've got it now. Thanks for letting me know you're safe on the other side. Now turn the darn thing off so I don't have to call the security company again.' And it went off!

She immediately called her priest to relay the good news. His response, 'Dear, if every time your father sends you a message, he sets off the smoke alarm, just where do you think he's calling from?!'

———————————— ¡ ¡ ¡ ————————————

A new priest at his first mass was so nervous he could hardly speak. After mass he asked the monsignor how he had done. The monsignor replied, 'When I am worried about getting nervous on the pulpit, I put a glass of vodka next to the water glass. If I start to get nervous, I take a sip.'

So next Sunday he took the monsignor's advice.

At the beginning of the sermon, he got nervous and took a drink. He proceeded to talk up a storm.

Upon his return to his office after the mass, he found the following note on the door:

1. Sip the vodka, don't gulp.
2. There are 10 commandments, not 12.
3. There are 12 disciples, not 10.
4. Jesus was consecrated, not constipated.
5. Jacob wagered his donkey, he did not bet his ass.
6. We do not refer to Jesus Christ as the late J.C.
7. The Father, Son, and Holy Ghost are not referred to as Daddy, Junior and the Spook.
8. David slew Goliath, he did not kick the shit out of him.
9. When David was hit by a rock and was knocked off his donkey, don't say he was stoned off his ass.
10. We do not refer to the cross as the 'Big T'.
11. When Jesus broke the bread at the last supper he said, 'Take this and eat it for it is my body.' He did not say 'Eat me.'

12. *The Virgin Mary is not called 'Mary with the Cherry'.*
13. *The recommended grace before a meal is not, 'Rub-A-Dub-Dub thanks for the grub, Yeah God'.*
14. *Next Sunday there will be a taffy pulling contest at St. Peter's not a peter pulling contest at St. Taffy's.*

───────────── ⁞⁞⁞ ─────────────

There was a preacher whose wife was expecting a baby. The preacher went to the congregation and asked for a raise. After much consideration and discussion, they passed a rule that whenever the preacher's family expanded, so would his pay cheque.

After six children, this started to get expensive and the congregation decided to hold another meeting to discuss the preacher's salary.

There was much yelling and bickering about how much the clergyman's additional children were costing the church.

'Having children is an act of God!' Silence fell upon the congregation.

In the back of the room a little old lady stood up and in her frail voice said, 'Snow and rain are also acts of God, but when we get too much, we wear rubbers!'

───────────── ⁞⁞⁞ ─────────────

After getting all of Pope John Paul's luggage loaded into the limo (and he doesn't travel light), the driver notices that the Pope is still standing on the curb.

'Excuse me, Your Eminence,' says the driver, 'would you please take your seat so we can leave?'

'Well, to tell you the truth,' says the Pope, 'they never let me drive at the Vatican, and I'd really like to drive today.'

'I'm sorry but I cannot let you do that. I'd lose my job! And what if something should happen?' protests the driver, wishing he'd never gone to work that morning.

'There might be something extra in it for you,' says the Pope. Reluctantly, the driver gets in the back as the Pope climbs in behind the wheel. The driver quickly regrets his decision when, after exiting the airport, the Supreme Pontiff floors it, accelerating the limo to 105 mph.

'Please slow down, Your Holiness!!!' pleads the worried driver, but the Pope keeps the pedal to the metal until they hear sirens.

'Oh, my God, I'm gonna lose my licence,' moans the driver. The Pope pulls over and rolls down the window as the cop approaches, but the cop takes one look at him, goes back to his motorcycle, and gets on the radio. 'I need to talk to the Chief,' he says to the dispatcher. The Chief gets on the radio and the cop tells him that he's stopped a limo going a hundred and five.

'So bust him,' said the Chief.

'I don't think we want to do that, he's really important,' said the cop.

Chief exclaimed, 'All the more reason!'

'No, I mean really important,' said the cop.

The Chief then asked, 'Who ya got there, the Mayor?'

Cop: 'Bigger.'

Chief: 'Governor?'

Cop: 'Bigger.'

'Well,' said the Chief, 'Who is it?'

Cop: 'I think it's God!'

Chief: 'What makes you think it's God?'

Cop: 'He's got the Pope for a limo driver!'

Three Italian nuns die and go to heaven where they are met at the Pearly gates by St. Peter. He says, 'Ladies, you all led such wonderful lives that I am granting you six months to go back to earth and be anyone you want.

The first nun, 'I want to be Sophia Loren' and *poof*, she's gone.

The second nun, 'I want to be Madonna' and *poof*, she's gone. The third nun says, 'I want to be Sara Pipalini.'

St. Peter looks perplexed. 'Who?' he asks.

'Sara Pipalini', replies the nun.

St. Peter shakes his head and says, 'I'm sorry but that name doesn't ring a bell.'

The nun then takes the newspaper out of her habit and hands it to St. Peter. He reads the paper and starts laughing. He hands the paper back to her and says ...

'No Sister, this headline says "Sahara Pipeline, laid by 1900 men in 6 months".'

————————— ⁛ —————————

God said, 'Adam, I want you to do something for me.'

Adam said, 'Gladly, Lord, what do you want me to do?'

God said, 'Go down into that valley.'

Adam said, 'What's a valley?'

God explained it to him.

Then God said, 'Cross the river.'

Adam said, 'What's a river?'

God explained that to him, and then said, 'Go over to the hill ...'

Adam said, 'What is a hill?'

So, God explained to Adam what a hill was.

He told Adam, 'On the other side of the hill you will find a cave.'

Adam said, 'What's a cave?'

After God explained, he said, 'In the cave you will find a woman.'

Adam said, 'What's a woman?'

So God explained that to him, too.

Then, God said, 'I want you to reproduce.'

Adam said, 'How do I do that?'

God first said (under his breath), 'Geez ...'

And then, just like everything else, God explained that to Adam, as well.

So, Adam goes down into the valley, across the river, and over the hill, into the cave, and finds the woman. Then, in about five minutes, he was back. God, his patience wearing thin, said angrily, 'What is it now?'

And Adam asked, 'What's a headache?'

A couple made a deal that whoever died first would come back and inform the other of the afterlife. The biggest fear was that there was no heaven. After a long life, the husband was the first to go, and true to his word, he made contact.

'Rose ... Rose ...'

'Is that you, Douglas?'

'Yes, I've come back like we agreed.'

'What's it like?'

'Well, I get up in the morning, I have sex. I have breakfast, I have sex. I bathe in the sun, then I have sex twice. I have lunch, then sex pretty much all afternoon. After supper, I have sex until late at night. The next day it starts again.'

'Oh, Douglas, you surely must be in heaven.'

'Not exactly. I'm a rabbit in Queensland.'

One Sunday morning, the pastor noticed little Alex was staring up at the large plaque that hung in the foyer of the church. It was covered with names, and small Australian flags were mounted on either side of it.

The seven-year-old had been staring at the plaque for some time, so the pastor walked up, stood beside the little boy, and said quietly, 'Good morning, Alex.'

'Good morning, Pastor,' replied the young man, still focused on the plaque.

'Pastor, what is this?'

'Well, son, it's a memorial to all the young men and women who died in the service.'

Soberly, they stood together, staring at the large plaque. Little Alex's voice was barely audible, trembling with fear, when he asked, 'Which service, the 9.45 or the 11.15?'

A new Monk arrives at the Monastery and is assigned to help the other monks in copying the old texts by hand. But soon he realises that the other monks are copying from copies and not from the original manuscripts. He goes to the Head Monk and points out that if there was an error in the first copy, that error would be continued in all the other copies.

The Head Monk says, 'We have been copying from the copies for centuries, but you make a good point my son.'

So the Head Monk goes down to the cellar with one of the copies to check it against the original manuscript. Hours go by and nobody sees him so the new Monk is sent downstairs to look for him. He hears sobbing coming from the back of the cellar and finds the old Head Monk leaning over one of the original books crying.

He asks the Head Monk what's wrong and in a choked voice came the reply ... 'The word is celebrate.'

Two old rugby players are on their last legs and discussing death and wether they play rugby in heaven or not.

'I'll tell you what Bob, if I die first, I'll find a way to come back and tell you if they play rugby in heaven,' says one.

'That's a good idea John, I'll tell you what, I'll do the same if I die first,' says Bob.

Low and behold, but two weeks later old Bob dies. RIP.

After the funeral, John is in his lounge room, knocking back a few drops of rum, when suddenly he hears a voice coming from the dark behind him. 'Don't turn around John, it's me, Bob. I can only stay a minute and you're not allowed to see me.'

John can't believe his ears and bursts out in tears. 'Me old mate Bob. Back from the dead. I can't believe it. I've missed you so much, old mate.'

'I have to go John, but I came back to fulfil my promise and tell you whether they play rugby in heaven,' says Bob.

'Well, do they?' John asks excitedly.

'I have both good and bad news for you old friend, which do you want first.'

'Stop screwing around just like you did for 70 years when you were alive and give me the good news mate,' snaps John.

'The good news,' starts Bob, 'is that they absolutely do play rugby in heaven. It's the number one sport and there is an international twice a day.'

'That's bloody fantastic,' exclaims John, 'but what's the bad news?'

'Well, I don't know how to tell you this John, but ...' There is a long silence.

'But what?' urges John.

'You've been selected to play next week!!!'

The elderly priest, speaking to the younger priest, said, 'It was a good idea to replace the first four pews with plush bucket theater seats. It worked like a charm. Now the front of the church fills first.'

The young priest nodded, and the old priest continued, 'And you told me a little more beat to the music would bring young people back to church, so I supported you when you brought in that rock 'n roll gospel choir. We are packed to the balcony.'

'Thank you, Father,' answered the young priest. 'I am pleased that you are open to the new ideas of youth.'

'Well,' said the elderly priest, 'I'm afraid you've gone too far with the drive-through confessional.'

'But, Father,' protested the young priest, 'my confessions have nearly doubled since I began that!'

'I know, son,' replied the elderly priest, 'but that flashing neon sign, "Toot 'n Tell or Go to Hell" can't stay on the church roof!'

An Australian dies and is sent to hell. He had been a horrible man throughout life and even the devil wanted to punish him, so he puts him to work breaking up rocks with a sledgehammer.

To make it worse he cranks up the temperature and the humidity. 'Love my kingdom!' laughs the devil.

After a couple of days the devil checks in on his victim to see if he is suffering adequately. The devil is aghast as he looks at the Aussie happily swinging his hammer and whistling a happy tune. The devil walks up to him and says, 'I don't understand this. I've turned the heat way up, it's humid, you're crushing rocks ... why are you so happy?'

The Aussie, smiling big, looks at the devil and replies, 'This is great! It reminds me of January in Australia. Hot, humid, a good place to work. It reminds me of home. This is fantastic!'

The devil, extremely perplexed, walks away to ponder the Aussie's remarks. Then he decides to drop the temperature, send down driving rain and torrential wind. Soon, hell is a wet, muddy mess. Walking in mud up to his knees with dust blowing into his eyes, the Aussie is happily slogging through the mud pushing a wheelbarrow full of crushed rocks.

Again, the devil asks how he can be happy in such conditions. The Aussie replies, 'This is great! Just like September in Darwin. It reminds me of working out in the fields with spring planting!'

The devil is now completely baffled. Angry, and desperate to make hell really hell, he tries one last ditch effort. He makes the temperature plummet. Suddenly hell is blanketed in snow and ice. Confident that this will surely make the Australian unhappy, the devil checks in on him.

He is aghast at what he sees. The Aussie is dancing, singing, and twirling his sledgehammer as he cavorts in glee.

'How can you be so happy? Don't you know it's 40 below zero!?' screams the devil.

Jumping up and down the Aussie throws a snowball at the devil and yells, 'Hell's frozen over!! This means the Wallabies won the World Cup!!!'

International

A construction site boss was interviewing people for a job, when along came an Italian.

I'm not hiring any Italians, the foreman thought to himself, so he made up a test to avoid hiring the Italian without getting into an argument.

'Here's your first question,' the foreman said. 'Without using numbers, represent the number 9.'

'Widout numbers?' the Italian says. 'Dat is easy,' and proceeds to draw three trees.

'What's this?' the boss asks.

'Ave you got no brain? Tree and tree and tree make nine,' says the Italian.

'Fair enough,' says the boss. 'Here is your second question. Use the same rules, but this time the number is 99.'

The Italian stares into space for a while, then picks up the picture that he has just drawn and makes a smudge on each tree. 'Ere you go.'

The boss scratches his head and says, 'How on earth do you get that to represent 99?'

'Each of da trees is dirty now! So it's dirty tree, and dirty tree, and dirty tree. Dat is 99.'

The boss is getting worried he's going to have to hire this Italian, so he says, 'All right, last question. Same rules again, but represent the number 100.'

The Italian stares into space some more, then he picks up the picture again and makes a little mark at the base of each tree, and says, 'Ere you go, 100.'

The boss looks at the attempt, and says 'You must be nuts if you think that represents a hundred.'

The Italian leans forward and points to the marks at the base of each tree, and says, 'A little dog come along and crap by each tree. So now you got dirty tree and a turd, dirty tree and a turd, and dirty tree and a turd, which make 100. So when I start?'

An officer in the US Naval Reserve was attending a conference that included admirals from both the U.S. Navy and the French Navy. At a cocktail reception, he found himself in a small group that included personnel from both Navies.

The French admiral started complaining that whereas Europeans learned many languages, Americans learned only English. He then asked, 'Why is it that we have to speak English in these conferences rather than you speak French?'

Without hesitation, the American Admiral replied, 'Maybe it's because the Brits, Canadians, Aussies, and the Americans have arranged it so you would not have to speak German.'

A Polish man married a Canadian girl after he had been in Canada a year or so and, although his English was far from perfect, they got on very well. Until the day he rushed into his lawyer's office and asked him if he could arrange a divorce for him – 'very quick'.

The lawyer said that the speed for getting a divorce would depend on the circumstances and asked him the following questions.

LAWYER: 'Have you any grounds?'

POLE: 'JA, JA, an acre and half and a nice little home with three bedrooms.'

LAWYER: 'No, I mean what is the foundation of this case?'

POLE: 'It is made of concrete, brick and mortar.'

LAWYER: 'Does either of you have a real grudge?'

POLE: 'No, he replied. We have a two-car carport and have never really needed one.'

LAWYER: 'I mean, what are your relations like?'

POLE: 'All my relations are in Poland.'

LAWYER: 'Is there any infidelity in your marriage?'

POLE: 'Yes, we have hi fidelity stereo set and DVD player with 6.1 sound. We don't necessarily like the music, but the answer to your questions is yes.'

LAWYER: 'No, I mean, does your wife beat you up?'

POLE: 'NO, I'm always up before her.'

LAWYER: 'Is your wife a nagger?'

POLE: 'NO, she white.'

LAWYER: 'WHY do you want this divorce?'

POLE: 'SHE going to kill me.'

LAWYER: 'What makes you think that?'

POLE: 'I got proof.'

LAWYER: 'What kind of proof?'

POLE: 'She going to poison me. She buy a bottle at the drug store and put on shelf in bathroom. I can read … it says, "Polish Remover".'

Two Mexican cops are investigating a murder.

Carlos turns to his partner and asks, 'So what do you think?' to which his partner replies, 'I think he's been shot by a golf gun.'

'I've never heard of a golf gun before,' said Carlos.

His partner replies, 'Well, it sure made a hole in Juan.'

A guy was sitting in an airplane when another guy took the seat beside him. The new guy was a wreck, pale, hands shaking, biting his nails and moaning in fear.

'Hey, pal, what's the matter?' said the first guy.

'I've been transferred to Los Angeles, California,' he answered nervously. 'They've got race riots, drugs, the highest crime rate in the country ...'

'Hold on,' said the first. 'I've been in L.A all my life, and it's not as bad as the media says. Find a nice home, go to work, mind your own business, enrol your kids in a good school and it's as safe as anywhere in the world.'

The second guy stopped shaking for a moment and said, 'Oh, thank God. I was worried to death! But if you live there and say it's OK, I'll take your word for it. By the way, what do you do for a living?'

'Me?' said the first, 'I'm the tail gunner on a bread truck.'

Charlie was a Chinese shop-keeper who used to pass Nick the Greek's shop every Friday to do his banking.

As he passed by, Nick and his mates would call out, 'What day is it Charlie?'

Charlie would reply 'It is FLIDAY.'

This would cause much laughter among Nick and his mates. Poor old Charlie got fed up with this so he took speech lessons to fix the problem.

Then one Friday as he passed Nick's shop and they called out, 'What day is it Charlie?'

He replied in the most eloquent and perfect English, 'Today is most certainly FRIDAY ... You GLEEK PLICKS!'

Three men, one German, one Japanese and a hillbilly were sitting naked in a sauna. Suddenly there was a beeping sound. The German pressed his forearm and the beep stopped. The others looked at him questioningly.

'That was my pager,' he said, 'I have a microchip under the skin of my arm.'

A few minutes later a phone rang. The Japanese fellow lifted his palm to his ear. When he finished he explained, 'That was my mobile phone. I have a micro chip in my hand.'

The hillbilly felt decidedly low tech, but not to be outdone he decided he had to do something just as impressive. He stepped out of the sauna and went to the bathroom. He returned with a piece of toilet paper hanging from his behind.

The others raised their eyebrows and stared at him. The hillbilly finally said ... 'Well, will you look at that, I'm getting a fax.'

An aircraft was about to crash; there were five passengers on board but only four parachutes.

The first passenger said, 'I'm Kobe Bryant, the best NBA basketball player, the Lakers need me, I can't afford to die ... ' So he took the first pack and left the plane.

The second passenger, Hillary Clinton, said, 'I am the wife of the former President of the United States, I am the most ambitious woman in the world, I am also a New York Senator and a potential future President.' She just took the second parachute and jumped out of the plane.

The third passenger, John Howard, said, 'I am the Prime Minister of Australia, I have a great responsibility being the leader of a great nation. And above all I'm the most intelligent Prime Minister in Australian history, so Australia's people won't let me die.' So he put on the pack next to him and jumped out of the plane.

The fourth passenger, the Pope, says to the fifth passenger, a 10-year-old school boy, 'I am old and frail and I don't have many years left, as a Christian I will sacrifice my life and let you have the last parachute.'

The boy said, 'It's OK, there's a parachute left for you. Australia's most intelligent Prime Minister has taken my school backpack.'

159

International Jokes

A language instructor was explaining to her class that in French, nouns, unlike their English counterparts, are grammatically designated as masculine or feminine.

'House,' in French, is feminine – 'la maison'.

'Pencil,' in French, is masculine – 'le crayon'.

One puzzled student asked, 'What gender is computer?'

The teacher did not know, and the word wasn't in her French dictionary. So for fun she split the class into two groups appropriately enough, by gender, and asked them to decide whether computer should be a masculine or feminine noun. Both groups were required to give four reasons for their recommendation.

The men's group decided that computers should definitely be of the feminine gender (la computer), because:

1. No one but their creator understands their internal logic,

2. The native language they use to communicate with other computers is incomprehensible to everyone else,

3. Even the smallest mistakes are stored in long-term memory for possible later retrieval, and

4. As soon as you make a commitment to one, you find yourself spending half your pay on accessories for it.

The women's group, however, concluded that computers should be masculine (le computer), because:

1. In order to do anything with them, you have to turn them on,

2. They have a lot of data but still can't think for themselves,

*3. They are supposed to help you solve problems, but half the time they **are** the problem, and*

4. As soon as you commit to one, you realise that if you'd waited a little longer, you could have gotten a better model.

The women won.

According to inside contacts, the Japanese banking crisis shows no signs of stopping. Following last week's news that Origami Bank had folded, we are hearing that Sumo Bank has gone belly up and Bonsai Bank plans to cut back some of its branches.

Karaoke Bank is up for sale and is (you guessed it!) going for a song.

Meanwhile, shares in Kamikaze Bank have nose-dived and 500 back-office staff at Karate Bank got the chop.

Analysts report that there is something fishy going on at Sushi Bank and staff fear they may get a raw deal.

One day the US President's wife Lady Bush died and went to Heaven. When she got there she was met by St. Peter at the Pearly Gates.

She saw lots of clocks, all moving at different speeds. She asked St, Peter what they are.

He replied, 'They are lie clocks and the hands tick every time a person lies.'

She saw one that had only moved twice. St. Peter told her that it was Mother Theresa's clock. Then she saw one that had moved eight times. St. Peter told her it was George Washington's clock.

Then she asked 'Where's George's clock?' to which St. Peter replied, 'It's in my office. I use it as a ceiling fan.'

Before the 2001 inauguration of George Bush, he was invited to a get acquainted tour of the White House. After drinking several glasses of iced tea, he asked Bill Clinton if he could use his personal bathroom.

When he entered Clinton's private toilet, he was astonished to see that President Clinton had a solid gold urinal.

That afternoon, George told his wife, Laura, about the urinal. 'Just think,' he said, 'when I am President, I could have a gold urinal, too. But I wouldn't do something that self-indulgent!'

Later, when Laura had lunch with Hillary at her tour of the White House, she told Hillary how impressed George had been at his discovery of the fact that, in the President's private bathroom, the President had a gold urinal.

That evening, when Bill and Hillary were getting ready for bed, Hillary smiled, and said to Bill, 'I found out who pissed in your saxophone.'

———————— ᛚᛘᛚ ————————

Air Force One arrives at Heathrow and President Bush strides to a warm and dignified handshake from the Queen.

They ride in a 1934 Bentley to the edge of central London where they board a magnificent 17th century carriage hitched to six magnificent white horses. They ride towards Buckingham Palace waving to the thousands of cheering Britons, and all is going well.

Suddenly the right rear horse lets fly with one of the most horrendous earth shattering farts ever heard in the British Empire and the smell was excruciating. Both the Queen and President Bush had to use handkerchiefs over their noses.

The fart shakes the coach but the two dignitaries of state do their best to ignore the incident.

The Queen turns to President Bush, 'Mr. President please accept my regrets ... I am sure you understand there are some things that even a Queen cannot control.'

George Bush, always trying to be 'presidential', replies, 'Your Majesty do not give the matter another thought ... If you had not mentioned it I would have thought it was one of the horses.'

———————— ᛚᛘᛚ ————————

A bus stops and two Italian men get on. They sit down and engage in an animated conversation. The lady sitting behind them ignores them at first, but her attention is galvanised when she hears one of the men say the following ...

'Emma come first. Den I come. Den two asses come together. I come once-a-more. Two asses, they come together again. I come again and pee twice. Then I come one lasta time.'

'You foul-mouthed sex-obsessed swine,' retorted the lady indignantly. 'In this country we don't speak out loud in public places about our sex lives!'

'Hey, coola down lady,' said the man. 'Who talkin' abouta sexa? I'm a justa tellin' my frienda how to spella Mississippi!'

A tourist, travelling through Italy, walks into a bar and notices a small man leaning on the bar, crying into his drink.

The tourist (not wanting to see someone in such a distressed state) walks up to the man and asks him why he was so upset.

The small man turns to the tourist and replies, 'You see that large cathedral out that window? For ten years I worked hard to build that cathedral with my bare hands. It is the greatest cathedral ever built in this country. But do you think they call me Luigi the great cathedral builder? NO!'

The tourist looks at the little man reassuringly as he continues. 'And you see that bridge out of that window over there? Fifteen years! Fifteen years I slaved away to build what is the longest bridge in all of Europe ... But do you think they call me Luigi the great bridge builder? No! But sleep with just one goat ...!'

Nelson Mandela is sitting at home watching TV and drinking a beer when he hears a knock at the door. When he opens it, he is confronted by a little Chinese man, clutching a clipboard and yelling, 'You sign, You sign.' Behind him is an enormous truck full of car exhausts.

Nelson is standing there in complete amazement when the Chinese man starts to yell louder, 'You sign, you sign.'

Nelson says to him, 'Look you've obviously got the wrong man,' and shuts the door.

The next day he hears a knock at the door again. When he opens it, the same little Chinese man is back with a huge truck of brake pads. He thrusts his clipboard under Nelson's nose yelling, 'You sign, you sign.'

Nelson is getting quite annoyed by now and yells back, 'You've got the wrong man, go away!' and slams the door shut.

The following day he hears another knock at the door and there again is the little Chinese man with two very large trucks full of car parts behind him and he is yelling, 'You sign, you sign,' while thrusting the clipboard at Nelson.

This time Nelson loses his temper completely, he picks up the little man by his shirt front and yells at him 'Look, I don't want these! Do you understand? You must have the wrong name! Who do you want to give these to?'

The little Chinese man looks at him very puzzled, consults his clipboard and says … 'You not Nissan Main Dealer?'

A bloke went to Mexico and watched a bullfight. After watching the bloke kill the bull he goes to a restaurant across the street. He is watching another bloke eat some soup and he asks the waiter what it is. The waiter tells him, 'It's bull testicles, 'cause every time the bull dies in the fight he is recycled for meat. And the testicles are the best tasting part.'

So the bloke says, 'Can I have one of that?'

The waiter answers, 'Sorry but there was only one bull today, tomorrow I can reserve some testicle soup for you.'

The bloke says, 'OK, I'll come back tomorrow.'

The next day he comes back for his soup and he eats it. He then remembers that the bloke from the restaurant had bigger testicles in his soup. So he asks the waiter, 'Why is my soup testicles smaller than the guy's soup yesterday?'

The waiter answers, 'Sir, sometimes the bull wins.'

Bill Clinton steps out onto the White House lawn in the dead of winter. Right in front of him, on the White House lawn, he sees 'The President Must Die' written in urine across the snow.

Well, old Bill is pretty pissed off. He storms into his security staff's HQ, and yells 'Somebody wrote a death threat in the snow on the front damn lawn! And they wrote it in urine! Son-of-a-bitch had to be standing right on the porch when he did it! Where were you guys?!'

The security guys stay silent and stare ashamedly at the floor. Bill hollers, 'Well dammit, don't just sit there! Get out and FIND OUT WHO DID IT! I want an answer, and I want it TONIGHT!'

The entire staff immediately jump up and race for the exits. Later that evening, his chief security officer approaches him and says, 'Well, Mr. President, we have some bad news and we have some really bad news. Which do you want first?'

Clinton says, 'Oh Hell, give me the bad news first.'

The officer says, 'Well, we took a sample of the urine and tested it. The results just came back, and it was Al Gore's.'

Clinton says, 'Oh my god, I feel so ... so ... betrayed! My own vice president! Damn! Well, what's the really bad news?'

The officer replies, 'Well, it's Hillary's handwriting.'

The only seat available on the train was directly adjacent to a well-dressed middle-aged French woman and the seat was being used by her dog.

The weary traveller asked, 'Ma'am, could you please move your dog. I need that seat.'

The French woman looked down her nose at the American, sniffed and said, 'You Americans. You are such a rude class of people. Can't you see my little FiFi needs that seat?'

The American walked away, determined to find a place to rest, but after another trip down to the end of the train, found himself again facing the woman with the dog.

Again he asked, 'Please, lady. May I sit there? I'm very tired.'

The French woman wrinkled her nose and snorted, 'You Americans! Not only are you rude, you are also arrogant. Imagine!'

The American didn't say anything else. He leaned over, picked up the dog, tossed it out the window of the train and sat down in the empty seat.

The woman shrieked and railed, and demanded that someone defend her honour and chastise the American.

An Englishman sitting across the aisle spoke up indignantly, 'You know, sir, you Americans do seem to have a penchant for doing the wrong thing. You eat holding the fork in the wrong hand. You drive your autos on the wrong side of the road. And now, sir, you've thrown the wrong bitch out the window.'

An Australian rugby fan, a Scottish rugby fan and a New Zealand rugby fan are all in Arabia, sharing a smuggled crate of booze when, all of a sudden, Saudi police rush in and arrest them. The mere possession of alcohol is a severe offence in Saudi Arabia, so for the terrible crime of actually being caught consuming the booze, they are all sentenced to death!

However, after many months and with the help of very good lawyers, they are able to successfully appeal their sentences down to life imprisonment.

By a stroke of luck, it was a Saudi national holiday the day their trial finished, and the extremely benevolent Sheikh decided they could be released after receiving just 20 lashes each of the whip.

As they were preparing for their punishment, the Sheikh announced, 'It's my first wife's birthday today, and she has asked me to allow each of you one wish before your whipping.'

The Scotsman was first in line, he thought for a while and then said, 'Please tie a pillow to my back.'

This was done, but the pillow only lasted ten lashes before the whip went through. When the punishment was done he had to be carried away bleeding and crying with pain.

The New Zealander was next up. After watching the Scotsman in horror he said smugly, 'Please fix two pillows to my back.' But even two pillows could only take 15 lashes before the whip went through again and the New Zealander was soon led away whimpering loudly (as they do).

The Australian was the last one up, but before he could say anything, the Sheikh turned to him and said, 'You are from a most beautiful part of the world and your culture is one of the finest in the world. For this, you may have two wishes!'

'Thank you, your Most Royal and Merciful Highness,' the Australian replied. 'In recognition of your kindness, my first wish is that you give me not 20 lashes but 100 lashes.'

'Not only are you an honorable, handsome and powerful man, you are also very brave,' the Sheikh said with an admiring look on his face. 'If 100 lashes is what you desire, then so be it. And your second wish?'

'Tie the New Zealander to my back.'

California (car lee four near)

The New California Governor has just announced an agreement whereby English will be the official language of the state, rather than German which was the other possibility.

International Jokes

As part of the negotiations, The Terminator's Government conceded that English spelling had some room for improvement and has accepted a 5-year phase-in plan that would become known as 'Austro-English' (or, if nobody will be offended, 'Austrionics').

In the first year, 's' will replace the soft 'c'. (Sertainly, this will make the sivil servants jump with joy.) The hard 'c' will be dropped in favor of the 'k'. (This should klear up konfusion, and keyboards kan have one less letter.)

There will be growing publik enthusiasm in the sekond year when the troublesome 'ph' will be replaced with the 'f'. (This will make words like fotograf 20% shorter.)

In the 3rd year, publik akseptanse of the new spelling kan be expekted to reach the stage where more komplikated changes are possible.

Governments will enkourage the removal of double letters, which have always ben a deterent to akurate speling. Also, al wil agre that the horibl mes of the silent 'e' in the languag is disgrasful and it should go away.

By the 4th yer peopl wil be reseptiv to steps such as replasing 'th' with 'z' and 'w' with 'v'.

During ze fifz yer, ze unesesary 'o' kan be dropd from vords kontaining 'ou' and after ziz fifz yer, ve vil hav a reil sensibl riten styl.

Zer vil be no mor trubl or difikultis and evrivun vil find it ezi tu understand ech oza. Ze drem of a united urop vil finali kum tru.

An Australian man was having coffee and croissants with butter and jam in a cafe, when an American tourist, chewing gum, sat down next to him.

The Australian politely ignored the American who, nevertheless, started up a conversation. The American snapped the gum in his mouth and said, 'Do you Australian folks eat the whole loaf?'

'The Australian frowned, annoyed with being bothered during his breakfast, and replied, 'Yeah, of course.'

The American blew a huge bubble. 'We don't. In the States we only eat what's inside. The crusts we collect in a container, recycle them, transform them into croissants and sell them to Australia.'

The American had a smirk on his face, the Australian listened in silence. The American persisted, 'D'ya eat jam with the bread?'

Sighing, the Australian replied, 'Yes.' Cracking his gum between his teeth, the American said, 'We don't. In the States we eat fresh fruit for breakfast, we collect all the peels, seeds and leftovers in containers, recycle them, transform them into jam, and sell it to Australia.'

The Australian then asked, 'Do you have sex in the States?'

The American smiled and said 'Yeah, of course we do.'

The Australian leant closer to him and asked, 'What do you do with the condoms once you've used them?'

'We throw them away of course,' replied the American. Now it was the Australian's turn to smile.

'We don't. In Australia, we put them in containers, recycle them, melt them down into chewing gum and sell them to the United States, that's why it's called Wrigley's!'

The radio station is running a contest and the grand prize is $50,000. The question is 'What does old Macdonald have?'

The American says ... 'That's easy, old Macdonald has a ranch, RANCH.'

'No that's incorrect,' says the announcer

The Aussie guy says ... 'That's easy, old Macdonald has a station, STATION.'

'No that's incorrect,' says the announcer

The Irishman says ... 'I know this one, old Macdonald has a farm, EIEIO!!'

Ira Goldberg was in front heading out of the Synagogue one day, and as always the rabbi was standing at the door shaking hands as the congregation departed.

The rabbi grabbed Ira by the hand and pulled him aside. 'You need to join the Army of God!'

Ira replied, 'I'm already in the Army of God, Rabbi.'

Rabbi questioned, 'How come I don't see you except for Rosh Hashanah and Yom Kippur?'

Ira whispered back, 'I'm in the secret service.'

A journalist is walking along the beach and notices a young boy in the surf being attacked by a shark. Then he sees a bloke rush in, swim out to the attack, pry the sharks mouth open, give it a flogging and ends up killing the beast. He swims back to shore with the youngster alive yet with some gashes out of his leg, then calls for help and makes sure the boy is ok.

The journo goes up to the brave rescuer and says, 'What an amazing heroic effort, I'm a journalist and can see the front page headlines already … "Aussie hero saves young boy from shark attack".'

The hero says, 'That's fantastic but I'm actually English.'

Journo says, 'Oh, that's ok, no worries.'

The next day the pom picks up the paper to see the following front page headline - POMMY BASTARD KILLS YOUNG BOY'S PET FISH.

Two families move from Pakistan to Australia. When they arrive the two fathers make a bet. In a year's time whichever family has become more Australian will win. A year later they meet again.

The first man says, 'I have changed my name to Trevor, my son is playing AFL football, I had a meat pie with sauce for breakfast and I'm just about to jump in my Commodore and go to the pub to pick up a slab of VB. How about you?'

The second man replies ... 'F@#$ off, towelhead!'

An American decided to write a book about famous churches around the world.

So he bought a plane ticket and took a trip to Orlando, thinking that he would start by working his way across the USA from South to North. On his first day he was inside a church taking photographs when he noticed golden telephone mounted on the wall with a sign that read '$10,000 per call'.

The American, intrigued, asked a priest who was strolling by what the telephone was used for. The priest replied that it was a direct line to heaven and that for $10,000 you could talk to God. The American thanked the priest and went on his way.

Next stop was in Atlanta. There, at a very large cathedral, he saw the same golden telephone with the same sign under it. He wondered if this was the same kind of telephone he saw in Orlando and he asked a nearby nun what its purpose was. She told him that it was a direct line to heaven and that for $10,000 he could talk to God. 'O.K., thank you,' said the American.

He then travelled to Indianapolis, Washington DC, Philadelphia, Boston, and New York. In every church he saw the same golden telephone with the same '$10,000 per call' sign under it.

The American decided to travel to AUSTRALIA to see if they had the same phone. He arrived in Australia, and again, in the first church he entered, there was the same golden telephone, but this time the sign under it read '40 cents per call'. The American was surprised so he asked the priest about the sign.

'Father, I've travelled all over America and I've seen this same golden telephone in many churches. I'm told that it is a direct line to Heaven, but in the US the price was $10,000 per call. Why is it so cheap here?'

The priest smiled and answered, 'You're in Australia now, son. It's a local call.'

The Irish

An Irishman walks into a bar in Dublin, orders three pints of Guinness and sits in the back of the room, drinking a sip out of each one in turn. When he finishes them, he comes back to the bar and orders three more. The bartender approaches and tells him, 'You know, a pint goes flat after I draw it, it would taste better if you bought one at a time.'

The Irishman replies, 'Well, you see, I have two brothers. One is in America, the other is in Australia, and I'm in Dublin. When we all left home, we promised that we'd drink this way to remember the days we drank together. So I drink one for each o'me brothers and one for me self.'

The bartender admits that this is a nice custom, and leaves it there. The Irishman becomes a regular in the bar, and always drinks the same way: He orders three pints and drinks them in turn.

One day, he comes in and orders two pints. All the other regulars take notice and fall silent. When he comes back to the bar for the second round, the bartender says, 'I don't want to intrude on your grief, but I wanted to offer my condolences on your loss.'

The Irishman looks quite puzzled for a moment, then a light dawns and he laughs, 'Oh, no, everybody's just fine,' he explains. 'It's just that me wife had us join that Baptist Church and I had to quit drinking. Hasn't affected me brothers though.'

In the pub Doug O'Reilly hoisted his beer and said, 'Here's to spending the rest o' me life, between the wide open legs o' me wife.' That won him the top prize for the best toast of the night. He went home and told his wife, Mary.

She asked, 'And what was yer toast, then?'

Doug replied, 'Here's to spending the rest o' me life, sitting in church beside me dear wife.'

'Oh, that's very nice indeed, Doug,' Mary said.

The next day, Mary bumped into one of Doug's drinking mates on the corner of the street. The man chuckled leeringly and said, 'Doug won first prize the other night with a toast about yerself, Mary.'

She said, 'Aye, I was a bit surprised meself. You know, he's only been there twice. Once he fell asleep and the other time I had to pull him by the ears to make him come.'

———————————— ⋮⋮⋮ ————————————

Into a Belfast pub comes Paddy Murphy, looking like he'd just been run over by a train. His arm is in a sling, his nose is broken, his face is cut and bruised and he's walking with a limp.

'What happened to you?' asks Sean, the bartender.

'Jamie O'Conner and me had a fight,' says Paddy.

'That little shit, O'Conner,' says Sean, 'he couldn't do that to you, he must have had something in his hand.'

'That he did,' says Paddy, 'a shovel is what he had, and a terrible lickin' he gave me with it.'

'Well,' says Sean, 'you should have defended yourself, didn't you have something in your hand?'

'That I did,' said Paddy ... 'Mrs. O'Conner's breast, and a thing of beauty it was, but useless in a fight.'

———————————— ⋮⋮⋮ ————————————

Mary Clancy goes up to Father O'Grady after his Sunday morning service, and she's in tears.

He says, 'So what's bothering you, Mary my dear?'

She says, 'Oh, Father, I've got terrible news. My husband passed away last night.'

The priest says, 'Oh, Mary, that's terrible. Tell me, Mary, did he have any last requests?'

She says, 'That he did, Father.'

The priest says, 'What did he ask, Mary?'

She says, 'He said, "Please Mary, put down that damn gun!"'

'Bless me Father, for I have sinned. I have been with a loose woman.'

The priest asks, 'Is that you, little Tommy Shaughnessy?'

'Yes, Father, it is.'

'And, who was the woman you were with?'

'I can't be tellin' you, Father. I don't want to ruin her reputation.'

'Well, Tommy, I'm sure to find out sooner or later, so you may as well tell me now. Was it Brenda O'Malley?'

'I cannot say.'

'Was it Patricia Kelly?'

'I'll never tell.'

'Was it Liz Shannon?'

'I'm sorry, but I can't name her.'

'Was it Cathy Morgan?'

'My lips are sealed.'

'Was it Fiona McDonald, then?'

'Please, Father, I cannot tell you.'

The priest sighs in frustration. 'You're a steadfast lad, Tommy Shaughnessy, and I admire that. But you've sinned, and you must atone. You cannot attend church mass for three months. Be off with you now.'

Tommy walks back to his pew. His friend Sean slides over and whispers, 'What'd you get?!'

'Three month's vacation and five good leads.'

Paddy and Mick worked together in the factory and were both laid off. At the unemployment office, Paddy was asked his occupation, 'Panty stitcher ... I stitch de elastic in ladies panties,' he replied.

Being unskilled labour, Paddy was given 100 euros a week. When Mick was asked the same question, he replied 'diesel fitter', and since this is skilled work he was given 200 euros a week. When Paddy found out Mick was getting 100 euros a week more than him he was furious. He stormed back into the unemployment office and demanded to know why his mate was getting more dosh.

The clerk explained that panty stitching is unskilled work, whereas diesel fitting was skilled work.

'What fecking skill???' yelled Paddy ... 'I sew the fecking elastic on the panties. Mick puts them over his head and says, "Yep diesel fitter".'

Two men were sitting next to each other at a bar. After a while, one bloke looks at the other and says, 'I can't help but think, from listening to you, that you're from Ireland.'

The other guy responds proudly, 'Yes, that I am!'

The first bloke says, 'So am I! And where about from Ireland might you be?'

The other bloke answers, 'I'm from Dublin, I am.'

The first bloke responds, 'Sure and begora, and so am I! And what street did you live on in Dublin?'

The other bloke says, 'A lovely little area it was, I lived on McCleary Street in the old central part of town.'

The first bloke says, 'Faith and it's a small world, so did I! And to what school would you have been going?'

The other guy answers, 'Well now, I went to St. Mary's of course.'

The first bloke gets really excited, and says, 'And so did I. Tell me, what year did you graduate?'

The other bloke answers, 'Well, now, I graduated in 1964.'

The first bloke exclaims, 'The Good Lord must be smiling down upon us! I can hardly believe our good luck at winding up in the same bar tonight. Can you believe it, I graduated from St. Mary's in 1964 my own self.'

About this time, another bloke walks into the bar, sits down, and orders a beer. The bartender walks over shaking his head and mutters, 'It's going to be a long night tonight, the Murphy twins are drunk again.'

An Englishman, a Scotsman, and an Irishman walk into a pub. They proceed to each buy a pint of Guinness.

Just as they were about to enjoy their creamy beverage three flies landed in each of their pints, and were stuck in the thick head.

The Englishman pushed his beer away in disgust.

The Scotsman fished the offending fly out of his beer and continued drinking it as if nothing had happened.

The Irishman too, picked the fly out of his drink, held it out over the beer and then started yelling, 'Spit it out, spit it out you bugger!!!'

Did you hear about the Irish newlyweds who sat up all night on their honeymoon waiting for their sexual relations to arrive?

An Irish girl went to London to work as a secretary and began sending home money and gifts to her parents.

After a few years they asked her to come home for a visit, as her father was getting frail and elderly. She pulled up to the family home in a Rolls Royce and stepped out wearing furs and diamonds.

As she walked into the house her father said, 'Hmmm, they seem to be paying secretaries awfully well in London.'

The girl took his hands and said, 'Dad, I've been meaning to tell you something for years but I didn't want to put it in a letter. I can't hide it from you any longer, I've become a prostitute.'

Her father gasped, put his hand on his heart and keeled over. The doctor was called but the old man had clearly lost the will to live. He was put to bed and the priest was called.

As the priest began to administer Extreme Unction, with the mother and daughter weeping and wailing, the old man muttered weakly, 'I'm a goner, killed by me own daughter! Killed by the shame of what you've become!'

'Please forgive me,' his daughter sobbed, 'I only wanted to have nice things! I wanted to be able to send you money and the only way I could do it was by becoming a prostitute.'

Brushing the priest aside, the old man sat bolt upright in bed, smiling.

'Did ye say prostitute? I thought ye said PROTESTANT!!'

Paddy and Paddy, two Irishmen, went out one day and each bought a pig. When they got home, Paddy turned to Paddy and said, 'Paddy, me ol' mate, how we gonna tell who owns which pig?'

Paddy says, 'Well Paddy, I'll cut one a ta' ears off my pig, and ten we can tell 'em apart.'

'Ah tat'd be grand,' says Paddy.

This worked fine until a couple of weeks later when Paddy stormed into the house.

'Paddy,' he said, 'your pig has chewed the ear off a my pig. Now we got two pigs with only one ear each. How we gonna tell who owns which pig?'

'Well Paddy,' said Paddy, 'I'll cut ta other ear off my pig. Ten we'll av two pigs and only one of them will av an ear.'

'Ah tat'd be grand,' says Paddy.

Again this worked fine until a couple of weeks later when Paddy again stormed into the house.

'Paddy' he said, 'your pig has chewed the other ear offa my pig. Now we got two pigs with no ears. How we gonna tell who owns which pig?'

'Ah tis is serious, Paddy,' said Paddy. 'I'll tell ya what I'll do. I'll cut ta tail offa my pig. Ten we'll av two pigs with no ears, and only one tail.'

'Ah tat'd be grand,' says Paddy.

Another couple of weeks went by, and you guessed it, Paddy stormed into the house once more.

'PADDY!' shouted Paddy, 'your pig has chewed the tail offa my pig and now we got two pigs with no ears and no tails!!! How the hell are we gonna tell 'em apart!!!!

'Ah booga it,' says Paddy. 'How's about you have the black one, and I'll have the white one.'

An Irishman, a Mexican and a blonde guy were doing construction work on scaffolding on the 20th floor of a building.

They were eating lunch and the Irishman said, 'Corned beef and cabbage! If I get corned beef and cabbage one more time for lunch I'm going to jump off this building.'

The Mexican guy opened his lunch box and exclaimed, 'Burritos again! If I get burritos one more time I'm going to jump off, too.'

The blond guy opened his lunch and said, 'Salami again. If I get a salami sandwich one more time, I'm jumping too.'

The next day the Irishman opened his lunch box, saw corned beef and cabbage and jumped to his death.

The Mexican guy opened his lunch, saw a burrito and jumped too.

The blonde guy opened his lunch, saw the salami sandwich and jumped to his death as well.

At the funeral the Irishman's wife was weeping. She said, 'If I'd known how really tired he was of corned beef and cabbage, I never would have given it to him again!'

The Mexican's wife also wept and said, 'I could have given him tacos or enchiladas! I didn't realise he hated burritos so much.'

Everyone turned and stared at the blonde's wife.

'Hey, don't look at me,' she said, 'He makes his own lunch.'

A young man goes to confession and says, 'Father, it has been one month since my last confession. I have had sex with Nookie Green every week for the last month.'

The priest tells the sinner, 'You are forgiven. Go out and say three Hail Mary's.'

Soon after, another man enters the confessional. 'Father, it has been two months since my last confession. I have had sex with Nookie Green twice a week for the last two months.'

This time the priest questions, 'Who is Nookie Green?'

'A new woman in the neighbourhood,' the sinner replies.

'Very well,' sighs the priest. 'Go and say ten Hail Mary's.'

At Mass the next morning, as the priest prepares to deliver his sermon, a tall, drop dead gorgeous woman enters the sanctuary. All the men's eyes fall upon her as she slowly sashays up the aisle and sits down right in front of the priest! Her dress is green and very short, with matching shiny emerald green shoes.

The priest and altar boy gasp, as the woman in the matching green shoes and dress sits with her legs slightly spread apart.

The priest turns to the altar boy and whispers, 'Is that Nookie Green?'

The bug-eyed altar boy can't believe his ears but replies, 'No, I think it's just the reflection off her shoes!'

Mick appeared on the Irish version of 'Who Wants to Be a Millionaire' and towards the end of the programme had already won $500,000.

'You've done very well so far,' said the show's presenter, 'but for $1 million you've only got one lifeline left - phone a friend. Everything is riding on this question … will you go for it?'

'Sure,' said Mick. 'I'll have a go!'

'OK. The question is: Which of the following birds does **not** build it's own nest?

(a) Robin, (b) Sparrow, (c) Cuckoo, or (d) Thrush.'

'I haven't got a clue,' said Mick, 'so I'll use my last lifeline and phone my friend Paddy back home in Ballygoon.'

Mick called up his mate, told him the circumstances and repeated the question to him.

'Bloody hell, Mick!' cried Paddy. 'Dat's simple … it's a cuckoo.'

'Are you sure, Paddy?' asked Mick.

'I'm bloody sure.'

Mick hung up the phone and told the TV presenter, 'I'll go with cuckoo as my answer.'

'Is that your final answer?' asked the host.

'Dat it is, Sir.'

There was a long, long pause, then the presenter screamed, 'Cuckoo is the correct answer! Mick, you've won $1 million!'

The next night, Mick invited Paddy to their local pub to buy him a drink.

'Tell me, Paddy? How in God's name did you know it was the cuckoo that doesn't build it's own nest? I mean you know nuffin about birds.'

'For Goodness sake!' laughed Paddy, 'everybody knows a bloody cuckoo lives in a clock!'

Two Irishmen in London looking for work were strolling down Oxford Street.

After walking for a few minutes, Paddy turns to Murphy with a look of amazement on his face and says, 'Murphy, will you have a look at that shop over there, I thought that London was supposed to be expensive but that shop is as cheap as chips!'

Murphy says, 'Paddy you're right so you are, will you have a look at that. Suits 10 pounds, Shirts 4 pounds, Trousers 5 pounds, I think that we should buy the lot and take them back to Ireland. We would make a tidy profit selling them in Dublin so we would.'

Paddy says in agreement, 'Murphy that is as good an idea as you'll ever have, but I'm pretty sure that you have to pay taxes and duty on things like that. The shopkeeper will never let us have them if he thinks we're gonna export them and make our fortune, so he won't.'

Murphy thinks and says: 'Paddy, I've got an idea! You can do the best English accent out of the pair of us. You go in there and do the talking and I'll just stand behind you and say nothing. He'll never guess we're Irish. No he won't.'

'OK Murphy,' agrees Paddy, 'I'll do the talking, you just stand there and look English.'

So the two visitors to the illustrious capital city go into the shop, where Paddy is greeted politely by the owner.

Paddy then proceeds to do his best Alf Garnet impression; 'Awwwight Guvnor, I'll 'ave 20 of yer Whistle 'un Flutes, 20 Dickie Dirts and 20 pairs of strides. And if yer don't mind I'll be paying with the 380 Pictures of the Queen in my Sky Rocket.'

Upon hearing this request from Paddy, the owner smiles, takes a look at Murphy as well then says to Paddy, 'You're Irish aren't you?'

Quite bemused, Paddy replies, 'Oh be'Jesus. Mary mother of Christ, if that ain't me best English accent? How in God's name did you know that we were Irish?'

The owner replies, 'This is a bloody Dry Cleaners.'

Tiger Woods is invited to play in the Irish Open. The promoter offers him the use of a BMW Z4 for the duration.

On his day off, Tiger is driving through the Irish countryside, when he pulls into a quaint Irish service station, in a quaint Irish village, and is served by a quaint old Irish geezer. As he pulls his wallet out of his pocket to pay for the fuel, two tees drop to the floor.

The Irish geezer says, 'By gaw, what are dey'?

Tiger responds, 'They're golf tees.'

'Yeah, but wad do ya use 'em for?' asks the Irish geezer.

'You rest your balls on them when you're driving,' responds Tiger getting more perplexed.

'By gaw,' says the Irishman, 'don't BMW tink of everything!'

Three Irishmen, Paddy, Sean and Seamus, were stumbling home from the pub late one night and found themselves on the road which led past the old graveyard.

'Come have a look over here,' says Paddy, 'it's Michael O'Grady's grave, God bless his soul. He lived to the ripe old age of 87.'

'That's nothing,' says Sean, 'here's one named Patrick O'Tool. It says here that he was 95 when he died.'

Just then, Seamus yells out, 'Good God, here's a fella that got to be 145!'

'What was his name?' asks Paddy.

Seamus stumbles around a bit, awkwardly lights a match to see what else is written on the stone marker, and exclaims, 'Miles, from Dublin.'

An Irishman who had a little too much to drink is driving home from the city one night and, of course, his car is weaving violently all over the road. A cop pulls him over.

'So,' says the cop to the driver, 'where have ya been?'

'Why, I've been to the pub of course,' slurs the drunk.

'Well,' says the cop, 'it looks like you've had quite a few to drink this evening.'

'I did all right,' the drunk says with a smile.

'Did you know,' says the cop, standing straight and folding his arms across his chest, 'that a few intersections back, your wife fell out of your car?'

'Oh, thank heavens,' sighs the drunk. 'For a minute there, I thought I'd gone deaf.'

Brenda O'Malley is home making dinner, as usual, when Tim Finnegan arrives at her door.

'Brenda, may I come in?' he asks. 'I've somethin' to tell ya.'

'Of course you can come in, you're always welcome, Tim. But where's my husband?'

'That's what I'm here to be tellin' ya, Brenda. There was an accident down at the Guinness brewery ...'

'Oh, God no!' cries Brenda. 'Please don't tell me ...'

'I must, Brenda. Your husband Seamus is dead and gone. I'm sorry.'

Finally, she looked up at Tim. 'How did it happen, Tim?'

'It was terrible, Brenda. He fell into a vat of Guinness Stout and drowned.'

'Oh my dear Jesus! But you must tell me true, Tim. Did he at least go quickly?'

'Well, no Brenda ... no. Fact is, he got out three times to pee.'

Drunk, Ole Mulvihill (From the Northern Irish Clan) staggers into a Catholic Church, enters a confessional box, sits down but says nothing.

The Priest coughs a few times to get his attention but the Ole just sits there.

Finally, the Priest pounds three times on the wall. The drunk mumbles, 'Ain't no use knockin', there's no paper on this side either.'

———— ⦂⦀⦂ ————

An Irishman's been drinking at a pub all night. The bartender finally says that the bar is closing. So the Irishman stands up to leave and falls flat on his face. He tries to stand one more time, same result. He figures he'll crawl outside and get some fresh air and maybe that will sober him up a bit.

Once outside he stands up and falls flat on his face. So he decides to crawl four blocks to his home and when he arrives at the door, he stands up and falls flat on his face. He crawls through the door and into his bedroom. When he reaches for his bed, he tries one more time to stand up.

This time he manages to pull himself upright but quickly falls right into bed. He awakens the next morning to his wife standing over him shouting, 'So, you've been out drinking again!!'

'What makes you say that?' he asks as he put on an innocent look.

'The pub called me, you left you wheelchair there again!'

———— ⦂⦀⦂ ————

KIDS

A man was talking to his daughter, a typical four-year-old girl, cute, inquisitive and bright as a new penny. Out of the blue she asked her Dad to explain what marriage was.

So Dad explained, but when the young girl appeared to be having difficulty grasping the concept, her father decided to pull out his wedding photo album, thinking perhaps visual images would help. One page after another, he pointed out the bride arriving at the church, the entrance, the wedding ceremony, and the reception.

'Now do you understand?' he asked.

'I think so,' she said. 'Is that when Mummy came to work for us?'

Little Johnny was attending his first wedding. After the service, his Uncle Rodney asked him, 'So Johnny, now that you've been to your first wedding, can you tell me how many women can a man marry?'

'Sixteen,' Johnny responded.

His Uncle was amazed that he had an answer so quickly and asked, 'How do you know that?'

'Easy,' Little Johnny said. 'All you have to do is add it up, like the preacher said, "4 better, 4 worse, 4 richer, 4 poorer".'

A young boy went up to his father and asked, 'What's the difference between potentially and realistically?'

The father ponders for a moment then answered, 'Go ask your mother if she would sleep with Robert Redford for a million quid and also ask your sister if she would sleep with Brad Pitt for a million quid, then come back and tell me what you learned.'

So the boy went to his mother and asked, 'Mum would you sleep with Robert Redford for a million quid?' The mother replied, 'Definitely, I wouldn't pass up an opportunity like that.'

The boy then went to his older sister and asked, 'Would you sleep with Brad Pitt for a million quid?' The girl replied 'Oh gosh, I would just love to do that, I would be nuts to pass up that opportunity.'

The boy then thought about it for a few days, and went back to his father. His father asked him, 'Did you find the difference between potentially and realistically?'

The boy replied, 'Yes, potentially we're sitting on 2 million quid, but realistically we're living with two slappers.'

The father replied, 'That's my boy!'

Two little boys went fishing and caught nothing. Discouraged, they decided to try again the next day. Again they caught nothing. Finally, on the third day, they caught a fish. Soon they were both pulling them in one after another. 'Hey, it's time to go home,' one little fellow finally said to the other. 'We'll come back again tomorrow now that we know where the fish are.' And he began to carve an 'X' in the bottom of the boat.

'What do you think you're doing?' the second kid asked.

'I'm making a mark so we'll know where to come back to,' was the reply.

The second kid said, 'That's dumb, we may not even get the same boat tomorrow.'

———————— ⚱ ————————

A sister and brother are talking to each other when the little boy gets up and walks over to his Grandpa and says, 'Grandpa, please make a frog noise.'

The Grandpa says, 'No.'

The little boy goes on, 'Please, please make a frog noise.'

The Grandpa says, 'No, now go play.'

The little boy then says to his sister, 'Go tell Grandpa to make a frog noise.'

So the little girl goes to her Grandpa and says, 'Please make a frog noise.'

The Grandpa says, 'I just told your brother no and I'm telling you no.'

The little girl says, 'Please, please Grandpa make a frog noise.'

The Grandpa says, 'Why do you want me to make a frog noise?'

The little girl replied, 'Because mommy said when you croak we can go to Disney World!'

———————— ⚱ ————————

A new teacher was trying to make use of her psychology courses. She started her class by saying, 'Everyone who thinks you're stupid, stand up!'

After a few seconds, Little Johnny stood up. The teacher said, 'Do you think you're stupid, Little Johnny?'

'No, ma'am, but I hate to see you standing there all by yourself!'

A mother was working in the kitchen, listening to her five-year-old son playing with his new electric train in the living room.

She heard the train stop and her son saying, 'All of you bastards who want off, get the hell off now, cause this is the last stop! And all of you bastards who are getting on, get your ass in the train, cause we're going down the tracks right now.'

The horrified mother went in and told her son, 'We don't use that kind of language in this house. Now I want you to go to your room and stay there for two hours. When you come out, you may play with the train, but I want you to use nice language.'

Two hours later, the son came out of the bedroom and resumed playing with his train. Soon the train stopped and the mother heard her son say, 'All passengers who are disembarking the train, please remember to take all of your belongings with you. We thank you for travelling with us today and hope your trip was a pleasant one.'

She hears the little boy continue, 'For those of you just boarding, we ask you to stow all of your hand luggage under your seat. Remember, there is no smoking on the train. We hope you will have a pleasant and relaxing journey with us today. '

As the mother began to smile, the child added, 'For those of you who are pissed off about the two hour delay, please see the fat bitch in the kitchen.'

What is a grandparent?

(taken from papers written by a class of 8-year-olds)

- Grandparents are a lady and a man who have no little children of their own. They like other people's.
- A grandfather is a man grandmother.
- Grandparents don't have to do anything except be there when we come to see them.
- They are so old they shouldn't play hard or run. It is good if they drive us to the shop and have lots of coins for us.
- When they take us for walks, they slow down past things like pretty leaves and caterpillars.
- They show us and talk to us about the colour of the flowers and also why we shouldn't step on cracks.
- They don't say, 'Hurry up.'
- Usually grandmothers are fat, but not too fat to tie your shoes.
- They wear glasses and funny underwear.
- They can take their teeth and gums out.
- Grandparents don't have to be smart.
- They have to answer questions like, 'Why isn't God married?' and 'How come dogs chase cats?'
- When they read to us, they don't skip. They don't mind if we ask for the same story over again.
- Everybody should try to have a grandmother, especially if you don't have television, because they are the only grown-ups who like to spend time with us.
- They know we should have snack-time before bedtime and they say prayers with us every time, and kiss us even when we've been bad.

A little boy opened the big family bible. He was fascinated as he fingered through the old pages. Suddenly, something fell out of the bible. He picked up the object and looked at it. What he saw was an old leaf that had been pressed in between the pages.

'Mummy, look what I found,' the boy called.

'What have you got there, dear?'

With astonishment in his voice, he answered, 'I think it's Adam's underpants!'

Attending a wedding for the first time, a little girl whispered to her mother, 'Why is the bride dressed in white?'

'Because white is the colour of happiness and today is the happiest day of her life.'

The child thought about this for a moment, then said, 'So why is the groom wearing black?'

Two boys were walking home from Sunday school after hearing a strong preaching on the devil.

One said to the other, 'What do you think about all this Satan stuff?'

The other boy replied, 'Well, you know how Santa Claus turned out. It's probably just your Dad.'

My 4-year-old girl picked up something off the ground and started to put it in her mouth. I asked her not to do that.

'Why?'

'Because it's been laying outside and it is dirty and probably has germs.'

At this point, she looked at me with total admiration and asked, 'Wow! How do you know all this stuff?'

'Uh,' I was thinking quickly, '... all mums know this stuff. Um, it's on the Mummy Test. You have to know it, or they don't let you be a Mummy.'

We walked along in silence for two or three minutes, but she was evidently pondering this new information. 'OH ... I get it!' she beamed. 'Then if you flunk, you have to be the Daddy.'

A little girl was talking to her teacher about whales. The teacher said it was physically impossible for a whale to swallow a human because even though it was a very large mammal its throat was very small.

The little girl stated that Jonah was swallowed by a whale. Irritated, the teacher reiterated that a whale could not swallow a human; it was physically impossible.

The little girl said, 'When I get to heaven I will ask Jonah.'

The teacher asked, 'What if Jonah went to hell?'

The little girl replied, 'Then you ask him.'

Parenthood
- You spend the first two years of your child's life teaching them to walk and talk. Then you spend the next sixteen telling them to sit down and shut up.
- Grandchildren are God's reward for not killing your own children.
- Mothers of teens now know why some animals eat their young.
- Children seldom misquote you. In fact, they usually repeat word for word what you shouldn't have said.

- The main purpose of holding children's parties is to remind yourself that there are children more awful than your own.
- We child proof our homes, but they are still getting in.

Moral of the story: Be nice to your kids. They will choose your nursing home.

The boss of a big company needed to call one of his employees about an urgent problem with one of the main computers. He dialled the employee's home phone number and was greeted with a child's whispered, 'Hello?'

Feeling put out at the inconvenience of having to talk to a youngster the boss asked, 'Is your Daddy home?'

'Yes', whispered the small voice.

'May I talk with him?' the man asked.

To the surprise of the boss, the small voice whispered, 'No.'

Wanting to talk with an adult, the boss asked, 'Is your Mommy there?'

'Yes', came the answer.

'May I talk with her?'

Again the small voice whispered, 'No.'

Knowing that it was not likely that a young child would be left home alone, the boss decided he would just leave a message with the person who should be there watching over the child.

'Is there any one there besides you?' the boss asked the child.

'Yes,' whispered the child, 'a policeman.'

Wondering what a cop would be doing at his employee's home, the boss asked, 'May I speak with the policeman?'

'No, he's busy,' whispered the child.

'Busy doing what?' asked the boss. 'Talking to Daddy and Mommy and the fireman,' came the whispered answer. Growing concerned and even worried as he heard what sounded like a helicopter through the earpiece on the phone the boss asked, 'What is that noise?'

'A hello-copper,' answered the whispering voice.

'What is going on there?' asked the boss, now alarmed.

In an awed whispering voice the child answered, 'The search team just landed the hello-copper.'

Alarmed, concerned, and more than just a little frustrated the boss asked, 'What are they searching for?'

Still whispering, the young voice replied along with a muffled giggle, 'Me.'

A little boy and girl are playing in a sandbox. The little boy has to go to take a pee and he was told by his mother to always be polite and don't talk about private matters in public.

At first he holds it in for a little while because he does not know what to say to the little girl to excuse himself. Then he remembers what his Mom had said at the restaurant to excuse herself from the table.

So he turns to the little girl and says, 'Will you excuse me. I have to go powder my nose,' leaps out of the sandbox and runs to the bathroom.

When he comes back the little girl looks up at him and asks 'Did you powder your nose?'

'Yes,' said the little boy stepping back into the sandbox.

'Well then,' says the little girl, 'you'd better close your purse because your lipstick is hanging out.'

A kindergarten teacher was observing her classroom of children while they drew. She would occasionally walk around to see each child's work. As she got to one little girl who was working diligently, she asked what the drawing was.

The girl replied, 'I'm drawing God.'

The teacher paused and said, 'But no one knows what God looks like.'

Without missing a beat, or looking up from her drawing, the girl replied, 'They will in a minute.'

A Sunday school teacher was discussing the Ten Commandments with her 6-year-olds. After explaining the commandment to 'honour' thy Father and thy Mother, she asked, 'Is there a commandment that teaches us how to treat our brothers and sisters?'

Without missing a beat one little boy (the oldest of a family) answered, 'Thou shalt not kill.'

One day a little girl was sitting and watching her mother do the dishes at the kitchen sink. She suddenly noticed that her mother has several strands of white hair sticking out in contrast on her brunette head. She looked at her mother and inquisitively asked, 'Why are some of your hairs white, Mum?'

Her mother replied, 'Well, every time that you do something wrong and make me cry or unhappy, one of my hairs turns white.'

The little girl thought about this revelation for a while and then said, 'Mum, how come ALL of grandma's hairs are white?'

The children were lined up in the cafeteria of a Catholic primary school for lunch. At the head of the table was a large pile of apples.

The nun made a note, and posted it on the apple tray: 'Take only ONE. God is watching.'

Moving further along the lunch line, at the other end of the table was a large pile of chocolate chip biscuits. A child had written a note, 'Take all you want. God is watching the apples.'

A boy and his father were playing catch in the front yard when the boy saw a honey-bee. He ran over and stomped it.

'That was a honey bee,' his father said, 'one of our friends. For stomping him you will do without honey for a week.'

Later the boy saw a butterfly, so he ran over and stomped it.

'That was a butterfly,' his father said, 'one of our friends, and for stomping him you will do without butter for a week.'

The next morning the family sat down for breakfast. The boy ate his plain toast with no honey or butter.

Suddenly a cockroach ran out from under the stove. His mother stomped it.

The boy looked at his father and said, 'Are you going to tell her, Dad, or should I?'

A young female teacher was giving an assignment to her 6th grade class one day. It was a large assignment so she started writing high up on the blackboard. Suddenly there was a giggle from one of the boys in the class. She quickly turned and asked, 'What's so funny, Pat?'

'I just saw one of your garters!'

'Get out of my classroom,' she yells, 'I don't want to see you for three days!'

The teacher turns back to the blackboard. Realising she had forgotten to title the assignment, she reaches to the very top of the blackboard. Suddenly there is an even louder giggle from another male student. She quickly turns and asks, 'What's so funny, Billy?'

'I just saw both of your garters!'

Again, she yells, 'Get out of my classroom! This time the punishment is more severe, I don't want to see you for three weeks!'

Embarrassed and frustrated, she drops the eraser when she turns around again. So she bends over to pick it up. This time there is a burst of laughter from another male student. She quickly turns to see Little Johnny leaving the classroom.

'Where do you think you're going?' she asks.

'From what I just saw, my school days are over!'

The 6th grade science teacher, Ms. Rock, asked her class, 'Which human body part increases to ten times its size when stimulated?'

No one answered until little Marcy stood up, angry, and said, 'You should not be asking 6th graders a question like that! I'm going to tell my parents, and they will go and tell the principal, who will then fire you!'

With a sneer on her face, she then sat back down. Ms. Rock ignored her and asked the question again, 'Which body part increases to ten times its size when stimulated?'

Little Marcy's mouth fell open; then she said to those around her, 'Boy is she gonna get in big trouble!'

The teacher continued to ignore and said to the class, 'Anybody?' Finally, Bruce stood up, looked around nervously, and said 'The body part that increases ten times its size when stimulated is the pupil of the eye.'

Ms. Rock said, 'Very good, Bruce', then turned to Marcy and continued, 'As for you, young lady, I have three things to say,

1. You have a dirty mind

2. You didn't read your homework, and

3. One day you are going to be very, very disappointed.

An honest 7-year-old admitted calmly to her parents that Billy Brown had kissed her after class.

'How did that happen?' gasped her mother.

'It wasn't easy,' admitted the young lady, 'but three girls helped me catch him.'

Little Johnny and his family were having dinner at his grandmother's house. Everyone was seated around the table as the food was being served. When little Johnny received his plate, he started eating right away.

'Johnny, wait until we say our prayer.'

'I don't have to,' the boy replied.

'Of course, you do,' his mother insisted. 'We always say a prayer before eating at our house.'

'That's at our house,' Johnny explained. 'But this is grandma's house and she knows how to cook.'

On the way to preschool, the doctor had left her stethoscope on the car seat, and her 4-year-old daughter picked it up and began playing with it.

'Wow!' thought the doctor, 'my daughter wants to follow in my footsteps!'

Then the child spoke into the instrument, 'Welcome to McDonald's. May I take your order?'

The nun teaching Sunday School was speaking to her class one Sunday morning and she asked the question, 'When you die and go to Heaven ... which part of your body goes first?'

Suzie raised her hand and said, 'I think it's your hands.'

'Why do you think it's your hands, Suzie?'

Suzie replied, 'Because when you pray, you hold your hands together in front of you and God just takes your hands first!'

'What a wonderful answer!' the Nun said.

Little Johnny raised his hand and said, 'Sister, I think it's your legs.'

The Nun looked at him with the strangest look on her face. 'Now, Little Johnny, why do you think it would be your legs?'

Little Johnny said, 'Well, when I walked into Mommy and Daddy's bedroom the other night, Mommy had her legs straight up in the air and she was saying, "Oh God, I'm coming!" If Dad hadn't had her pinned down, we'd have lost her.'

Little Johnny keeps asking his Dad for a television in his bedroom, to which his Dad keeps saying 'No'. After all the nagging, he agrees and says, 'OK'.

Several nights later Johnny comes downstairs and asks, 'Dad, what's Love Juice?'

Dad is horrified, and after looking at Mum who's also gob smacked, proceeds to give his son the whole works, warts and all. Johnny now sits on the sofa with his mouth open in amazement.

Dad asks, 'So, what is it you've been watching then, son?'

Johnny replies, 'Australian Open'.

A little boy got on the bus, sat next to a man reading a book and noticed he had his collar on backwards. The little boy asked why he wore his collar that way.

The man, who was a priest, said, 'I am a Father.'

The little boy replied, 'My Daddy doesn't wear his collar like that.'

The priest looked up from his book and answered, 'I am the Father of many.'

The boy said, 'My Dad has four boys, four girls, and two grandchildren and he doesn't wear his collar that way.'

The priest, getting impatient, said, 'I am the Father of hundreds,' and went back to reading his book.

The little boy sat quietly ... but on leaving the bus, he leaned over and said, 'Well, maybe you should wear your pants backwards instead of your collar.'

A couple had two little boys, ages eight and ten, who were excessively mischievous. They were always getting into trouble and their parents knew that if any mischief occurred in their town, their sons were probably involved.

The boys' mother heard that a clergyman in town had been successful in disciplining children, so she asked if he would speak with her boys. The clergyman agreed, but asked to see the boys individually. So the mother sent her 8-year-old first, in the morning, with the older boy to see the clergyman in the afternoon.

The clergyman, a huge man with a booming voice, sat the younger boy down and asked him sternly, 'Where is God?'

The boy's mouth dropped open, but he made no response, sitting there with his mouth hanging open, wide-eyed. So the clergyman repeated the question in an even sterner tone, 'Where is God!!?'

Again the boy made no attempt to answer. So the clergyman raised his voice even more and shook his finger in the boy's face and bellowed, 'WHERE IS GOD!?'

The boy screamed and bolted from the room, ran directly home and dove into his closet, slamming the door behind him. When his older brother found him in the closet, he asked, 'What happened?'

The younger brother, gasping for breath, replied, 'We are in BIG trouble this time, dude. God is missing, and they think we did it!'

A small boy was lost at a large shopping mall. He approached a policeman and said, 'I've lost my dad!'

The cop asked, 'What's he like?'

The little boy replied, 'Beer and women with big tits.'

Children's science exam answers

Q.: Name the four seasons.
A.: Salt, pepper, mustard and vinegar.

Q.: Explain one of the processes by which water can be made safe to drink.
A.: Flirtation makes the water safe to drink because it removes large pollutants like grit, sand, dead sheep and canoeists.

Q.: How is dew formed?
A.: The sun shines down on the leaves and makes them perspire.

Q.: How can you delay milk turning sour?
A.: Keep it in the cow.

Q.: What causes the tides in the oceans?
A.: The tides are a fight between Earth and the Moon. All water tends to flow towards the moon, because there is no water on the moon, and nature hates a vacuum. I forget where the sun joins in this fight.

Q.: What are steroids?
A.: Things for keeping carpets still on the stairs.

Q.: What happens to your body as you age?
A.: When you get old, so do your bowels and you get intercontinental.

Q.: What happens to a boy when he reaches puberty?
A.: He says good-bye to his boyhood and looks forward to his adultery.

Q.: Name a major disease associated with cigarettes.
A.: Premature death.

Q.: What is artificial insemination?
A.: When a farmer does it to the bull instead of the cow.

Q.: How are the main parts of the body categorised? (e.g. abdomen.)
A.: The body consists of three parts - the brainium, the borax and the abdominal cavity. The brainium contains the brain, the borax contains the heart and lungs, and the abdominal cavity contains the five bowels, A, E, I, O and U.

Q.: What is the fibula?
A.: A small lie.

Q.: What does 'varicose' mean?
A.: Nearby.

Q.: What does the word 'benign' mean?
A.: Benign is what you will be after you be eight.

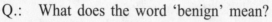

There was a city cop sitting on his horse waiting to cross the street when a little boy on his shiny, new bike stopped beside him.

'Nice bike,' the cop said. 'Did Santa bring it to you?'

'Yep,' the little boy said. 'He sure did!'

The cop looked the bike over, and handed the little boy a $20 ticket for a safety violation. The cop said, 'Next year, tell Santa to put a reflector light on the back of it.'

The young boy looked up at the cop and said, 'Nice horse you got there, sir. Did Santa bring it to you?'

'Yes, he sure did,' chuckled the cop.

The little boy looked up at the cop and said, 'Next year, tell Santa the dick goes underneath the horse, not on top.'

A little girl is in line to see Santa. When it's her turn, she climbs up on Santa's lap. Santa asks, 'What would you like Santa to bring you for Christmas?'

The little girl replies, 'I want a Barbie and Action Man.'

Santa looks at the little girl for a moment and says, 'I thought Barbie comes with Ken.'

'No,' said the little girl. 'She comes with Action Man, she fakes it with Ken.'

One day the first grade teacher was reading the story of Chicken Little to her class. She came to the part of the story where Chicken Little tried to warn the farmer.

She read, '... and so Chicken Little went up to the farmer and said, "The sky is falling, the sky is falling!"'

The teacher paused then asked the class, 'And what do you think that farmer said?' One little girl raised her hand and said, 'I think he said, "Holy Crap! A talking chicken!"'

A ten-year-old Jewish boy was failing his math exams. His parents tried everything from tutors to hypnosis, but to no avail. Finally, at the insistence of a family friend, they decided to enrol their son in a private Catholic school.

After the first day, the boy's parents were surprised when he walked in after school with a stern, focused and very determined look on his face. He went straight past them, right to his room and quietly closed the door. For nearly two hours he toiled away in his room with maths, books strewn about his desk and the surrounding floor.

He emerged long enough to eat, and after quickly cleaning his plate, went straight back to his room, closed the door and worked feverishly at his studies until bedtime.

This pattern of behaviour continued until it was time for the first term's report card. The boy walked in with it unopened, laid it on the dinner table and went straight to his room. Cautiously, his mother opened it and to her amazement, she saw a large red 'A' under the subject of Maths. Overjoyed, she and her husband rushed into their son's room, thrilled at his remarkable progress.

'Was it the nuns that did it?' the father asked. The boy shook his head and said ,'No.'

'Was it the one-to-one tutoring? The textbooks? The teachers? The curriculum?'

'No,' said the son. 'On that first day, when I walked in the front door and saw that guy nailed to the plus sign, I KNEW they were serious!'

A little girl asked her mother, 'Mum, may I take the dog for a walk around the block?'

Mum replies, 'No, because she is on heat.'

'What's that mean?' asked the child.

'Go ask your father. I think he's in the garage.'

The little girl goes to the garage and says, 'Dad, may I take Belle for a walk around the block? I asked Mum, but she said the dog was on heat, and to come to you'.

Dad said, 'Bring Belle over here.' He took a rag, soaked it with petrol, and scrubbed the dog's backside with it and said, 'Okay, that should take care of that problem. You can go now, but keep Belle on the leash and only go one time around the block.'

The little girl left, and returned a few minutes later with no dog on the leash. Surprised, Dad asked, 'Where's Belle?'

The little girl said, 'She ran out of petrol about halfway around the block, so another dog is pushing her home.'

A father watched his precious 6-year-old daughter playing in the garden. He smiled as he reflected on how sweet and innocent his little girl was. Suddenly she just stopped and stared at the ground. He went over to her and noticed she was looking at two spiders mating.

'Daddy, what are those two spiders doing?' she asked.

'They're mating,' her father replied.

'What do you call the spider on top, Daddy?' she asked.

'That's a Daddy Longlegs,' her father answered.

'So, the other one is a Mummy Longlegs?' the little girl asked.

'No,' her father replied. 'Both of them are Daddy Longlegs.'

The little girl thought for a moment, then took her foot and stomped them flat.

'Well, we're not having any of that queer shit in our garden.'

Male

A lady came home one day to find her husband in bed with a strange woman. As she storms out, he chased after her and cries, 'Don't you at least want to know why I did it?'

Wife sobs, 'OK.'

'I'm driving along the street when I saw this lass in torn clothes and no shoes, all muddy and crying,' he begins. 'I took pity on her and took her to our place to clean up. Once there she took a shower, then I gave her the underwear that doesn't fit you any more, the $150 Nike running shoes you bought but never used. I even gave her the roast beef you had in the fridge but didn't serve me. She thanked me and was about to leave when she turned and asked me, "Is there anything else your wife doesn't use anymore?"'

The owner of a golf course in Queensland misplaced his calculator and was confused about the correct amount to pay on an invoice, so he decided to ask his secretary for some mathematical help. He called her into his office and said, 'You graduated from the University of Queensland and I need some help. If I were to give you $20,000 minus 14%, how much would you take off?'

The secretary thought a moment, then replied ... 'Everything but my earrings.'

An Amish boy and his father were visiting a mall. They were amazed by almost everything they saw, but especially by two, shiny silver walls that could move apart and then slide back together again. The boy asked, 'What is this, Father?'

The father (never having seen an elevator) responded, 'Son, I have never seen anything like this in my life, I don't know what it is.'

While the boy and his father were watching with amazement, a fat old lady strolled up to the moving walls and pressed a button. The walls opened and the lady strolled between them into a small room. The walls closed and the boy and his father watched the small circular numbers above the walls light up sequentially.

They continued to watch until it reached the last number and then the numbers began to light in the reverse order. Finally the walls opened up again and a gorgeous, voluptuous 24-year-old blonde woman stepped out.

The father, not taking his eyes off the young woman, said quietly to his son, 'Go get your mother.'

Two dwarfs go into a bar, where they pick up two women and took them to their separate hotel rooms.

The first dwarf, however, is unable to get it up. His depression is made worse by the fact that, from the next room, he hears his little friend shouting out cries of, 'Here I go again ... one, two, three ... Uh,' all night long.

In the morning, the second dwarf asks the first, 'How did it go?'

The first mutters, 'It was so embarrassing. I simply couldn't get it up.'

The second dwarf shook his head. 'You think that's embarrassing? I couldn't even get on the bed.'

———————— ⸎ ————————

Two women friends had gone for a girls' night out, but had been decidedly over-enthusiastic on the Bacardi Breezers. Incredibly drunk and walking home they needed to pee, so they stopped in the cemetery. One of them had nothing to wipe with so she thought she would take off her panties and use them.

Her friend however was wearing a rather expensive pair of panties and did not want to ruin them, but was lucky enough to salvage a large ribbon from a wreath that was on one of the graves and she proceeded to wipe with that. After the girls did their business they proceeded to go home.

The next day one of the women's husbands phoned the other husband and said, 'These damn girls' nights have to stop. My wife came home with no panties.'

'That's nothing,' said the other husband. 'Mine came back with a card stuck between the cheeks of her bottom that said "From all of us at the Fire Station. We will never forget you!"'

———————— ⸎ ————————

A man walks into doctor's office. 'What seems to be the problem?' asks the doctor.

'It's ... um ... well ... I have five penises,' replies the man.

'Blimey!' says the doctor, 'How do your trousers fit?'

'Like a glove.'

Men know ...   that Mother Nature's best aphrodisiac is still a naked woman.

Men know ...   that PMS is Mother Nature's way of telling you to get out of the house.

Men know ...   that if she looks like your mother, run.

Men know ...   that there are at least three sides to every story: His, hers, and the truth.

Men know ...   never to run away from a fight that you know you can win.

Men know ...   how to change the toilet paper, but to do so would ruin the game.

Men know ...   exactly how much gas is left in the tank and how far that gas will get them.

Men know ...   that from time to time, it is absolutely necessary to adjust oneself.

Men know ...   that a woman will wear a low-cut dress and expect the man to stare at her cleavage. Men also know that the woman will get ticked off when they do, for reasons not totally clear to them.

Men know ...   that there is no such thing as a sure thing, unless her name is Bambi.

Men know ...   that it's never a good idea to tell your father-in-law how good his daughter is in bed.

Men know ... that men are from here, and women are from way the hell over there.

Q.:   Why do men pass wind more than women?
A.:   Because women won't shut up long enough to build up pressure.

One day, Jimmy Joe was walking down Main Street when he saw his buddy Bubba driving a brand new pickup. Bubba pulled up to him with a wide grin.

'Bubba, where'd you get that truck?!?'

'Bobby Sue gave it to me,' Bubba replied.

'She gave it to you? I knew she was kinda sweet on ya, but a new truck?'

'Well, Jimmy Joe, let me tell you what happened. We were driving out on County Road 6, in the middle of nowhere. Bobby Sue pulled off the road, put the truck in 4-wheel drive, and headed into the woods. She parked the truck, got out, threw off all her clothes and said, "Bubba, take whatever you want!" So I took the truck!'

'Bubba, you're a smart man! Them clothes woulda never fit you!'

A young Scottish lad and lass were sitting on a low stone wall, holding hands, gazing out over the loch. For several minutes they sat silently, then finally the girl looked at the boy and said, 'A penny for your thoughts, Angus.'

'Well, uh, I was thinkin' ... perhaps it's aboot time for a wee kiss.'

The girl blushed, then leaned over and kissed him lightly on the cheek. Then he blushed. The two turned once again to gaze out over the loch. Minutes passed, then the girl spoke again, 'Another penny for your thoughts, Angus.'

'Well, uh I was thinkin' ... perhaps it's noo aboot time for a wee cuddle.'

The girl blushed, then leaned over and cuddled him for a few seconds. Then he blushed. Then the two turned once again to gaze out over the loch. After a while, she again said, 'Another penny for your thoughts, Angus.'

'Well, uh I was thinkin' ... perhaps its aboot time you let me pewt ma hand on yer leg.'

The girl blushed, then took his hand and put it on her knee. Then he blushed. Then the two turned once again to gaze out over the loch before the girl spoke again. 'Another penny for your thoughts, Angus.'

The young man glanced down with a furled brow. 'Well, noo,' he said, 'my thoughts are a wee bit more serious this time.'

'Really?' said the girl in a whisper, filled with anticipation.

'Aye,' said the lad, nodding. The girl looked away in shyness, began to blush, and bit her lip in anticipation of the ultimate request.

Then he said, 'Dae ye nae think it's aboot time ye paid me the first three pennies?'

A man is lying in bed in the hospital with an oxygen mask over his mouth. A young nurse appears to sponge his hands and feet.

'Nurse,' he mumbles from behind the mask, 'Are my testicles black?'

Embarrassed, the young nurse replies, 'I don't know, I'm only here to wash your hands and feet.'

He struggles again to ask, 'Nurse, are my testicles black?'

Finally, she pulls back the covers, raises his gown, holds his penis in one hand and his testicles in her other hand and takes a close look, and says, 'There's nothing wrong with them!'

Finally, the man pulls off his oxygen mask and replies, 'That was very nice but, are ... my ... test ... results ... back?'

If your wife puts you in the dog house, don't go and bury your bone next door.

A guy rings up a home delivery pizza place and orders a 'thin crusty supreme' ...
So they sent him Diana Ross!!!!

MALE JOKES

An Aberdonian goes to the dentist and asks how much it is for an extraction.

'$85 for an extraction, sir,' was the dentist's reply.

'Och huv ye nay got unyhin cheaper,' replies the Aberdonian getting agitated.

'But that's the normal charge for an extraction, sir,' said the dentist.

'Fit aboot if ye dinae use uny anaesthetic?' asked the Aberdonian hopefully.

'Well it's highly unusual sir, but if that's what you want, I suppose I can do it for $70,' said the dentist.

'Hmmmm, fit aboot if ye used one of the dentist trainees and still wi' oot anaesthetic,' said the Aberdonian.

'Well it's possible but they are only training and I can't guarantee their level of professionalism and it'll be a lot more painful, but I suppose in that case we can bring the price down to say $40,' said the dentist.

'Och that's still a bit much. How aboot if ye make it a training session and have a student do the extraction and the other students watchin and learnin,' said the Aberdonian hopefully.

'Hmmmmm, well OK it'll be good for the students I suppose, I'll charge you only $5 in that case,' said the dentist.

'Wonderful, it's a deal,' said the Aberdonian ... 'Can ye book the wife in for next Tuesday?'

———————— ¡♦¡ ————————

Three men were sitting together bragging about how they had given their new wives duties.

The first man had married a woman from Albania, and bragged that he had told his wife she was going to do all the dishes and house cleaning that needed to be done at their house. He said that it took a couple days but on the third day he came home to a clean house and the dishes were all washed and put away.

The second man had married a woman from Korea. He bragged that he had given his wife orders that she was to do all the cleaning, dishes, and the cooking. He told them that the first day he didn't see any results, but the next day it was better. By the third day, his house was clean, the dishes were done, and he had a huge dinner on the table.

The third man had married an Australian girl. He boasted that he told her that her duties were to keep the house cleaned, dishes washed, lawn mowed, laundry washed and hot meals on the table for every meal. He said the first day he didn't see anything, the second day he didn't see anything, but by the third day most of the swelling had gone down and he could see a little out of his left eye.

Got to love them Australian girls!

———————— ¡♦¡ ————————

A young man was sentenced to jail. Every lunch-time in the exercise yard these lifers would say a number, like 13, 24, 8, and everybody would laugh. This went on for days, so our young fellow thought he would get into the act, so blurts out, SEVENTEEN. Stony silence followed.

Later on in his cell he asked his lifer room-mate what happened in the yard. His mate said, 'Well, we have been here so long, and heard the jokes so many times that we have given them numbers, so instead of telling the joke again we just call out a number.'

'Well what was wrong with my joke?' the young fellow asked.

The old lifer said, 'Son it is not just the joke, but the way you tell it that makes it funny.'

A Queenslander is drinking in a NSW bar when he gets a call on his mobile phone. He hangs up, grinning from ear to ear and orders a round of drinks for everyone in the bar because, he announces, his wife has just produced a typical baby boy weighing 25 pounds.

Nobody can believe that any baby can weigh in at 25 pounds, but the Queenslander just shrugs, 'That's about average in Queensland ... like I said, my boy is a typical Queensland baby boy.'

Congratulations showered him from all around, and many exclamations of 'Strewth!' were heard. One woman actually fainted due to sympathy pains.

Two weeks later he returns to the bar. The bartender says, 'You're the father of that typical Queensland baby that weighed 25 pounds at birth. Everybody's been having bets about how big he'd be in two weeks. We were going to call you, so how much does he weigh now?'

The proud father answers, '17 pounds.'

The bartender is puzzled, and concerned. 'What happened? He weighed 25 pounds the day he was born.'

The Queensland father takes a slow swig from his XXXX beer, wipes his lips on his shirt sleeve, leans onto the bar and proudly says ... 'Had him circumcised!!'

On a recent transpacific flight, a plane passes through a severe storm. The turbulence is awful, and things go from bad to worse when one wing is struck by lightning. One woman in particular loses it. Screaming, she stands up in the front of the plane. 'I'm too young to die,' she wails.

Then she yells, 'Well, if I'm going to die, I want my last minutes on earth to be memorable! Is there anyone on this plane who can make me feel like a WOMAN?'

For a moment there is silence. Everyone has forgotten their own peril. They all stared, riveted, at the desperate woman in the front of the plane.

Then an Aussie bloke stands up in the rear of the plane. He is gorgeous ... tall, well-built, with sun-bleached blond hair and blue eyes. He starts to walk slowly up the aisle, unbuttoning his shirt ... one button at a time.

No-one moves. Everyone is transfixed. He removes his shirt. Muscles ripple across his chest.

She gasps ... He whispers ...

'Here ya go, luv. Iron this and then go get me a beer ...'

The father of five children had won a toy at a raffle. He called his kids together to ask which one should have the present.

'Who is the most obedient?' he asked. 'Who never talks back to mother? Who does everything she says?'

Five small voices answered in unison, 'Okay, dad, you get the toy.'

One day a man, stranded on a desert island for over ten years, sees an unusual speck on the horizon.

'It's certainly not a ship,' he thinks to himself. As the speck gets closer and closer, he begins to rule out the possibilities of a small boat, then even a raft. Suddenly, emerging from the surf comes a drop dead gorgeous blonde woman wearing a wetsuit and scuba gear.

She approaches the stunned guy and says to him, 'Tell me, how long has it been since you've had a cigarette?'

'Ten years,' replies the stunned man. With that, she reaches over and unzips a waterproof pocket on her left sleeve and pulls out a pack of fresh cigarettes. He takes one, lights it, takes a long drag and says, 'Man, oh Man! Is that good!'

'And how long has it been since you've had a sip of bourbon?' she asks him. Trembling, the castaway replies, 'Ten years.'

She reaches over, unzips her right sleeve, pulls out a flask and hands it to him. He opens the flask, takes a long swig and says, 'Wow, that's absolutely fantastic!'

At this point she starts slowly unzipping the long zipper that runs down the front of her wetsuit, looks at the man seductively and asks, 'And how long has it been since you've played around?'

With tears in his eyes, the guy falls to his knees and sobs, 'Oh, sweet Jesus! Don't tell me you've got golf clubs in there too?!?'

MALE JOKES

———— ░░░ ————

A policeman pulls over a driver who has a VB label stuck to his forehead. The policeman says, 'Have you been drinking?'

The driver replies, 'No, I've given up. I'm on the patches now.'

———— ░░░ ————

A sailor stationed overseas received a 'Dear John' letter from his girlfriend back home. It read as follows:

Dear Ricky,
I can no longer continue our relationship. The distance between us is just too great. I must admit that I have cheated on you twice, since you've been gone, and it's not fair to either of us. I'm sorry. Please return the picture of me that I sent to you.
Love,
Becky

The sailor, with hurt feelings, asked his fellow sailors for any snapshots they could spare of their girlfriends, sisters, ex-girlfriends, aunts, cousins etc. In addition to the picture of Becky, Ricky included all the other pictures of the pretty gals he had collected from his buddies. There were 57 photos in that envelope ... along with this note:

Dear Becky,
I'm so sorry, but I can't quite remember who you are. Please take your picture from the pile, and send the rest back to me.
Take Care,
Ricky

A man walks into a pharmacy and wanders up and down the aisles. The sales girl notices him and asks him if she can help him. He answers that he is looking for a box of tampons for his wife.

She directs him down the correct aisle. A few minutes later, he deposits a huge bag of cotton balls and a ball of string on the counter. She says, confused, 'Sir, I thought you were looking for some tampons for your wife?'

He answers, 'You see, it's like this, yesterday, I sent my wife to the store to get me a carton of cigarettes and she came home with a tin of tobacco and some rolling papers. Because it is soooooo much cheaper. So, I figure that if I have to roll my own, so does she!!

Four men went golfing one day. Three of them headed to the first tee and the fourth went into the clubhouse to take care of the bill. The three men started talking and bragging about their sons.

The first man told the others, 'My son is a home builder, and he is so successful that he gave a friend a new home for free. Just gave it to him!'

The second man said, 'My son was a car salesman, and now he owns a multi-line dealership. He's so successful that he gave one of his friends a new Mercedes, fully loaded.'

The third man, not wanting to be outdone, bragged, 'My son is a stockbroker and he's doing so well that he gave his friend an entire portfolio.'

After a few minutes of taking care of business, the fourth man joined them on the tee. The first man mentioned, 'We were just talking about our sons. How is yours doing?'

The fourth man replied, 'Well, my son is gay and a go-go dancer in a gay bar. I'm not totally thrilled about his preferences and the dancing job, but he must be doing well. His last three boyfriends gave him a house, a brand new Mercedes, and a stock portfolio.'

Once upon a time, there was a female brain cell which, by mistake, happened to end up in a man's head. She looked around nervously, but it was all empty and quiet. 'Hello?' she cried ... but no answer. 'Is there anyone here?' she cried a little louder, but still no answer ...

Now the female brain cell started to feel alone and scared and yelled, 'Hello, is there anyone there?'

Then she heard a voice from far, far away ... 'Hello, hello, we're all down here ...'

If men got pregnant
1. Morning sickness would rank as the nation's number one health problem.
2. Maternity leave would last for two years with full pay.
3. Children would be kept in the hospital until toilet trained.
4. Natural childbirth would become obsolete.
5. All methods of birth control would become 100% effective.
6. Men would be eager to talk about commitment.
7. There would be a cure for stretch marks.
8. They would serve beer instead of coffee at antenatal classes.
9. Men wouldn't think twins were so cute.
10. Sons would have to come home from dates by 10pm.

Men's No 1 Rules
- Learn to work the toilet seat. You're a big girl. If it's up, put it down. You can handle it. We need it up, you need it down. You don't hear us complaining about you leaving it down, do you?
- Sunday = sports. It's like the full moon. Let it be.
- Crying is blackmail.
- Ask for what you want. Let us be clear on this one. Subtle hints do not work! Strong hints do not work! Obvious hints do not work! Just say it!
- Yes and No are perfectly acceptable answers to almost every question.
- Come to us with a problem only if you want help solving it. That's what we do. Sympathy is what your girlfriends are for.

- A headache that lasts for 17 months is a problem. See a doctor.
- Anything we said six months ago is inadmissible in an argument. In fact, all comments become null and void after seven days.
- If you won't dress like the Victoria's Secret girls, don't expect us to act like soap opera guys.
- If you think you're fat, you probably are. Don't ask us.
- If something we said can be interpreted two ways, and one of the ways makes you sad or angry, we meant the other one.
- You can either ask us to do something or tell us how you want it done. Not both. If you already know best how to do it, just do it yourself.
- Whenever possible, please say whatever you have to say during commercials.
- Christopher Columbus did not need directions, and neither do we.
- ALL men see in only 16 colours, like Windows default settings. Peach, for example, is a fruit, not a colour. We have no idea what mauve is.
- If it itches, it will be scratched. We do that.
- If we ask what is wrong and you say 'nothing,' we will act like nothing's wrong. We know you are lying, but it is just not worth the hassle.
- If you ask a question you don't want an answer to, expect an answer you don't want to hear.
- Don't ask us what we're thinking about unless you are prepared to discuss such topics as football, fast cars, or horse racing.
- You have enough clothes.
- You have too many shoes.
- I am in shape. ROUND is a shape.

A man and a young and very beautiful woman walk into a posh upmarket furrier. 'Show the lady your finest mink!' the fellow exclaims. So the owner of the shop goes in back and comes out with an absolutely gorgeous full-length coat. As the lady tries it on, the furrier discreetly whispers to the man, 'Ah, sir, that particular fur goes for $165,000.'

'No problem! I'll write you a cheque!'

'Very good, sir,' says the shop owner. 'Today is Saturday. You may come by on Monday to pick it up, after the cheque has cleared.'

So the man and the woman leave. On Monday, the fellow returns. The store owner is outraged, 'How dare you show your face in here?! There wasn't a single penny in your cheque account!!'

'I know, but I just had to come by,' grinned the guy, 'to thank you for the most wonderful weekend of my life!'

A man is driving down a road. A woman is driving down the same road from the opposite direction. As they pass each other, the woman leans out the window and yells 'PIG!' The man immediately leans out his window and yells, 'BITCH!!'

They each continue on their way and as the man rounds the next bend he crashes into a huge pig in the middle of the road.

Who understands men?
- The nice men are ugly.
- The handsome men are not nice.
- The handsome and nice men are gay.
- The handsome, nice and heterosexual men are married.

- The men who are not so handsome, but are nice men, have no money.
- The men who are not so handsome, but are nice men with money think we are only after their money.
- The handsome men without money are after our money.
- The handsome men, who are not so nice and somewhat heterosexual, don't think we are beautiful enough.
- The men who think we are beautiful, that are heterosexual, somewhat nice and have money, are pigs.
- The men who are somewhat handsome, somewhat nice and have some money and thank God are heterosexual, are shy and never make the first move!
- The men who never make the first move, automatically lose interest in us when we take the initiative. Now, who in the world understands men?
- Men are like a fine wine. They all start out like grapes, and it's our job to stomp on them and keep them in the dark until they mature into something you'd like to have dinner with.

Driving to the office this morning on the motorway, I looked over to my right and there was a woman in a brand new silver Mercedes doing 110km per hour with her face up close to her rear view mirror putting on her eyeliner! I looked away for a couple of seconds and when I looked back she was halfway over in my lane still working on that makeup!!

It scared me so much that I dropped my electric shaver, which knocked the bacon roll out of my other hand. In all the confusion of trying to straighten out the car using my knees against the steering wheel, it knocked my mobile from my ear, which fell into the coffee between my legs, causing it to splash and burn Big Jim and The Round Twins, causing me to scream, which made me drop the cigarette butt out of my mouth, ruined my shirt and disconnected an important call!!!

Bloody women drivers!

A man is driving down a deserted stretch of highway when he notices a sign out of the corner of his eye ... It reads: SISTERS OF ST. FRANCIS HOUSE OF PROSTITUTION - 10 KM.

He thinks it was a figment of his imagination and drives on without a second thought. Soon he sees another sign, which says: SISTERS OF ST. FRANCIS HOUSE OF PROSTITUTION - 5 KM.

Suddenly, he begins to realise that these signs are for real ... Then he drives past a third sign saying: SISTERS OF ST. FRANCIS HOUSE OF PROSTITUTION - NEXT RIGHT.

His curiosity gets the best of him and he pulls into the drive. On the far side of the parking lot is a stone building with a small sign next to the door reading: SISTERS OF ST. FRANCIS.

He climbs the steps and rings the bell. The door is answered by a nun in a long black habit who asks, 'What may we do for you, my son?'

He answers, 'I saw your signs along the highway, and was interested in possibly doing business.'

'Very well, my son. Please follow me.'

He is led through many winding passages and is soon quite disoriented. The nun stops at a closed door and tells the man, 'Please knock on this door.'

He does as he is told and another nun in a long habit, holding a tin cup answers the door. This nun instructs, 'Please place $100 in the cup, then go through the large wooden door at the end of this hallway.'

He gets $100 out of his wallet and places it in the second nun's cup. He trots eagerly down the hall and slips through, out the door, pulling it shut behind him.

As the door locks behind him, he finds himself back in the parking lot, facing another small sign:

GO IN PEACE. YOU HAVE JUST BEEN SCREWED BY THE SISTERS OF ST. FRANCIS. SERVES YOU RIGHT, YOU SINNER!

———————— ⚭ ————————

Marital Bliss

A woman accompanied her husband to the doctor's office. After his checkup, the doctor called the wife into his office alone.

He said, 'Your husband is suffering from a very severe disease, combined with horrible stress. If you don't want him to die, each morning, fix him a healthy breakfast. Be pleasant, and make sure he is in a good mood. For lunch make him a nutritious meal. For dinner prepare an especially nice meal for him. Don't burden him with chores, as he probably had a hard day. Don't discuss your problems with him, it will only make his stress worse. And most importantly, make love with your husband several times a week and satisfy his every whim. If you can do this for the next ten months to a year, I think your husband will regain his health completely.'

On the way home, the husband asked his wife, 'What did the doctor say?'

'You're going to die,' she replied.

A long married couple came upon a wishing well. The husband leaned over, made a wish and threw in a penny.

The wife decided to make a wish too. But she leaned over too much, fell into the well, and drowned.

The husband was stunned for a moment but then smiled, 'Hey, it really works!'

A husband read an article to his wife about how many words women use a day - 30,000 to a man's 15,000.

The wife replied, 'The reason has to be because we have to repeat everything to men.'

The husband turned to his wife and asked, 'What?'

Husband and wife were in the midst of a violent quarrel, and hubby was losing his temper. 'Be careful,' he said to his wife, 'you will bring out the animal in me.'

'So what?' his wife shot back, 'who is afraid of a mouse?'

A woman awakes during the night to find that her husband was not in their bed. She puts on her robe and goes downstairs to look for him. She finds him sitting at the kitchen table with a cup of coffee in front of him. He appears deep in thought, just staring at the wall. She watches as he wipes a tear from his eye and takes a sip of coffee.

'What's the matter, dear?' she whispers as she steps into the room. 'Why are you down here at this time of night?'

The husband looks up, 'Do you remember 20 years ago when we were dating, and you were only 16?' he asks solemnly.

The wife is touched to tears thinking that her husband is so caring and sensitive. 'Yes, I do' she replies.

The husband pauses. The words are not coming easily. 'Do you remember when your father caught us in the back seat of my car making love?'

'Yes, I remember,' says the wife, lowering herself into a chair beside him. The husband continues …

'Do you remember when he shoved a shotgun in my face and said, "Either you marry my daughter, or I will send you to jail for 20 years?"'

'I remember that too,' she replies softly.

He wipes another tear from his cheek and says … 'I would have gotten out today.'

A woman standing naked in front of the bedroom mirror says to her husband, 'I feel fat, saggy and ugly. Pay me a compliment.'

Her husband says, 'Your eyesight is blooming spot on.'

On their honeymoon the new husband told his bride, 'I have a confession that I should have made before, but I was concerned that it might affect our relationship.'

'What is it?' she asked.

'I'm a golfer,' he said.

'What's the big deal about that?' she asked.

He replied, 'When I say I'm a golfer, I mean that I'll be on the course Saturday, Sunday, Wednesday afternoon, and any holidays. If it comes to a choice between your wishes and golf … golf wins.'

She pondered a moment and said, 'I thank you for your honesty. In the same spirit of honesty, I should tell you that I've concealed something about my own past that you should know about. I'm a hooker.'

'No problem,' was his response, 'just widen your stance a little and overlap your grip and that should clear right up.'

A man and his wife were having an argument about who should brew the coffee each morning. The wife said, 'You should do it, because you get up first, and then we don't have to wait as long to get our coffee.'

The husband said, 'You are in charge of cooking around here and you should do it, because that is your job, and I can just wait for my coffee.'

Wife replies, 'No, you should do it, and besides, it is in the Bible that the man should do the coffee.'

Husband replies, 'I can't believe that, show me.'

So she fetched the Bible, and opened the New Testament and showed him at the top of several pages, that it indeed says ... 'HEBREWS'.

———— ⋮⋮⋮ ————

WIFE: 'What would you do if I died? Would you get married again?'

HUSBAND: 'Definitely not!'

WIFE: 'Why not - don't you like being married?'

HUSBAND: 'Of course I do.'

WIFE: 'Then why wouldn't you remarry?'

HUSBAND: 'Okay, I'd get married again.'

WIFE: 'You would? (with a hurtful look on her face).'

HUSBAND: (makes audible groan).

WIFE: 'Would you sleep with her in our bed?'

HUSBAND: 'Where else would we sleep?'

WIFE: 'Would you replace my pictures with hers?'

HUSBAND: 'That would seem like the proper thing to do.'

WIFE: 'Would you play golf with her?'

HUSBAND: 'I guess so.'

WIFE: 'Would she use my golf clubs?'

HUSBAND: 'No, she's left-handed.'
WIFE: - - - - silence - - - -
HUSBAND: 'Sh* t!'

He said, 'I don't know why you wear a bra, you've got nothing to put in it.' She said, 'You wear pants don't you?'

He said, 'Shall we try swapping positions tonight?' She said, 'That's a good idea - you stand by the ironing board while I sit on the couch.'

He said, 'What have you been doing with all the grocery money I gave you?' She said 'Turn sideways and look in the mirror!'

One evening Mary arrived home from work to find the children bathed, a load of clothes in the washing machine and another in the dryer, dinner on the stove and a beautifully set table, complete with flowers. She was astonished, and she immediately wanted to know what was going on.

It turned out that her husband Charlie had read a magazine article that suggested working wives would be more romantically inclined if they weren't so tired from having to do all the housework in addition to holding down a full-time job.

The next day, she couldn't wait to tell her friends in the office. 'How did it work out?' they asked.

'Well, it was a great dinner,' Mary said. 'Charlie even cleaned up, helped the kids with their homework, folded the laundry and put everything away.'

'But what about afterward?' her friends wanted to know.

'Oh, that part didn't work out,' Mary said. 'Charlie was too tired.'

At the cocktail party, one woman said to another, 'Aren't you wearing your wedding ring on the wrong finger?'

The other women replied, 'Yes I am, I married the wrong man.'

The other night I was invited out for a night with 'the girls'. I told my husband that I would be home by midnight ... 'I promise!' Well, the hours passed and the champagne was going down way too easy. Around 3am, drunk as a skunk, I headed for home.

Just as I got in the door, the cuckoo clock in the hall started up and cuckooed three times. Quickly, realising he'd probably wake up, I cuckooed another nine times. I was really proud of myself for coming up with such a quick-witted solution (even when smashed), in order to escape a possible conflict with him.

The next morning my husband asked me what time I got in, and I told him midnight. He didn't seem disturbed at all. Whew! Got away with that one!

Then he said, 'We need a new cuckoo clock.'

When I asked him why, he said, 'Well, last night our clock cuckooed three times, then said, 'Oh shit,' cuckooed four more times, cleared its throat, cuckooed another three times, giggled, cuckooed twice more, and then tripped over the cat and farted.'

A man went to see a wizard about removing a curse that was placed upon him. The wizard said to the man that he could remove the curse if he knew what words were used to place the curse?

The man replied, 'I now pronounce you man and wife.'

A couple drove down a country road for several miles, not saying a word. An earlier discussion had led to an argument and neither of them wanted to concede their position.

As they passed a barnyard of mules, goats and pigs, the husband asked sarcastically, 'Relatives of yours?'

'Yep,' the wife replied, 'in-laws.'

Jack and Joan were having some problems at home and were giving each other the 'silent treatment'.

But then Jack realised that he would need his wife to wake him at 5am for an early morning drive with his friends to play golf. Not wanting to be the first to break the silence - and so lose the war, he wrote on a piece of paper, 'Please wake me at 5am,' and gave it to his wife.

The next morning, Jack woke up, to discover it was already 9am. He knew that his friends would have left for the golf course without him. Furious, he was about to go and see why his wife hadn't awakened him when he noticed a piece of paper by the bed.

The paper said, 'It is 5am. Wake up.'

Marital Bliss Jokes

While attending a marriage seminar on communication, David and his wife listened to the instructor declare, 'It is essential that husbands and wives know the things that are important to each other.'

He addressed the men, 'Can you describe your wife's favourite flower?'

David leaned over, touched his wife's arm gently and whispered, 'Black & Gold, self-raising, isn't it?'

A 50-ish woman was at home happily jumping on her bed and squealing with delight. Her husband watches her for a while and asks, 'Do you have any idea how ridiculous you look? What's the matter with you?'

The woman continues to bounce on the bed and says, 'I don't care. I just came from a mammography and the doctor says I have the breasts of an 18-year-old.'

The husband said, 'What did he say about your 55 year old arse?'

'Your name never came up, dear,' she replied.

A woman is standing in front of her bedroom mirror trying on her new dress she turns to her hubby and asks, 'Does this dress make my bum look big?'

Hubby replies, 'Of course not, it's all those chocolates you eat that does that.'

During a recent publicity outing, Jennifer snuck off to visit a fortune teller of some local repute. In a dark and hazy room, peering into a crystal ball, the mystic delivered grave news.

'There's no easy way to say this, so I'll just be blunt. Prepare yourself to be a widow. Your husband will die a violent and horrible death this year.'

Visibly shaken, Jennifer stared at the woman's face, then at the single flickering candle, and then down at her hands. She took a few deep breaths to compose herself. She simply had to know. She met the fortune teller's gaze, steadied her voice, and asked, 'Will I be acquitted?'

A husband and wife were having dinner at a very fine restaurant when this absolutely stunning young woman comes over to their table, gives the husband a big open-mouthed kiss, then says she'll see him later and walks away.

The wife glares at her husband and says, 'Who the hell was that?'

'Oh,' replies the husband, 'she's my mistress.'

'Well, that's the last straw,' says the wife. 'I've had enough, I want a divorce!'

'I can understand that,' replies her husband, 'but remember, if we get a divorce it will mean no more shopping trips to Paris, no more wintering in Barbados, no more summers in Tuscany, no more Infiniti or Lexus in the garage and no more yacht club. But the decision is yours.'

Just then, a mutual friend enters the restaurant with a gorgeous babe on his arm. 'Who's that woman with Jim?' asks the wife.

'That's his mistress,' says her husband.

'Ours is prettier,' she replies.

There was a man who had worked all of his life and had saved all of his money. He was a real miser when it came to his money. He loved money more than just about anything, and just before he died, he said to his wife, 'Now listen, when I die, I want you to take all my money and place it in the casket with me. I want to take my money to the afterlife.'

So he got his wife to promise him with all her heart that

when he died, she would put all the money in the casket with him.

Well, one day he died. He was stretched out in the casket, the wife was sitting there in black next to her closest friend.

When they finished the ceremony, just before the undertakers got ready to close the casket, the wife said, 'Wait just a minute!' She had a shoe box with her, she came over with the box and placed it in the casket.

Then the undertakers locked the casket down and rolled it away.

Her friend said, 'I hope you weren't crazy enough to put all that money in the casket.' She said, 'Yes, I promised. I'm a good Christian, I can't lie. I promised him that I was going to put that money in that casket with him.'

'You mean to tell me you put every cent of his money in the casket with him?'

'I sure did,' said the wife. 'I got it all together, put it into my account and I wrote him a cheque.'

A man walks into his bedroom and sees his wife packing a suitcase. He says, 'What are you doing?'

She answers, 'I'm moving to Sydney. I heard prostitutes there get paid $400 for doing what I do for you for free.'

Later, on her way out, the wife walks into the bedroom and sees her husband packing his suitcase.

When she asks him where he's going, he replies, 'I'm going to Sydney too, I want to see you live on $800 a year.'

A woman stopped by unannounced at her recently married son's house. She rang the doorbell and walked in.

She was shocked to see her daughter-in-law lying on the couch, totally naked. Soft music was playing, and the aroma of perfume filled the room.

'What are you doing?' she asked.

'I'm waiting for my husband to come home from work,' the daughter-in-law answered.

'But you're naked!' the mother-in-law exclaimed.

'This is my love dress,' the daughter-in-law explained.

'Love dress? But you're naked!'

'My husband loves me to wear this dress,' she explained. 'It excites him no end. Every time he sees me in this dress, he instantly becomes romantic and ravages me for hours on end. He can't get enough of me.'

The mother-in-law left. When she got home, she undressed, showered, put on her best perfume, dimmed the lights, put on a romantic CD, and laid on the couch waiting for her husband to arrive. Finally, her husband came home. He walked in and saw her laying there so provocatively.

'What are you doing?' he asked.

'This is my love dress,' she whispered, sensually.

'Needs ironing,' he said. 'What's for dinner?'

A married couple is driving along a highway doing a steady 60 km per hour. The wife is behind the wheel. Her husband suddenly looks across at her and speaks in a clear voice. 'Darling,' he says. 'I know we've been married for twenty years, but I want a divorce.'

The wife says nothing, keeps looking at the road ahead but slowly increases her speed to 70 km/h.

The husband speaks again. 'I don't want you to try and talk me out of it,' he says, 'because I've been having an affair with your best friend, and she's a far better lover than you are.'

Again the wife stays quiet, but grips the steering wheel more tightly and slowly increases the speed to 80km/h.

He pushes it. 'I want the house,' he says insistently. Up to 90km/h.

'I want the car, too,' he continues. 100 km/h.

'And,' he says, 'I'll have the bank accounts, all the credit cards and the boat.'

The car slowly starts veering towards a massive concrete flyover. This makes him a wee bit nervous, so he asks her: 'Isn't there anything you want?'

The wife at last replies … in a quiet and controlled voice, 'No, I've got everything I need,' she says.

'Oh, really?' he inquires, 'so what have you got?'

Just before they slam into the wall at 120 km/h, the wife turns to him and smiles saying, 'The airbag!'

A man approached a very beautiful woman in the large supermarket and said, 'I've lost my wife here in the supermarket. Can you talk to me for a couple of minutes?'

The woman looked puzzled. 'Why talk to me?' she asked.

'Because every time I talk to a woman with tits like yours, my wife appears out of nowhere.'

Several men are in the locker room of a golf club. A mobile phone on a bench rings and a man engages the hands free speaker function and begins to talk. Everyone else in the room stops to listen.

Man: 'Hello.'

Woman: 'Honey it's me. Are you at the Club?'

Man: 'Yes.'

Woman: 'I am at the mall now and found this beautiful leather coat. It's only $1,000. Is it OK if I buy it?'

Man: 'Sure ... go ahead if you like it that much.'

Woman: 'I also stopped by the Mercedes dealership and saw the new 2005 models. I saw one I really liked.'

Man: 'How much?'

Woman: '$60,000.'

Man: 'OK, but for that price I want it with all the options.'

Woman: 'Great. Oh, and one more thing. The house we wanted last year is back on the market. They're asking $950,000.'

Man: 'Well then go ahead and give them an offer - but just an offer mind you of $900,000.'

Woman: 'OK, I'll see you later and I love you.'

Man: 'Bye darl, I love you too!'

The man hangs up, and the other men in the locker room are looking at him in astonishment. Then he asks, 'Does anyone know who this mobile belongs to?'

A man is getting into the shower just as his wife is finishing up her shower when the doorbell rings. After a few seconds of arguing over which one should go and answer the doorbell, the wife gives up, quickly wraps herself up in a towel and runs downstairs.

When she opens the door, there stands Bob, the next door neighbour. Before she says a word, Bob says, 'I'll give you $800 to drop that towel you have on.'

After thinking for a moment, the woman drops her towel and stands naked in front of Bob. After a few seconds, Bob hands her $800 and leaves.

Confused, but excited about her good fortune, the woman wraps back up in the towel and goes back upstairs. When she gets back to the bathroom, her husband asks from the shower, 'Who was that?'

'It was Bob our neighbour,' she replies.

'Great,' the husband says, 'did he say anything about the $800 he owes me?'

A young couple are on their way to Las Vegas to get married.

Before getting there, the girl said to the guy that she had a confession to make. The reason that they had not been intimate was because she was very flat-chested. If he wished to cancel the wedding, it would be OK with her.

The guy thought about it for a while and said he did not mind if she was flat, and sex is not the most important thing in a marriage.

Several miles down the road, the guy turned to the girl and said that he also wanted to make a confession. He said that below his waist he was just like a baby, and if the girl wished to cancel the wedding, it'd be fine by him.

The girl thought about it for a while and said that she did not mind and she also believed there were other things far more important in a marriage than sex. Both were happy that they'd been honest with each other.

They went on to Vegas and got married. On the wedding night the girl took off her clothes and she was as flat as a washboard. Finally, the guy took off his clothes and one look at the guy's naked body made the girl faint and fall to the floor.

After she came to, the guy asked, 'I told you before we got married, why did you still faint?'

The girl said, 'You told me it was just like a baby.'

The guy replied, 'Yes, eight pounds and 21 inches.'

A woman's husband had been slipping in and out of a coma for months yet she stayed by his bedside every day. At last when he came to he motioned for her to come closer. Painfully he whispered to her, eyes full of tears, 'Darling you've always been with me all through the bad times . When I got fired, you stayed by me, when my business failed, you were there, when we lost the house and when my health began to fail, you stayed beside me. Do you know what?'

'What dear,' she said gently smiling as her heart began to fill with warmth.

'I think you're bad luck,' was his response.

A man was sitting on a bus looking ashamed. The man next to him noticed and asked what the matter was. He said that when he went to buy the bus ticket, the woman serving him had the most unbelievable breasts, so he got flustered and asked for two tickets to Tittsburgh instead of Pittsburgh.

The man next to him laughed and said, 'Don't worry about that. We all make Freudian slips. This morning I was having breakfast with my wife. I meant to say, "Pass the sugar," but I accidentally said, "You stupid woman, you've ruined my life".'

A man turns up at the emergency department of the Royal Hobart Hospital with bruises all over his head and a seven iron wrapped around his neck.

'You're in such a mess, what happened?' asked the medic.

'Well my wife and I were having a leisurely game of golf and on the 4th green we both spliced our ball into a paddock of cows.'

'I climbed the fence and noticed a cow wagging its tail and saw something white.'

'When I lifted its tail I saw my wife's ball and shouted to her, "This looks like yours"! Quite frankly that's about the last thing I remember.'

For the whole of their 50-year marriage, Bob kept a shoe box, under the bed, as his 'personal space'.

Jane was respectful of this and never opened it.

One day when tidying Jane accidentally bumped it and the lid fell off. There inside were two golf balls and $1,000 in cash. Since they'd always been honest, she confessed that night at dinner. She told Bob that she accidentally bumped the lid and saw what was inside.

Bob said, 'That's OK, never mind.'

Jane was curious, so she asked Bob about the golf balls.

'Every time I was unfaithful to you, I put a golf ball in the box.'

Jane was a bit upset, but thought that two golf balls in 50 years is not too bad. 'And where did all the money come from?' she asked.

'Each time I got a dozen golf balls, I sold them.'

John was going to be married to Jill, so his father sat him down for a little fireside chat.

He says 'John, let me tell you something. On my wedding night in our honeymoon suite, I took off my pants and handed them to your mother, and said, "Here try these on". So, she did and said, "These are too big, I can't wear them". So I replied, "Exactly! I wear the pants in this family and I always will". Ever since that night we have never had any problems.'

'Hmmm,' says John. He thinks that might be a good thing to try. So, on his honeymoon, John takes off his pants and says to Jill, 'Here, try these on.'

So she does and says, 'These are too large, they don't fit me.'

So John says, 'Exactly. I wear the pants in this family and I always will, and I don't want you to ever forget that.'

Then Jill takes off her pants and hands them to John and says, 'Here you try on mine.' So he does and says, 'I can't get into your pants.'

Jill says, 'Exactly. And if you don't change your smartass attitude, you never will!'

A man took his wife to the Royal Easter Show and one of the exhibits is that of breeding bulls. They went up to the first pen and there was a sign that said, 'This bull mated 50 times last year.' The wife poked her husband in the ribs and said, 'He mated 50 times last year.'

They walked a little further and saw another pen with a sign that said, 'This bull mated 120 times last year.' The wife hit her husband and said, 'That's more than twice a week! You could learn a lot from him.'

They walked further and a third pen had a bull with a sign saying, 'This bull mated 365 times last year.' The wife got really excited and said, 'That's once a day. You could REALLY learn something from this one.'

The husband looked at her and said, 'Go up and ask him if it was with the same cow.'

One morning while making breakfast, a man walked up to his wife and pinched her on the butt and said, 'If you firmed this up, we could get rid of your control top pantyhose.'

While this was on the edge of intolerable, she kept silent.

The next morning, the man woke his wife with a pinch on each of her breasts and said, 'You know, if you firmed these up, we could get rid of your bras.'

This was beyond a silent response, so she rolled over and

grabbed him by his penis. With a death grip in place, she said, 'You know, if you firmed this up, we could get rid of the gardener, the postman, the pool man, and your brother.'

A married man was having an affair with his secretary. One day, their passions overcame them and they took off for her house, where they made passionate love all afternoon.

Exhausted from the wild session, they fell asleep, awakening around 8pm. As the man threw on his clothes, he told the woman to take his shoes outside and rub them through the grass and dirt. Mystified, she nonetheless complied. He slipped into his shoes and drove home.

'Where have you been!' demanded his wife when he entered the house.

'Darling, I can't lie to you. I've been having an affair with my secretary, and I've been making love to her all afternoon. I fell asleep and didn't wake up until 8pm.'

The wife glanced down at his shoes and said, 'You lying b@#$%^d! You've been playing golf!!'

There was a middle-aged couple that had two stunningly beautiful teenage daughters. They decided to try one last time for the son they always wanted.

After months of trying, the wife finally became pregnant, and sure enough, delivered a healthy baby boy nine months later. The joyful father rushed into the nursery to see his new son. He took one look and was horrified to see the ugliest child he had ever seen.

He went to his wife and said that there was no way he could be the father of that child.

'Look at the two beautiful daughters I fathered!' Then he gave her a stern look and asked, 'Have you been fooling around on me?'

The wife just smiled sweetly and said, 'Not this time!'

A man walks into a bar one night. He goes up to the bar and asks for a beer.

'Certainly Sir, that'll be 1 cent.'

'ONE CENT?' exclaimed the man.

The barman replied, 'Yes.'

So the man glances over at the menu and asks, 'Could I have a nice juicy T-bone steak, with fries, peas and a fried egg?'

'Certainly, Sir,' replies the barman, 'but that comes to real money.'

'How much money?' inquires the man.

'4 cents,' he replied.

'FOUR CENTS?' exclaims the man. 'Where's the guy who owns this place?'

The barman replies, 'Upstairs, with my wife.'

The man says, 'What's he doing upstairs with your wife?'

The bartender replies, 'The same thing I'm doing to his business!!'

A man and a woman, who have never met before, find themselves assigned to the same sleeping room on a transcontinental train.

Though initially embarrassed and uneasy over sharing a room, the two are tired and fall asleep quickly - he in the upper bunk and she in the lower.

At 1am, he leans over and gently wakes the woman saying, 'Ma'am, I'm sorry to bother you, but would you be willing to reach into the closet to get me a second blanket? I'm awfully cold.'

'I have a better idea,' she replies. 'Just for tonight, let's pretend that we're married.'

'Wow! That's a great idea!!' he exclaims.

'Good,' she replies. 'Get your own bloody blanket.'

Jake was dying. His wife, Becky, was maintaining a candlelight vigil by his side. She held his fragile hand, tears running down her face. Her praying roused him from his slumber.

He looked up, and his pale lips began to move slightly. 'Becky, my darling,' he whispered.

'Hush, my love,' she said. 'Rest, don't talk.'

He was insistent.

'Becky,' he said in his tired voice. 'I have something that I must confess.'

'There isn't anything to confess,' replied the weeping Becky, 'everything's alright, go to sleep.'

'No, no, I must die in peace, Becky. I, I ... I slept with your sister, your best friend, her best friend, and your mother!'

'I know,' whispered Becky, 'that's why I poisoned you.'

A man returns home early from a business trip to find his wife making passionate love to a total stranger in their bedroom.

Goggle eyed, he asks, 'What on earth are you doing?'

His wife then turns to the other man and says, 'See I told you he is as dumb as a post.'

God may have created man before woman but there is always a rough draft before the masterpiece.

Dave works hard at the plant and spends most evenings bowling or playing basketball at the gym. His wife thinks he is pushing himself too hard, so for his birthday she takes him to a local strip club.

The doorman at the club greets them and says, 'Hey, Dave! How ya doin?' His wife is puzzled and asks if he's been to this club before. 'Oh no,' says Dave. 'He's on my bowling team.'

When they are seated, a waitress asks Dave if he'd like his usual and brings over a VB.

His wife is becoming increasingly uncomfortable and says, 'How did she know that you drink VB?' 'She's in the Ladies' Bowling Team, honey. We share lanes with them.'

A stripper then comes over to their table, throws her arms around Dave, starts to rub herself all over him and says, 'Hi Davey. Want your usual table dance, big boy?'

Dave's wife, now furious, grabs her purse and storms out of the club. Dave follows and spots her getting into a cab. Before she can slam the door, he jumps in beside her.

Dave tries desperately to explain how the stripper must have mistaken him for someone else, but his wife is having none of it. She is screaming at him at the top of her lungs, calling him every four-letter word in the book.

The cabby turns his head and says, 'Looks like you picked up a real bitch tonight, Dave.'

A guy came into a bar one day and said to the barman 'Give me six double vodkas.'

The barman says 'Wow! You must have had one hell of a day.'

'Yes, I've just found out my older brother is gay.'

The next day the same guy came into the bar and placed the same order for drinks. When the bartender asked what the problem was today the answer came back, 'I've just found out that my younger brother is gay too!'

On the third day the guy came into the bar and ordered another six double vodkas. The bartender said 'Darn! Doesn't anybody in your family like women?'

'Yeah, my wife ...'

Typical macho man married typical good-looking lady and after the wedding, he laid down the following rules, 'I'll be home when I want, if I want and at what time I want and I don't expect any hassles from you. I expect a great dinner to be on the table unless I tell you that I won't be home for dinner. I'll go hunting, fishing, boozing and card playing when I want with my old buddies and don't you give me a hard time about it. Those are my rules. Any comments?'

His new bride said, 'No, that's fine with me. Just understand this ... there will be sex here at seven o'clock every night ... whether you're here or not.'

Husband and wife had a bitter quarrel on the day of their 40th wedding anniversary.

'When you die, I'm getting you a headstone that reads, Here Lies My Wife - Cold As Ever.'

'Yeah?' she replies, 'When you die, I'm getting you a headstone that reads, Here Lies My Husband - Stiff At Last.'

Husband and his wife are having a fight at the breakfast table.

Husband gets up in a rage and says, 'And you are no good in bed either,' and storms out of the house.

After some time he realises he was nasty and decides to make amends and calls her. She comes to the phone after many rings and the irritated husband says, 'What took you so long to answer the phone?'

She says, 'I was in bed.'

He said, 'In bed this early, doing what?'

'Getting a second opinion!'

A man has six children and is very proud of his achievement. He is so proud of himself, that he starts calling his wife, 'Mother of Six' in spite of her objections.

One night, they go to a party. The man decides it's time to go home and wants to find out if his wife is ready to leave as well.

He shouts at the top of his voice 'Shall we go home, Mother of Six?'

His wife, irritated by her husband's lack of discretion shouts right back, 'Anytime you're ready, Father of Four.'

A man wakes up with a huge hangover. He forces himself to open his eyes, and the first thing he sees is a couple of aspirins and a glass of water on the side table. He sits down, sees his clothing in front of him, all clean and pressed. He looks around the room and sees it is in perfect order. So is the rest of the house.

He takes the aspirins and notices a note on the table, 'Honey, breakfast is on the stove, I left early to go shopping. Love you.'

He goes to the kitchen. Sure enough, a hot breakfast and the morning newspaper await him. His son is also at the table, eating. The man asks, 'Son, what happened last night?'

His son says, 'Well, you came home after 3am, drunk and delirious. You broke some furniture, puked in the hallway, gave yourself a black eye when you walked into the door.'

Confused, the man asks, 'So, why is everything in order and also clean, with breakfast on the table waiting for me?'

His son replies, 'Oh that! Mom dragged you to the bedroom, when she tried to take your pants off you shouted, "Hey, lady, get your hands off me! I'm MARRIED!"'

A husband and his wife had a bitter quarrel on the day of their 40th wedding anniversary. The husband yells, 'When you die, I'm getting you a headstone that reads: "Here Lies My Wife - Cold As Ever".'

'Yeah, ' she replies, 'When you die, I'm getting you a headstone reads: "Here Lies My Husband - Stiff At Last".'

Need to know

Did you know ...

- If you yelled for 8 years, 7 month and 6 days you would have produced enough sound energy to heat one cup of coffee.
- If you farted consistently for 6 years and 9 months, enough gas is produced to create the energy of an atomic bomb.
- The human heart creates enough pressure when it pumps to squirt blood 30 feet.
- A pig's orgasm lasts 30 minutes.
- A cockroach will live 9 days without its head before it starves to death.
- The flea can jump 350 times its body length. It's like a human jumping the length of a football field.
- The catfish has over 27,000 taste buds.
- Some lions mate over 50 times a day.
- Butterflies taste with their feet.
- The strongest muscle in the body is the tongue.
- Right-handed people live, on average, 9 years longer than left-handed people.
- Elephants are the only animals that cannot jump.
- A cat's urine glows under a black light.
- Polar bears are left-handed.
- Humans and dolphins are the only species that have sex for pleasure.

If you're like most people, common everyday items look inert to you. But what you may not know is that many have a gender. For example ...

Freezer bags - Male, because they hold everything in but you can see right through them.

Photocopier - Female, because once turned off, it takes a while to warm up. It's an effective reproductive device if the right buttons are pushed, but can wreak havoc, if the wrong buttons are pushed.

Tyre - Male, because it goes bald and often it's over-inflated.

Hot Air Balloon - Male, because to get it to go anywhere you have to light a fire under its arse and, of course, there's the hot air part.

Sponges - Female, because they're soft and squeezable and retain water.

Web page - Female, because they're always getting hit on.

Underground - Male, because it uses the same old lines to pick people up.

Hourglass - Female, because over time, the weight shifts to the bottom.

Hammer - Male, because it hasn't evolved much over the last 5,000 years, but it's handy to have around.

Remote control - Female ... You probably thought it'd be male. But consider ... It gives a man pleasure, he'd be lost without it, and while he doesn't always know the right buttons to push, he keeps trying!

Seven bartenders were asked if they could identify a woman's personality based on what she drinks. Though interviewed separately, they concurred on almost all counts.

The results were:

Beer
Personality: Casual, low-maintenance; down to earth.
Your Approach: Challenge her to a game of pool.

Blender Drinks with umbrella
Personality: Flaky, annoying; ditzy, and a pain in the ass.
Your Approach: Avoid her, unless you want to be her cabin boy.

Mixed Drinks - no umbrellas
Personality: Mature, has picky taste, knows what she wants.
Your Approach: If she wants you, she'll send YOU a drink.

Wine - (bottled not 4 litre cask)
Personality: Conservative and classy, sophisticated.
Your Approach: Try and weave Paris and clothing into the conversation.

Lemon Ruski
Personality: Easy, thinks she is trendy and sophisticated, actually has absolutely no clue.
Your approach: Make her feel smarter than she is ... and you're in.

Shots
Personality: Hanging with frat-boy pals or looking to get drunk ... and naked.
Your Approach: Easiest hit in the joint. Nothing to do but wait.

Then there is the male drink analysis ... The deal with guys is, as always, very simple and clear cut.

Cheap Domestic Beer: He's poor and wants to get laid.
Premium Local Beer: He likes good beer and wants to get laid.
Imported Beer: He likes expensive beer and wants to get laid.

Wine: He's hoping that the wine thing will give him a sophisticated image to help him get laid.

Whisky: He doesn't give two shits about anything and will hit anyone who will get in his way of getting laid.

Lemon Ruski: He's gay.

Coke: Has to be an accountant.

Think you know everything ...?

- A dime has 118 ridges around the edge.
- A cat has 32 muscles in each ear.
- A crocodile cannot stick out its tongue.
- A dragonfly has a life span of 24 hours.
- A goldfish has a memory span of three seconds.
- A 'jiffy' is an actual unit of time for 1/100th of a second.
- A shark is the only fish that can blink with both eyes.
- A snail can sleep for three years.
- Al Capone's business card said he was a used furniture dealer.
- Almonds are a member of the peach family.
- Cats have over one hundred vocal sounds. Dogs only have about 10.
- 'Dreamt' is the only English word that ends in the letters 'mt'.
- February 1865 is the only month in recorded history not to have a full moon.
- In the last 4,000 years, no new animals have been domesticated.
- If the population of China walked past you, in single file, the line would never end because of the rate of reproduction.
- It's impossible to sneeze with your eyes open.
- Leonardo Da Vinci invented the scissors.
- No word in the English language rhymes with month, orange, silver, or purple.
- Our eyes are always the same size from birth, but our nose and ears never stop growing.
- Peanuts are one of the ingredients of dynamite.
- Rubber bands last longer when refrigerated.

- 'Stewardesses' is the longest word typed with only the left hand, 'lollipop' with your right. The average person's left hand does 56% of the typing.
- The Bible does not say there were three wise men; it only says there were three gifts.
- The cruise liner, QE2, moves only six inches for each gallon of diesel that it burns.
- The microwave was invented after a researcher walked by a radar tube and a chocolate bar melted in his pocket.
- The sentence: 'The quick brown fox jumps over the lazy dog' uses every letter of the alphabet.
- The winter of 1932 was so cold that Niagara Falls froze completely solid.
- The words 'racecar,' 'kayak' and 'level' are the same whether they are read left to right or right to left (palindromes).
- There are more chickens than people in the world.
- There are only four words in the English language which end in 'dous' - tremendous, horrendous, stupendous, and hazardous.
- There are two words in the English language that have all five vowels in order, 'abstemious' and 'facetious.'
- Tigers have striped skin, not just striped fur.
- 'Typewriter' is the longest word that can be made using the letters only on one row of the keyboard.
- Winston Churchill was born in a ladies' room during a dance.
- Women blink nearly twice as much as men.
- Your stomach has to produce a new layer of mucus every two weeks; otherwise it will digest itself.

Now you know everything!

Things to say when you're stressed

1. Okay, okay! I take it back. Unf@#k you.
2. You say I'm a bitch like it's a bad thing.
3. Well this day was a total waste of make-up.
4. Well, aren't we a damn ray of sunshine?
5. Don't bother me, I'm living happily ever after.

6. Do I look like a people person?
7. This isn't an office. It's hell with fluorescent lighting.
8. I started out with nothing and still have most of it left.
9. Therapy is expensive. Popping bubble wrap is cheap. You choose.
10. Why don't you try practicing random acts of intelligence and senseless acts of self-control?
11. I'm not crazy. I've been in a very bad mood for 30 years.
12. Sarcasm is just one more service I offer.
13. Do they ever shut up on your planet?
14. I'm not your type. I'm not inflatable.
15. Stress is when you wake up screaming and you realise you haven't gone to sleep yet.
16. Back off!! You're standing in my aura.
17. Don't worry. I forgot your name too.
18. I work 45 hours a week to be this poor.
19. Not all men are annoying. Some are dead.
20. Wait … I'm trying to imagine you with a personality.
21. Chaos, panic and disorder ... my work here is done.
22. Ambivalent? Well, yes and no.
23. You look like shit. Is that the style now?
24. Earth is full. Go home.
25. Aw, did I step on your poor little bitty ego?
26. I'm not tense, just terribly, terribly alert.
27. A hard-on doesn't count as personal growth.
28. You are depriving some village of an idiot.
29. If assholes could fly, this place would be an airport

———————— ⚱ ————————

Respect is worked for
Trust is earned
Friendship's hard to find
Miracles are easy, AND
Life is full of small surprises

Reasons why English is so hard to understand:

1. The bandage was wound around the wound.
2. The farm used to produce produce.
3. The dump was so full that it had to refuse more refuse.
4. We must polish the Polish furniture.
5. He could lead if he could get the lead out of his feet.
6. The soldier decided to desert his dessert in the desert.
7. Since there is no time like the present, he thought it was time to present the present.
8. A bass was painted on the head of the bass drum.
9. When shot at, the dove dove into the bushes.
10. I did not object to the object.
11. The insurance was invalid for the invalid.
12. There was a row among the oarsmen about how to row.
13. They were too close to the door to close it.
14. A seamstress and a sewer fell down the sewer line.
15. To help him with planting, the farmer taught his sow to sow.
16. The wind was too strong to wind the sail.
17. After a number of injections, my jaw got number.
18. Upon seeing the tear in the painting, I shed a tear.
19. I had to subject the subject to a series of tests.
20. How can I intimate this to my most intimate friend.

Questions & Answers

- Can you cry under water?
- When I was young we used to go 'skinny dipping' now I just 'chunky dunk'.
- How important does a person have to be before they are considered assassinated instead of just murdered?
- If money doesn't grow on trees then why do banks have branches?
- Since bread is square, then why is sandwich meat round?
- Why do you have to 'put your two cents in '... but it is only a 'penny for your thoughts'?
- Where is that extra penny going? Taxes?
- Once you're in heaven, do you get stuck wearing the clothes you were buried in for eternity?
- Why does a round pizza come in a square box?
- How is it that we put a man on the moon before we figured out it would be a good idea to put wheels on luggage?
- Why is it that people say they 'slept like a baby' when babies wake up like every two hours?
- If a deaf person has to go to court, is it still called a hearing?
- If you drink Pepsi at work in the Coke factory, will they fire you?
- Why are you IN a movie, but you are ON TV?
- Why do people pay to go up tall buildings and then put money in binoculars to look at things on the ground?
- Why do doctors leave the room while you change? They are going to see you naked anyway.

- I signed up for an exercise class and was told to wear loose-fitting clothing. If I had loose-fitting clothing, I wouldn't have signed up in the first place!
- Wouldn't it be nice if whenever we messed up our life we could simply press Ctrl-Alt-Delete and start all over?
- Stress is when you wake up screaming and then you realise you haven't fallen asleep yet.
- If raising children was going to be easy, it never would have started with something called labour!!!

Q.: How many men does it take to wallpaper a room?
A.: Depends on how thinly you slice them!!

Q.: Did you hear Boris Yeltsin reshuffled his cabinet?
A.: He moved the vodka to the front.

Q.: What do Telstra and a bad hooker have in common?
A.: They charge heaps for an STD!

Q.: Why do bagpipe players walk when they play?
A.: To get away from the sound!

Q.: What do Tupperware products and a walrus have in common?
A.: They both like a tight seal!

Q.: What's the difference between Dolly Parton running for a bus and a sewing machine?
A.: A sewing machine only has one bobbin!

Q.: Did you hear about the bloke who went into a shoe shop and bought some tortoise-shell boots?
A.: It took him four hours to leave!

Q.: Why do women have small feet?
A.: So they can stand closer to the sink!

Q.: What should a bloke do if his missus tells him to be more affectionate?
A.: Get a girlfriend!

Q.: What do you call it when a man talks dirty to a woman?
A.: Harassment.

Q.: What do you call it when a woman talks dirty to a man?
A.: $5.99 per minute.

Q.: Did you hear about the new condoms with crosswords printed on them?
A.: They're for clever dicks!

Q.: What's the difference between pink and purple?
A.: Your grip!

Q.: Did you hear about the chick who went fishing with six males?
A.: She went home with a red snapper!

Q.: What's the difference between a solar-powered car and a politician?
A.: A solar-powered car works during the day.

Q.: Where did Linda Lovelace get her start in movies?
A.: Tonsiltown!

Q.: Where are the Andes?
A.: At the end of your armies!

Q.: What do you get if you cross a penis and a potato?
A.: A dicktater!

Q.: Why can't Barbie get pregnant?
A.: Cause Ken comes in a different box.

Q.: What did the officer say to his colleague after discovering the deceased man had a straw laying on his chest?
A.: 'Someone must have sucked the life out of this one!'

Q.: Why is Turtle Wax so expensive?
A.: Because turtles have really tiny ears.

Q.: Why do men have their best ideas when they're having sex?
A.: Because they are plugged into a genius.

Q.: What do you get when you wipe your bottom with a newspaper?
A.: A news update!

Q.: How do butchers introduce their wives?
A.: Meet Pattie.

———————————— ⫯⫯⫯ ————————————

- The Post Office just recalled their latest stamps. They weren't working ... *They had pictures of lawyers on them, and people couldn't figure out which side to spit on.*
- How can a pregnant woman tell that she's carrying a future lawyer? *She has an uncontrollable craving for baloney.*
- How does an attorney sleep? *First he lies on one side, and then he lies on the other.*
- How many lawyer jokes are there? *Only three ... the rest are true stories.*
- How many lawyers does it take to change a light bulb? *How many can you afford?*
- How many lawyers does it take to screw in a light bulb? *Three ... one to climb the ladder, one to shake it, and one to sue the ladder company.*

- If a lawyer and the taxman were both drowning, and you could save only one of them, would you, *(a) go to lunch, or (b) read the newspaper?*
- What did the lawyer name his daughter? *Sue.*
- What do you call 25 skydiving lawyers? *Skeet.*
- What do you call a lawyer gone bad? *'Senator'*
- What do you call a lawyer with an IQ of 50? *'Your Honour.'*
- What do you throw to a drowning lawyer? *His partners.*
- What does a lawyer use for birth control? *His personality.*
- What happens when you cross a pig with a lawyer? *Don't know. (There are some things a pig just won't do.)*
- What's the difference between a lawyer and a vulture? *The lawyer gets frequent flyer miles.*
- What's another difference between a lawyer and a vulture? *Removable wing tips.*

Q.: What's the best way to kill a man?
A.: Put a naked woman and a six-pack in front of him. Then tell him to pick only one.

Q.: What do men and pantyhose have in common?
A.: They either cling, run or don't fit right in the crotch!

Q.: What is the difference between men and women ...
A.: A woman wants one man to satisfy her every need, a man wants every woman to satisfy his one need.

Q.: How does a man keep his youth?
A.: By giving her money, furs and diamonds.

Q.: How do you keep your husband from reading your e-mail?
A.: Rename the mail folder to 'instruction manuals'.

Q.: How do you circumcise a whale?
A.: You send in four skin divers.

Q.: How many psychologists does it take to change a light bulb?
A.: One, as long as the bulb is willing to change.

Q.: What's the difference between a porcupine and a BMW?
A. : A porcupine has the pricks on the outside.

Q.: What's the best form of birth control after 50?
A.: Nudity.

Q.: What's the difference between a girlfriend and a wife?
A.: 45 kilos.

Q.: What's the difference between a boyfriend and a husband?
A.: 45 minutes.

Q.: Why are men and parking spaces alike?
A.: Because all the good ones are gone and the only ones left are disabled.

Q.: What have men and floor tiles got in common?
A.: If you lay them properly the first time, you can walk all over them for life.

Q.: Why do men want to marry virgins?
A. They can't stand criticism.

Q.: Why is it so hard for women to find men that are sensitive, caring and good looking?
A.: Because those men already have boyfriends.

Q.: What's the difference between a new husband and a new dog?
A.: After a year, the dog is still excited to see you.

Q.: What makes men chase women they have no intention of marrying?

A.: The same urge that makes dogs chase cars they have no intention of driving.

Q.: What is the biggest problem for an atheist?

A.: No-one to talk to during orgasm.

Q.: Why does the bride always wear white?

A.: Because it's good for the dishwasher to match the stove and refrigerator.

Q.: Which sexual position produces the ugliest children?

A.: Ask your Mum.

Q.: How do you know when you're really ugly?

A.: Dogs hump your leg with their eyes closed.

Q.: How do you know when you're leading a sad life?

A.: When a nymphomaniac tells you, 'Lets just be friends.'

Q.: Why don't bunnies make noise when they have sex?

A.: Because they have cotton balls.

Q.: What does a 75-year-old woman have between her breasts?

A.: Her navel.

Q.: What has a whole bunch of little balls and screws old ladies?

A.: A Bingo machine.

Q.: Why did God create alcohol?

A.: So ugly people could have sex too.

Q.:   What three two-letter words mean small?
A.:   'Is it in?'

Q.:   If you are having sex with two women and one more walks in, what do you have?
A.:   Divorce proceedings most likely.

Q.:   Did you hear about the Chinese couple who had an injured baby?
A.:   They named him Sum Ting Wong.

Q.:   What would you call it when an Italian has one arm shorter than the other?
A.:   A speech impediment.

Q.:   Why do men find it difficult to make eye contact?
A.:   Breasts don't have eyes.

Q.:   Did you hear about the dyslexic Rabbi?
A.:   He walks around saying 'Yo.'

Q.:   What do you call a New Zealand farmer with a sheep under each arm?
A.:   A Pimp.

Q.:   What's the difference between a Japanese zoo, and an Australian zoo?
A.:   A Japanese zoo has a description of the animal on the front the cage, along with a recipe.

Q.:   How do you know when a woman is about to say something smart?
A.:   When she starts her sentence with 'A man once told me...'

Q.:   Why do men break wind more than women?
A.:   Because women can't shut up long enough to build up the required pressure.

Q.: If your dog is barking at the back door and your wife is yelling at the front door, who do you let in first?

A.: The dog, of course. He'll shut up once you let him in.

- I married Miss Right. I just didn't know her first name was Always.
- I haven't spoken to my wife for 18 months ... I don't like to interrupt her.
- Scientists have discovered a food that diminishes a woman's sex drive by 90% ... It's called a wedding cake.
- Marriage is a 3-ring circus: Engagement Ring, Wedding Ring, Suffering.
- Our last fight was my fault: My wife asked me 'What's on the TV?' ... I said, 'Dust!'
- The most effective way to remember your wife's birthday is to forget it once.
- Women will never be equal to men until they can walk down the street with a bald head and a beer gut, and still think they are beautiful.

A beggar walked up to a well-dressed woman shopping on Toorak Road and said, 'I haven't eaten anything for days.'

She looked at him and said, 'God, I wish I had your willpower.'

A man inserted an advertisement in the classified – 'Wife Wanted.' The next day he received a hundred letters. They all said the same thing: 'You can have mine.'

Q.: What is a mixed feeling?
A.: When you see your mother-in-law backing off a cliff in your new car.

Q.: What is the definition of macho?
A.: A guy jogging home after a vasectomy.

Q.: What is the difference between an Aussie male and a pig
A.: A pig doesn't turn into an Aussie male after a few drinks!!

Q.: What do most blondes get on an IQ test?
A.: Drool.

Q.: What's invisible and smells like carrots?
A.: A rabbit's fart.

Q.: What do you call a woman who knows where her husband is every night?
A.: A widow.

Q.: Why is a Christmas tree better than a bloke?
A.: It's always erect, it stays up 12 days and nights, has cute balls and it looks good with the lights on.

Q.: What do you do for a drowning New Zealand Rugby player?
A.: Nothing. You could drag him to the top, but he'll choke anyway.

Q.: What's the difference between the All Blacks and an arsonist?
A.: An arsonist wouldn't waste five matches.

- If you take an Oriental person and spin him around several times, does he become disoriented?
- If people from Poland are called Poles, why aren't people from Holland called Holes?
- Why do we say something is out of whack? What's a whack?
- Do infants enjoy infancy as much as adults enjoy adultery?
- If a pig loses its voice, is it disgruntled?
- If love is blind, why is lingerie so popular?
- Why is the man who invests all your money called a broker?
- When cheese gets its picture taken, what does it say?
- Why is a person who plays the piano called a pianist but a person who drives a race-car not called a racist?
- Why are a wise man and a wise guy opposites?
- Why do overlook and oversee mean opposite things?
- Why isn't the number 11 pronounced onety one?
- 'I am' is reportedly the shortest sentence in the English language. Could it be that 'I do' is the longest sentence?
- If lawyers are disbarred and clergymen defrocked, doesn't it follow that electricians can be delighted, musicians denoted, cowboys deranged, models deposed, tree surgeons debarked, and drycleaners depressed?
- Do Lipton Tea employees take coffee breaks?
- What hair colour do they put on the driver's licences of bald men?
- I was thinking about how people seem to read the Bible a whole lot more as they get older; then it dawned on me … they're cramming for their final exam.
- I thought about how mothers feed their babies with tiny little spoons and forks so I wondered what do Chinese mothers use? Toothpicks?
- If it's true that we are here to help others, then what exactly are the others here for?
- You never really learn to swear until you learn to drive.
- No-one ever says, 'It's only a game' when their team is winning.
- Ever wonder what the speed of lightning would be if it didn't zigzag?

- Do people who spend $2 apiece on those little bottles of Evian water know that if you spell it backwards, it is NAIVE?
- Isn't making a smoking section in a restaurant like making a peeing section in a swimming pool?
- If four out of five people SUFFER from diarrhoea ... does that mean the fifth one enjoys it?

How long did the Hundred Years War last? ... *116 years.*
Which country makes Panama hats? ... *Ecuador.*
From which animal do we get cat gut? ... *Sheep and Horses.*
In which month do Russians celebrate the October Revolution? ... *November.*
What is a camel's hair brush made of? ... *Squirrel fur.*
The Canary Islands in the Pacific are named after what animal? ... *Dogs.*
What was King George VI's first name? ... *Albert.*
What color is a purple finch? ... *Crimson.*
Where are Chinese gooseberries from? ... *New Zealand.*
What is the color of the black box in a commercial airplane? ... *Orange.*

Q.: What's the difference between a nine-month pregnant woman and a super-model?
A.: Nothing (if the pregnant woman's husband knows what's good for him).

Q.: What do you call a lady with one leg shorter than the other?
A:: Eilene.

Q.: What do you call a lady with both legs
the same length?
A.: Noelene.

Q.: What do you call someone in the sea
who has no arms or legs?
A.: Bob.

Q.: Should I have a baby after 35?
A.: No, 35 children is enough.

Q.: I'm two months pregnant now. When
will my baby move?
A.: With any luck, right after he finishes high
school.

Q.: What is the most reliable method to
determine a baby's sex?
A.: Childbirth.

Q.: My wife is five months pregnant and so moody that sometimes
she's borderline irrational.
A.: So what's your question?

Q.: My childbirth instructor says it's not pain I'll feel during labor,
but pressure. Is she right?
A.: Yes, in the same way that a tornado might be called an air
current.

Q.: When is the best time to get an epidural?
A.: Right after you find out you're pregnant.

Questions & Answers

Man says to God, 'God, why did you make woman so beautiful?'

God says, 'So you would love her.'

'But God,' the man says, 'why did you make her so dumb?'

'So she would love you.'

———————— ❦ ————————

Sport

An Irishman moves to the USA and finally attends his first baseball game. The first batter approached the batters box, took a few swings and then hits a double. Everyone was on their feet screaming, 'Run, Run …'

The next batter hits a single and the Irishman listened as the crowd again cheered, 'Run, Run.' The Irishman enjoyed the game and began screaming with the fans.

The fifth batter came up and four balls went by. The umpire called a walk and the batter started his slow trot to first base.

The Irishman stood up and screamed, 'R-R-Run ye bastard, run.'

The people around him began laughing. Embarrassed, the Irishman sat back down. A friendly fan noted the man's embarrassment, leaned over and explained, 'He can't run - he's got four balls.'

The Irishman stood up and screamed, 'Walk with pride, lad.'

I was at the golf store comparing different kinds of golf balls. I was unhappy with the women's type I had been using. After browsing for several minutes, I was approached by one of the good-looking gentlemen who worked at the store.

He asked if he could help me. Without thinking, I looked at him and said, 'I think I like playing with men's balls.'

A woman goes into Rebel sports to buy a rod and reel for her grandson's 21st. She doesn't know which one to get, so she just grabs one and goes over to the counter. A Rebel check-out clerk is standing there wearing dark shades.

She says, 'Excuse me, sir. Can you tell me anything about this rod and reel?'

He says, 'Ma'am, I'm completely blind, but if you'll drop it on the counter, I can tell you everything you need to know about it from the sound it makes.'

She doesn't believe him but drops it on the counter anyway.

He says, 'That's an eight-foot surf caster Shakespeare Graphite 667 Model rod fitted with a Shimano Calcutta 400 reel spooled with 20lb Berkley Fireline. It's a good all around combination and it's on sale this week for only $199.'

She says, 'It's amazing that you can tell all that just by the sound of it dropping on the counter. I'll take it!'

As she opens her purse, her credit card drops on the floor. She bends down to pick it up and accidentally breaks wind. At first she is really embarrassed, but then realises it's not likely that the blind clerk could tell it was she who farted. He may not know that she was the only person around.

The man rings up the sale and says, 'That'll be $254.50 please.'

The woman is totally confused by this and asks, 'Didn't you tell me it was on sale for $199? How did you get $254.50?'

He replies, 'Yes, Ma'am, the rod and reel is $199.00, but the duck caller is $36 and the fishing bait is $19.50.'

The Pope was driving in his Pope-mobile on the beach when he saw a poor unfortunate Englishman wearing an English Lions Rugby jumper in the jaws of a 20 foot shark.

All of a sudden three bronzed Aussies wearing the Australian Wallaby Rugby jumpers raced up in a boat, one thrust a harpoon into the shark and killed it, and the other two rescued the 'pom'.

The Pope was extremely impressed because all the hatred between the poms and Aussies over the loss of the Webb Ellis Cup was over by rescuing the pom and called a blessing to the three brave chaps and then drove off.

One of the Aussie blokes said it was nice that the Pope understood race relations, but it shows that he knows nothing about shark fishing.

A man calls home to his wife and says, 'Honey I have been asked to go fishing at a big lake up in the high country with my boss and several of his friends. We'll be gone for a week. This is a good opportunity for me to get that promotion I've been wanting so would you please pack me enough clothes for a week and set out my rod and tackle box. We're leaving from the office and I will swing by the house to pick my things up.

'Oh, yeah! Please pack my new blue silk pyjamas.'

The wife thinks this sounds a little fishy but being a good wife she does exactly what her husband asked. The following weekend he comes home a little tired but otherwise looking good. The wife welcomes him home and asks if he caught many fish?

He says, 'Yes! Lots of trout, some salmon, and a few pike. But why didn't you pack my new blue silk pyjamas like I asked you to do?'

The wife replies, 'I did, they were in your tackle box.'

Sport Jokes

Four married guys go fishing. After an hour, the following conversation took place.

First guy: 'You have no idea what I had to do to be able to come out fishing this weekend. I had to promise my wife that I will paint every room in the house next weekend.'

Second guy: 'That's nothing, I had to promise my wife that I will build her a new deck for the pool.'

Third guy: 'Man, you both have it easy! I had to promise my wife that I will remodel the kitchen for her.'

They continue to fish when they realised that the fourth guy has not said a word. So they asked him, 'You haven't said anything about what you had to do to be able to come fishing this weekend. What's the deal?'

Fourth guy: 'I just set my alarm for 5.30am. When it went off, I shut off my alarm, gave the wife a nudge and said, "Fishing or Sex" and she said, "Wear a jumper".'

An Australian family of rugby supporters head out one Saturday to do their Christmas shopping. While in the sports shop the son picks up a New Zealand rugby shirt and says to his sister, 'I've decided to be a New Zealand supporter and I would like this for Christmas.'

His sister is outraged by this and promptly whacks him round the head and says, 'Go talk to your mother.'

Off goes the little lad with the Kiwi rugby shirt in hand and finds his mother. 'Mum? I've decided I'm going to be a New Zealand supporter and I would like this shirt for Christmas.'

The mother is outraged at this, promptly whacks him around the head and says, 'Go talk to your father.'

Off he goes with the rugby shirt in hand and finds his father.

'Dad?'

'Yes son?'

'I've decided I'm going to be a New Zealand supporter and would like this shirt for Christmas.'

The father is outraged and promptly whacks his son around the head and says 'No son of mine is ever going to be seen in THAT!'

About half an hour later they're all back in the car and heading towards home. The father turns to his son and says 'Son, I hope you've learned something today?'

The son says, 'Yes dad I have.'

'Good son, what is it?'

The son replies, 'I've only been a New Zealand supporter for an hour and already I hate you Aussie bastards.'

Ten things that sound dirty in golf but aren't:
10. Nuts ... My shaft is bent.
9. After 18 holes I can barely walk.
8. You really whacked the hell out of that sucker.
7. Look at the size of that putter.
6. Keep your head down and spread your legs a bit more.
5. Mind if I join your threesome?
4. Stand with your back turned and drop it.
3. My hands are so sweaty I can't get a good grip.
2. Nice stroke, but your follow through has a lot to be desired.

And the No. 1 thing that sounds dirty in golf but isn't:
1. Hold up ... I need to wash my balls!

Two Englishmen in Australia for the Rugby World Cup were drinking in a bar, talking rugby, one said to his mate, 'The Welsh are a race of prostitutes and rugby players.'

He felt a tap on his shoulder and turned around to see a bloke about six foot six standing behind him!

The bloke said 'I heard that, my Mother is Welsh.'

The Pom answered, 'Oh yes, and what position does she play?'

A man had great tickets for the Grand Final. As he sits down, another man comes down and asks if anyone is sitting in the seat next to him.

'No,' he says. 'The seat is empty.'

'This is incredible!' said the man. 'Who in their right mind would have a seat like this for the Grand Final, the biggest sporting event in Australia, and not use it?'

He says, 'Well, actually, the seat belongs to me. My wife was supposed to come with me, but she passed away. This is the first Grand Final we haven't been to together since we got married.'

'Oh ... I'm sorry to hear that. That's terrible. But couldn't you find someone else, a friend or relative, or even a neighbour to take the seat?'

The man shakes his head. 'No. They're all at the funeral.'

Two hunters are out in the woods when one of them collapses. He doesn't seem to be breathing and his eyes are glazed. The other guy whips out his mobile phone and calls the emergency services. He gasps, 'My friend is dead! What can I do?'

The operator says, 'Calm down, I can help. First, let's make sure he's dead.'

There's a silence, then a shot is heard. Back on the phone, the guy says, 'OK, now what?'

Girl's diary
Saturday 16th August

Saw John in the evening and he was acting really strangely. I went shopping in the afternoon with the girls and I did turn up a bit late so I thought it might be that. The bar was really crowded and loud so I suggested we go somewhere quieter to talk. He was still very subdued and distracted so I suggested we go somewhere nice to eat. All through dinner he just didn't seem himself; he hardly laughed, and didn't seem to be paying any attention to me or to what I was saying. I just knew that something was wrong. He dropped me back home and I wondered if he was going to come in; he hesitated, but followed. I asked him again if there was something the matter but he just half shook his head and turned the television on. After about 10 minutes of silence, I said I was going upstairs to bed. I put my arms around him and told him that I loved him deeply. He just gave a sigh, and a sad sort of smile. He didn't follow me up, but later he did, and I was surprised when we made love. He still seemed distant and a bit cold, and I started to think that he was going to leave me, and that he had found someone else.

I cried myself to sleep.

Boy's diary
Saturday 16th August

Wallabies lost to New Zealand. Got a root though ...

A couple of women were playing golf one Saturday morning. The first of the twosome teed off and watched in horror as her ball headed directly toward a foursome of men playing the next hole. Indeed, the ball hit one of the men, and he immediately clasped his hands together at his crotch, fell to the ground and proceeded to roll around in evident agony.

The woman rushed down to the man and immediately began to apologise. She explained that she was a physical therapist.

'Please allow me to help. I am a physical therapist and I know I could relieve your pain if you'd just allow me!' she told him earnestly.

'Oh no, I'll be all right. I will be fine in a few minutes,' he replied breathlessly, as he remained in the foetal position still clasping his hands together at his crotch. But she persisted, and he finally allowed her to help him. She gently took his hands away and laid them to the side. She loosened his pants and put her hands inside.

After a short massage, she asked him, 'How does that feel?'

To which he replied, 'It feels great, but my thumb still hurts like hell!'

The seven dwarfs went off to work in the mine one day, while Snow White stayed at home to do the housework and cook their lunch. However when she went to the mine to deliver their lunches, she found there had been a cave-in, and there was no sign of the dwarfs. Tearfully she yelled in to the mine entrance, 'Hello, is anyone there. Can anyone hear me?'

A voice floated up from the bowels of the mine, 'England will win the Rugby World Cup.'

'Thank God,' said Snow White, 'at least Dopey's still alive.'

The England team's training session was delayed today for nearly two hours at Telstra Stadium.

One of the players, while on his way back to the dressing room happened to look down and notice a suspicious looking, unknown white powdery substance at the end of the field.

Coach Clive Woodward immediately suspended practice while the police were called in to investigate.

After a complete field analysis, the police determined that the white substance, unknown to the players, was the try line. Practice was resumed when the officials decided that it was unlikely that the team would encounter the substance again.

A guy walks into a bar with a dachshund under his arm. The dog is wearing an England rugby jersey and is festooned with England pom-poms. The bartender says, 'Hey! No pets are allowed! You'll have to leave.'

The guy begs him, 'Look, I'm desperate! We're both big fans, the TV's broken at home, and this is the only place around where we can see the game.'

After securing a promise that the dog will behave, and warning him that he and the dog will be thrown out if there's any trouble, the bartender relents and allows them to stay in the bar and watch the game. The big game begins with the poms receiving the kickoff. They march down field, get stopped at the 22, and kick a penalty goal.

Suddenly, the dog jumps up on the bar and begins walking up and down the bar giving high-fives to everyone. The bartender says, 'Wow, that is the most amazing thing I've seen! What does the dog do if they score a try?'

The owner replies, 'I don't know, I've only had him for three years.'

work

You know you work in the 21st Century if ...

- You've sat at the same desk for four years and worked for three different companies.
- Your company welcome sign is attached with Velcro.
- Your CV is on a CD in your briefcase.
- You really get excited about a 1.7% pay raise.
- You learn about your redundancy on the 9 o'clock news.
- Your biggest loss from a system crash is that you lose all your best jokes.
- Your supervisor doesn't have the ability to do your job.
- Contractors outnumber permanent staff and are more likely to get long-service awards.
- Board members' salaries are higher than all the Third World countries annual budgets combined.
- It's dark when you drive to and from work, even in the summer.
- You know exactly how many days you've got left until you retire.
- Interviewees, despite not having the relevant knowledge or experience, terminate the interview when told of the starting salary.
- You see a good-looking, smart person and you know it must be a visitor.

work jokes

- Free food left over from meetings is your staple diet.
- The work experience person gets a brand new state-of-the-art laptop with all the features, while you have time to go for lunch while yours powers up.
- Being sick is defined as you can't walk or you're in hospital.
- You're already late on the assignment you just got.
- There's no money in the budget for the extra five permanent staff your department needs, but they can afford four full-time management consultants advising your boss's boss on strategy.
- A holiday is something you roll over to next year or a cheque you get in January.
- Every week another brown collection envelope comes round because someone you didn't know had started, is leaving.
- You wonder who's going to be left to put into your 'leaving' collection.
- Your relatives and family describe your job as 'works with computers.'
- The only reason you recognise your kids is because their pictures are on your desk.
- You only have make-up for fluorescent lighting.
- Your boss's favourite lines are:
    When you've got a few minutes ...
    Could you fit this in ...
    In your spare time ...
    When you're freed up ...
    I know you're busy but ...
    I have an opportunity for you ...

You've read this entire list, kept nodding and you understood it!

You know you have been on the computer too long when ...
- You forgot how to work the TV remote control.
- You see something funny and scream, 'LOL, LOL!'

- You meet the mailman at the curb and swear he said 'You've to mail!'
- You sign off and your screen says you were on for six days and 45 minutes.
- You buy a laptop and a mobile so you can have AOL in your car.
- Tech support calls YOU for help.
- You beg your friends to get an account so you can 'hang out'.
- You get a second phone line just to call out for pizza.
- You purchase a vanity car licence plate with your screen name on it.
- You say 'he he he he' or 'heh heh heh' instead of laughing.
- You say 'SCROLL UP' when someone asks what it was you said.
- You sneak away to your computer when everyone goes to sleep.
- You talk on the phone with the same person you are sending an instant message to.
- You look at an annoying person off-line and wish that you had your ignore button handy.
- You sit on MSN for six hours for that certain special person to sign on.
- You get up in the morning and go online before getting your coffee.
- You end your sentences with ... three or more periods ...!
- You're on the phone and say 'BRB'.

When NASA began the launch of astronauts into space, they found out the pens wouldn't work at zero gravity. (Ink won't flow down to the writing surface.)

In order to solve this problem, they hired a consulting firm, and they spent one decade and $12M on the project. They developed a pen that worked at zero gravity, upside down, under water, in practically any surface including crystal and in a temperature range from below freezing to over 300 degrees

The Russians used a pencil ...!

A young man suffered brain damage in an accident. It was decided to offer him a brain transplant. He was shown the brain of a young 25-year-old laborer @ $70,000.

Then the brain of a middle aged professional man @ $40,000.

Finally a 70-year-old politician's brain @ $25,000.

When he asked why the 25-year-old's brain was $25,000 and the 70-year-old politician's brain was $70,000, the reply was, 'It has actually been used …!'

Usually the staff of the company plays Football.

The middle level managers are more interested in Tennis.

The top management usually has a preference for Golf.

Finding: As you go up the corporate ladder, the balls reduce in size.

A sales rep, an administration clerk and the manager are walking to lunch when they find an antique oil lamp.

They rub it and a genie comes out in a puff of smoke. The genie says, 'I usually only grant three wishes, so I'll give each of you just one.'

'Me first! Me first!' says the admin clerk. 'I want to be in the Bahamas, driving a speedboat, without a care in the world.' Poof! She's gone.

In astonishment, 'Me next! Me next!' says the sales rep. 'I want to be in Hawaii, relaxing on the beach with my personal masseuse, an endless supply of pina coladas and the love of my life.' Poof! He's gone.

'OK, you're up,' the genie says to the manager.

The manager says, 'I want those two back in the office after lunch.'

A man in a hot air balloon realised he was lost. He reduced altitude and spotted a woman below. He descended a bit more and shouted, 'Excuse me, can you help me? I promised a friend I would meet him an hour ago, but I don't know where I am.'

The woman below replied, 'You're in a hot air balloon hovering approximately 30 feet above the ground. You're between 40 and 41 degrees north latitude and between 59 and 60 degrees west longitude.'

'You must be in Information Technology,' said the balloonist.

'I am,' replied the woman, 'How did you know?'

'Well,' answered the balloonist, 'everything you told me is, technically correct, but I've no idea what to make of your information, and the fact is I'm still lost. Frankly, you've not been much help at all. If anything, you've delayed my trip.'

The woman below responded, 'You must be in management.'

'I am,' replied the balloonist, 'but how did you know?'

'Well,' said the woman, 'you don't know where you are or where you're going. You have risen to where you are, due to a large quantity of hot air. You made a promise, which you've no idea how to keep, and you expect people beneath you to solve your problems. The fact is you are in exactly the same position you were in before we met, but now, somehow, it's my fault.'

The local bar is so sure that its bartender is the strongest man around that they offer a standing $1,000 bet.

The bartender squeezes a lemon until all the juice runs into a glass, and hands the lemon to a patron. Anyone who can squeeze one more drop of juice out of it wins the money. Over time many people have tried, but nobody has succeeded.

One day a scrawny little man comes in, wearing thick glasses and a polyester, and says in a tiny, squeaky voice, 'I'd like to try the bet.'

After the laughter has died down, the bartender says, 'OK', grabs a lemon, and squeezes away. He then hands the wrinkled remains of the rind to the little man.

But the crowd's laughter turns to total silence as the man clenches his fist around the lemon and six drops fall into the glass.

As the crowd cheers, the bartender pays the $1,000 and asks the little man, 'What do you do for a living? Are you a logger, a weightlifter, or what?'

The man replies, 'I work for the tax office.'

A cocky young man on the first day in a big multi-national firm thought he would try out his authority and dialled the kitchen.

'Get me my coffee immediately,' he thundered down the phone.

The voice from the other side responded, 'You fool you have dialled the wrong extension. Do you know who you are talking to??'

Still being cocky the trainee said, 'NO, who am I talking to?'

'It's the managing director of the company you idiot!!!'

The trainee then shouted back, 'Well do you know who the hell you are talking to?'

'No,' replied the managing director.

'Thank God for that,' replied the trainee.

A man was in a taxi when he reached across and tapped the taxi driver on the shoulder.

At that, the taxi driver screamed! He pressed down both the break and accelerator at once spinning the taxi around in front of oncoming traffic before finally ending in front of a bus stop halfway over the curb.

Ashen faced the driver turned to the shaken passenger and said, 'Don't ever do that again.'

Stuttering, the passenger apologised and so the taxi driver calmed a little and also apologised saying, 'It's my fault, I only started this job yesterday. For the last 25 years I've been driving hearses.'

I think I'm coming down with something

There is a new virus: Code name is 'work'.

If you receive 'work', from your colleagues, your boss, via e-mail or anywhere else, do not open it under any circumstances!!

This virus wipes out your private life completely. If you should come into contact with this virus, put on your jacket and take two good friends and go straight to the nearest pub. Order three beers and after repeating 14 times, you will find that 'work' has been completely deleted from your brain.

Forward this warning immediately to at least five friends. Should you realise that you do not have five friends, this means that you are already infected by this virus and 'work' already controls your whole life.

This virus is deadly. Please make every effort to stop it and prevent it spreading.

My first job was working in an orange juice factory, but I got canned ... couldn't concentrate.

After that I tried to be a tailor, but I just wasn't suited for it ... mainly because it was a so-so job.

Then I tried to be a chef. Figured it would add a little spice to my life, but I just didn't have the thyme.

Next I tried working in a muffler factory but that was too exhausting.

I managed to get a good job working for a pool maintenance company, but the work was just too draining.

I attempted to be a deli worker, but anyway I sliced it, I couldn't cut the mustard.

Then I worked in the woods as a lumberjack, but I just couldn't hack it, so they gave me the axe.

Next was a job in a shoe factory, I tried but I just didn't fit in.

So then I got a job in a gym, but they said I wasn't fit for the job.

After many years of trying to find steady work I finally got a job as a historian until I realised there was no future in it.

I studied a long time to become a doctor, but I didn't have any patience.

My best job was being a musician, but eventually I found I wasn't noteworthy.

I became a professional fisherman, but discovered that I couldn't live on my net income.

My last job was working at Starbucks, but I had to quit because it was always the same old grind.

So I retired ... and found I'm perfect for the job!

Hung Chow calls in to work and says, 'Hey, boss I no come work today, I really sick. I got headache, stomach ache and my legs hurt. I no come work.'

The boss says, 'You know Hung Chow, I really need you today. When I feel like this I go to my wife and tell her to give me sex. That makes everything better and I can go to work. You should try that.'

Two hours later Hung Chow calls again. 'Boss, I do what you say and feel great. I be at work soon. You got nice house.'

Today's reading is from the Book of Corporate Life, Chapter 1 , Verses 1-15:

1. In the beginning there was the Plan.
2. And then came the Assumptions.
3. And the Assumptions were without form.
4. And the Plan was without Substance.
5. And darkness was upon the face of the Workers.
6. And the Workers spoke among themselves saying, 'It is a crock of shit and it stinks.'
7. And the Workers went unto their Supervisors and said, 'It is a crock of dung and we cannot live with the smell.'
8. And the Supervisors went unto their Managers saying, 'It is a container of organic waste, and it is very strong, such that none may abide by it.'
9. And the Managers went unto their Directors, saying, 'It is a vessel of fertilizer, and none may abide its strength.'
10. And the Directors spoke among themselves, saying to one another, 'It contains that which aids plant growth, and it is very strong.'
11. And the directors went to the Vice Presidents, saying unto them, 'It promotes growth, and it is very powerful.'
12. And the Vice Presidents went to the President, saying unto him, 'It has very powerful effects.'

13. And the President looked upon the Plan and saw that it was good.
14. And the Plan became Policy.
15. And that is how shit happens.

Word Perfect

'Rich Hall computer assistance; may I help you?'

'Yes, well, I'm having trouble with WordPerfect.'

'What sort of trouble?'

'Well, I was just typing along, and all of a sudden the words went away.'

'Went away?'

'They disappeared.'

'Hmmm. So what does your screen look like now?'

'Nothing.'

'Nothing?'

'It's a blank; it won't accept anything when I type.'

'Are you still in WordPerfect, or did you get out?'

'How do I tell?'

'Can you see the C: prompt on the screen?'

'What's a sea-prompt?'

'Never mind, can you move your cursor around the screen?'

'There isn't any cursor: I told you, it won't accept anything I type.'

'Does your monitor have a power indicator?'

'What's a monitor?'

'It's the thing with the screen on it that looks like a TV. Does it have a little light that tells you when it's on?'

'I don't know.'

'Well, then look on the back of the monitor and find where the power cord goes into it. Can you see that?'

'Yes, I think so.'

'Great. Follow the cord to the plug, and tell me if it's plugged into the wall.'

'Yes, it is.'

'When you were behind the monitor, did you notice that there were two cables plugged into the back of it, not just one?'

'No.'

'Well, there are. I need you to look back there again and find the other cable.'

'Okay, here it is.'

'Follow it for me, and tell me if it's plugged securely into the back of your computer.'

'I can't reach.'

'Well, can you see if it is?'

'No.'

'Even if you maybe put your knee on something and lean way over?'

'Oh, it's not because I don't have the right angle it's because it's dark.'

'Dark?'

'Yes - the office light is off, and the only light I have is coming in from the window.'

'Well, turn on the office light then.'

'I can't.'

'No? Why not?'

'Because there's a power failure.'

'A power … a power failure? … Aha, Okay, we've got it licked now. Do you still have the boxes and manuals and packing stuff your computer came in?'

'Well, yes, I keep them in the closet.'

'Good. Go get them, and unplug your system and pack it up just like it was when you got it. Then take it back to the store you bought it from.'

'Really? Is it that bad?'

'Yes, I'm afraid it is.'

'Well, all right then, I suppose. What do I tell them?'

'Tell them you're too bloody stupid to own a computer.'

This is a bricklayer's accident report, which was printed in the newsletter of the Australian equivalent of the Workers' Compensation Board. This is a true story. Had this guy died, he'd have received a Darwin Award for lack of logic/common sense.

'Dear Sir:

I'm writing in response to your request for additional information in Block 3 of the accident report form I filed. I put 'poor planning' as the cause of my accident. You asked for a fuller explanation, and I trust the following details will be sufficient.

I am a bricklayer by trade. On the day of the accident, I was working alone on the roof of a new six story building. When I completed my work, I found that I had some bricks left over which, when weighed later, were found to be slightly more than 500 pounds. Rather than carry the bricks down by hand, I decided to lower them in a barrel by using a pulley which was attached to the side of the building on the sixth floor. Securing the rope at the ground level, I went up to the roof, swung the barrel out and loaded the bricks into it. Then I went down and untied the rope, holding it tightly to ensure a slow descent of the bricks.

You will note in Block 11 of the accident report form that I weigh approximately 135 pounds.

Due to my surprise of being jerked off the ground so suddenly, I lost my presence of mind and forgot to let go of the rope. Needless to say, I proceeded upward at a rapid rate up the side of the building. In the vicinity of the third floor, I met the barrel, which was now proceeding downward at an equally impressive speed. This explains the fractured skull, minor abrasions and the broken collarbone, as listed in Section 3 of the accident report form.

Slowed down slightly by my impact with the barrel of bricks, I continued my rapid ascent, not stopping until the fingers on my right hand (which was still holding the rope) were two knuckles deep into the pulley.

Fortunately, by this time I had regained my presence of mind and was able to hold tightly to the rope, in spite of beginning to experience a great deal of pain. At approximately the same time, however, the barrel of bricks hit the ground and the bottom fell out of the barrel. Now devoid of the weight of the bricks, (the barrel weighed approximately 50 pounds), again I refer you to my weight, I began a rapid descent, down the side of the building. In the vicinity of the third floor, I met the barrel coming up.

This accounts for the fractured ankles, broken tooth and several lacerations of my legs and lower body. Here my luck began to change slightly. The encounter with the barrel seemed to slow me enough to lessen my injuries when I fell into the pile of bricks on the ground, and fortunately, only three vertebrae were cracked. I am sorry to report, however, as I lay there on the pile of bricks, in pain, unable to move, I again lost my composure and presence of mind and let go of the rope. I lay there watching the empty barrel beginning its journey back down to me. This explains the two broken legs.

I hope this answers your inquiry.'